With Sky News since its beginning, its Political Editor Adam Boulton is a previous winner of the Royal Television Society's supreme Judges' Award and was elected 2007 Chairman of the Parliamentary Lobby. Having long campaigned for televised Leaders' Debates, in 2010 Adam served as moderator for the second debate before leading Sky News' coverage of the new Coalition Government.

After more than ten years reporting for Sky News, Joey Jones was appointed Deputy Political Editor. He was nominated as specialist journalist of the year in the 2010 Royal Television Society Awards having forged a reputation as a respected analyst of the Westminster scene with his unique way of scrutinising Prime Minister's Questions and other set-piece events. He broke the stories of the resignations of Jacqui Smith and Hazel Blears, and shadowed David Cameron throughout the 2010 General Election.

HUNG TOGETHER

The Cameron-Clegg Coalition

ADAM BOULTON &
JOEY JONES

**SIMON &
SCHUSTER**

London · New York · Sydney · Toronto · New Delhi

A CBS COMPANY

First published in Great Britain by Simon & Schuster UK Ltd, 2010
This edition published by Simon & Schuster UK Ltd, 2012
A CBS Company

1 3 5 7 9 10 8 6 4 2

Simon & Schuster UK Ltd
1st Floor
222 Gray's Inn Road
London
WC1X 8HB

www.simonandschuster.co.uk

Simon & Schuster Australia
Sydney

Simon & Schuster India
New Delhi

Photos © PA Photos

A CIP catalogue for this book is available from the British Library.
ISBN: 978-1-84983-381-3

Typeset by Hewer Text UK Ltd, Edinburgh
Printed and bound in Great Britain by CPI Group (UK) Ltd,
Croydon, CR0 4YY

For Muriel
and
For Anji

'Gentlemen, we must all hang together, or assuredly we shall all hang separately.'

Benjamin Franklin (attributed) on the signing of the Declaration of Independence, 1776

CONTENTS

Illustrations

PROLOGUE by Joey Jones

Time to step up. As a politician, there are moments you realise your life is changing. When armed police officers appear at your side like magic for example, as happened to David Cameron on the morning of the 6th of April 2010. Right on cue, no ceremony, at 10.45 he was a protected person – the very instant that Prime Minister Gordon Brown returned from his audience with the Queen and announced in Downing Street the election would take place a month later. That's the machinery of state for you.

As opposition leader, Cameron had come to enjoy the company of a tight, informal coterie of friends and advisors. From that mid-morning on, things would be different. Bodyguards and armoured Jaguars meant sacrificing independence and having to accept much less freedom to dictate agendas. The subliminal message? – that he was but a player now in a piece of British theatre. And what a pantomime it would prove to be.

David Cameron told me that day that my voice had woken him – broadcasting outside his front door at six. I was more worried about the neighbours. Any guilt was assuaged by the knowledge that he had slept only fitfully. There were a few nerves, an aide told me. The election date might indeed have been the 'worst-kept secret in politics', as Gordon Brown joked, but for the Conservative leader, the chance to prove himself and his revamped party at the ballot box had been a long time coming.

Knowing I would be at Cameron's side for the duration of the campaign, it felt right to be the first journalist to arrive in the street. It was still dark but mild. (The weather smiled on us that April.) Chez Cameron is not flash. An unremarkable, mud-coloured brick residential street, around the corner from BBC TV Centre. Entirely free of stucco, porticos and the slightest hint of black wrought iron. In short, not the Notting Hill palace people often expect. (Several weeks back, a colleague sent to stake out the PM-to-be telephoned me, perplexed. 'Is this it? Are you sure? Doesn't feel right,' he complained. 'Does it have two olive trees out front . . . ?' I asked. 'Paving . . . a moped, probably under a tarpaulin . . . ? A glass panel in the front door through which you can see right back into the kitchen? That's the one.')

That morning at 5.30, anyone passing would have had no inkling of what was afoot. The hush was striking. There was little birdsong and no wind. Only the small Sky News satellite van, an engineer, Geppetto-like with half-moon glasses, twiddling knobs in the light of a small torch. As we were setting up for a first live report, a tramp walked past heading east. Not too long after he turned the corner, two Conservative press officers emerged with the sun rising at their backs, weighed down with newspapers.

When David Cameron opened the door, complete with bed-head and jogging shorts at 6.30, the four cups of tea he prof-fered were generous but insufficient. Photographers and TV camera crews had gathered. Cameron had taken to running with a vengeance over the past few months, and had lost weight as a result. But this half-hour trot was all about clearing his head, and allowing nervous energy to dissipate.

Later on (at points of uncertainty or disappointment during the campaign), the Tory leader told us how he would strive to step back, not to get caught up in the setbacks or frustrations of any one day, to 'keep focused on the end of the road'. This morning, as he paced around a local park, rehearsing lines for the campaign launch speech in his head, the end of the road would have seemed distant, but at last it was within view. Thirty more days like this one. Come on, keep going. One foot in front of the other . . .

PART I

CAMPAIGN

1

DAY ONE

'We're all feeling cautiously optimistic'

Downing Street under Gordon Brown was a place for early risers. Knowing that 'The Boss' would be up and at 'em this morning of all mornings, several among his staff arrived at work before seven o'clock. They found Brown in ebullient mood, already at his computer on what they called the horseshoe – the desk that had been set up in Number 12 with space for all his key advisors nearby. With the usual breakfast beside the keyboard (Gordon Brown's morning meal consisted of bacon alone, bacon sandwich or sausage and bacon in large quantities), he tapped away, occasionally barking out requests for information to weave into the speech he would make on returning from the Palace.

Brown was fizzing, full of ideas for the days ahead. As well as Cabinet and an audience with the Queen, there would be Prime Minister's Questions the next day, and then a speech on 'constitutional renewal' that he fully expected to be the 'game-changer' of the first part of the campaign. Determined to make a splash, and seize the agenda at the outset, Brown had been obsessed with the thought of making this occasion a spectacular throw of the dice. He wanted to tie his own future to a referendum on electoral reform and indicate his preparedness to go once the grand cause of constitutional renewal was won. The message to the electorate would be, in effect, 'I'll be here for you, to see you through the economic crisis, to manage political reform. And then I'll step aside.'

During a weekend of wrangling, Brown had been persuaded to think better of it – frankly, you would think some advisors imagined the whole thing to be a bit of a folly! – but there was surely enough meat and vision in his speech to make the Tories sit up and think? (Unfortunately for the PM, the whole thing would prove to be a damp squib, swamped by George Osborne's 'Jobs Tax' broadside and widely ignored. From that point on, Gordon Brown's campaign mood would darken quickly.)

Nick Clegg had planned a limited itinerary. A speech to party workers, an event with young people . . . and that was pretty much it. Leaving his home in Putney not long after seven, Clegg gave the assembled media an upbeat word or two before he jumped in a car – 'Wasn't that a minicab?' reporters wondered – and headed for the Work Foundation, the building in Westminster that the party had hired for its regular press conferences. The neighbours in Clegg's corner of south-west London were much less used to the media hullabaloo than Cameron's. A good many peered over their hedges to catch the scene, or paused on the opposite pavement with their dogs, waiting to see what was going on.

On day one, there was no suspicion of the freight train that would hit the Lib Dems just a week or so later, after Nick Clegg had wowed the nation. 'Cleggmania', as we would come to know it after the first televised debate, was the stuff of fantasy. Wearing the first of a collection of gold ties that had been purchased in bulk from M&S for the election, Clegg geed up party workers in the campaign nerve centre with a speech about 'real change' and 'real choice', delivered just before eight o'clock. (So different from David Cameron! The Tory party leader's speech, delivered a couple of hours later at County Hall on the South Bank of the Thames, was all about change and choice, choice and change.) Then, emerging into bright sunlight with Vince Cable, who was at that point the party's best-known and most trusted figure, Clegg headed north, out of London.

The Labour Cabinet, which gathered in Downing Street at nine o'clock, expected almost to a man and woman that this would be their last such meeting. Superficially, the mood was upbeat. There were straws worth clinging to. The Tories, it was agreed, were not as far ahead as they needed to be. Just four points, according to one poll. You couldn't tell for sure. It was worth giving it a try.

Having completed the formalities of an audience with the Queen; a speech flanked by smiling colleagues in Downing Street (the most resonant phrase? 'I come from an ordinary middle-class family in an ordinary middle-class town'), this ordinary Prime Minister was joined by his wife. Together they headed for the not altogether far-flung reaches of north Kent. It was no ordinary train though. The high-speed 'Javelin' that the Labour team boarded at St Pancras was chosen to showcase the sort of investment the Blair/Brown government had committed to the country's infrastructure. It was the sort of investment that could not be afforded in future, whoever won the election.

Gordon Brown's campaigning activities would become depressingly familiar over the coming weeks. Glad-handing, embarrassing small talk, handpicked 'real people'. No spontaneity, but no disasters. At least, not this time.

The young people that greeted Nick Clegg in Watford had been rounded up by the local YMCA. They cheered journalists emerging from the gleaming Lib Dem battle bus before realising the leader was not on board. In any case, many in the audience readily confessed to not knowing who Clegg was. That would change.

Making the journey by car was an exception. As the campaign progressed, it became unusual for Nick Clegg to travel apart from the small retinue of hacks assigned to the Liberal Democrat tour. Most of the time he seemed to relish their company. Solitude sat ill with the Lib Dem leader. The absence of his wife, and particularly his three sons, on holiday at the in-laws in Spain (and later stranded by the Icelandic ash cloud) was to become a constant cause for complaint. The on-board reporters would be frequently invited forward on the Lib Dem plane for a chat – some interviews for the papers or radio even took place in the back of his state-sponsored Jaguar, something the other parties would never have contemplated.

For David Cameron's accompanying press pack, the illusion of proximity to the man himself lasted until arrival at Euston Station for the midday train to Birmingham. A quick glimpse of the opposition leader on the concourse waiting for a coffee, and then the hacks were ushered into a carriage midway down the train, Cameron and his advisors into another, two or three back. The next sighting was not to be until they reached the Queen Elizabeth Hospital in Birmingham a couple of hours later. It was a venue chosen for David Cameron to trumpet his commitment to the NHS, and to reclaiming the local constituency, the ultra-marginal Birmingham Edgbaston.

From Kent, Gordon Brown returned to Downing Street, and to business. Straight into the Cabinet Room where he would prepare for the next day's Prime Minister's Questions, and take a call from the American President. Barack Obama was full of expressions of solidarity. He told Brown he had been looking at the numbers and, 'We're all feeling cautiously optimistic.' There was talk of coordinating plans to bring forward a levy on banks with the French and Germans. (This would have embarrassed the Tories, who were intent on proceeding with their own similar plan unilaterally.) As the conversation closed, the Democrat President told Gordon Brown, 'If there is anything symbolically we can do, you let me know.' Both men would have known that in reality, there was not. When it comes to an election, you are on your own.

Nevertheless, Gordon Brown was buoyed by his sense that 'friends' on the international stage were rooting for him. Among those taking what one of Brown's supporters described as an 'almost unhealthy' interest in the election were José Luis Rodríguez Zapatero of Spain ('Zap' was a useful Downing Street shorthand), and French President Nicolas Sarkozy. Though when it came to Sarko, it was widely believed he was most likely to be just as emollient with the other bunch.

As for the Conservative leader, having chatted to a small group of consultants, then a small group of nurses in Birmingham (both were in the same room, but segregated according to NHS protocol, one assumed), he headed on to a rally in the centre of Leeds. There was music, there were videos, the jacket came off as it would for the final event of most campaigning days but, shirt-sleeved, pumped and ready to increase the volume, the Tory leader encountered an audience a touch too 'British' in their politeness and reserve. Applause lines went by unmarked; nationally the speech went unnoticed, too late for most media deadlines. No matter. It was the major party launch at County Hall that morning that mattered to the Conservatives, the shots of David and Samantha, backs to a glittering Thames, Big Ben in the distance smiling and surrounded by optimistic supporters, that would adorn the next day's newspapers.

Flying back into Heathrow after dark took the Conservative leader low over the heart of London. Earlier that day, in the one theatrical gesture of his big speech, Cameron had pointed back over his right shoulder to the Palace of Westminster a few hundred metres across the river. He told the audience, 'I want to make people proud of that place again.' Heading home to his family, a little weary but satisfied with the first day on the trail, David Cameron could look out of the aeroplane window and see the Houses of Parliament once again, below him, as though within touching distance, a dull, rusty glow.

2

HITTING THE TRAIL

'Labour had gifted us a little opening which we held in our back pocket.

We waited . . . and deployed it'

Was it worth it? All that effort? The trains, planes and battle buses; soapboxes and walkabouts; the gaffes, the clasp and smile, cameras in tight; the half-eaten sandwiches and snatched sleep? Looking back, as they must from time to time, will not be pleasant for any of them – David Cameron, Gordon Brown or Nick Clegg. They would be forgiven for wondering whether the sweat and tears expended during the election campaign of 2010 made a jot of difference.

As the starting gun sounded, each of the three parties had reason to worry, and for all their attempts at forestalling the worst, on polling day those very worries would be realised in triplicate. Labour under Gordon Brown proved to be as unappealing to the electorate as most within the party had expected . . . David Cameron never did 'seal the deal' . . . and Nick Clegg got a hearing during the campaign, but a hiding on election night.

There has been much knowing talk since of how the voting public 'wanted' a hung parliament. But there were no done deals. Any politician who was on the stump that April will tell you the reality was people did not know what they wanted. David Cameron was well aware of it. With less than 48 hours before the polls opened, as he was standing in the lobby of a Blackpool hotel waiting to get his day's campaigning underway, people were coming up to talk to the man most likely to become Prime Minister. The question that most wanted answered was, 'Why should I vote for you?' They never quite seemed to get the answer they wanted. Voters were, in the end, unable to summon any great enthusiasm for the options confronting them, but there were moments – moments that were tantalising for the politicians seeking to govern – when the electorate seemed to intimate they could be wooed, and won. 'Volatile' hardly does it justice.

Politicians learned to be wary of the great British voter during the 2010 campaign. The eerie sense of dislocation between electors and those aspiring to be elected was profoundly unsettling even to those that have since made it into high office. The mood of the voters felt like a great unknown, and it has become no easier to categorise even with the benefit of time. After the whole expenses debacle, a heavy dose of suspicion and raw anger were inevitable. With a period of retrenchment and austerity looming, a fear of commitment was understandable. But all the parties found it much easier to identify grievances than to offer a convincing remedy. In the end, no politician – not Gordon Brown, not David Cameron, not even Nick Clegg, standard-bearer of the 'new politics' – escaped the sense that they were part of the problem, not the solution.

Back in October 2009, as parliament was just beginning to come to terms with the *Daily Telegraph*'s expenses revelations unleashed that spring, David Cameron's Head of Communications, Andy Coulson, was engaged in a spot of soul-searching. Persistent public apathy was an issue, clouding his party's hopes for the election. Voters had not yet 'tuned in' was Coulson's verdict. When might they though? His own hope and anticipation was that the turn of the year, 'election year', would be critical – the 'Year for Change'. Accordingly, the Conservatives had prepared a blitz of speeches and media announcements to cash in. With David Cameron to the fore, they flung themselves into a frenzy of New Year activity. But there was no traction. Not a sniff. The hype surrounding the 'first day of the election campaign' dissipated swiftly. Election fever would have to wait. And wait. The failure to inspire a positive engagement with Cameron's message was to be a persistent bugbear of the campaign. The questions for Andy Coulson and his colleagues never went away.

It remains true that the underlying mood among David Cameron's team was of confidence. But there was a deal of caution mixed in too. Cameron kept a chart always close at hand which showed the variations in the polls since his installation as leader of the opposition in September 2005. There were wild fluctuations, and one particular cautionary tale was often mulled over in leadership circles.

Cameron has never forgotten how, in the late spring of 2007, he allowed himself to be sidetracked by a row over whether the Conservative education policy should continue to support grammar schools – a tiny number of the nation's educational establishments, but of totemic importance to party figures including the former leader Michael Howard, who had either taken themselves or seen others take the 'grammar school route' from relative poverty to educational betterment.

It should have been a marginal issue. David Cameron's own impatience at the protectors of what he plainly viewed as an anachronistic institution was poorly disguised. But his humiliation when forced to change tack was not disguised at all. It was a classic internal party dispute, with nothing like the resonance of the 10p tax affair a year later that tore apart the Labour party, but which at least had its roots in a decision that would affect large numbers of people. Nevertheless, the Conservative poll rating tanked – a 10 point lead was lost, and within the space of a month or two, the Tories were trailing by almost the same margin. The 'Brown bounce' following his accession to the party leadership was undoubtedly a factor, but Cameron was inclined to blame himself for allowing a Tory family feud to muddy the message.

But the Tories of 2010 navigated between two emotional poles. Caution and anxiety prompted by the 'Grammargate' poll catastrophe, and at the other extreme, a perpetual sense of the proximity, indeed the imminence of triumph, brought on by the Crewe and Nantwich by-election of May 2008. Who could forget how a Labour majority of 7,000 was overturned? (The Conservative candidate won by nearly 8,000 votes.) Combined with Boris Johnson's success in the London mayoral poll, hugely successful local elections and a national lead of more than 20 points, it was this period that cemented the expectation of success come the real thing. The Conservatives believed they could recreate this halcyon period, stoke the Tory fever again, but this time on the bigger stage of the general election itself. The voters might be sleeping still, but when they awoke, this, they thought, is what the Tory love-in would feel like.

Rather than having been a springboard to greater things, Conservative strategists must ruefully acknowledge that Crewe and Nantwich proved to be the high watermark in enthusiasm among the electorate for the Cameron project. The balloons, the high hopes, the bright-faced, badge-wearing Tory on every corner. It was a long time ago.

Ultimately there were flashes of the same kind of spirit on the 2010 campaign – a sunny walkabout in Tamworth where smiles widened and the '*Mirror* Chicken' (a man in a chicken suit sent to harry the Conservative leader at every turn) was unmasked for the cameras, then left trailing and bedraggled. ('What about your Ashdown money?' a rather confused Lib Dem supporter could be heard shouting from behind the scrum of well-wishers.) Moments like Holywell in North Wales. Not natural Tory territory, this – 'Where is that arsehole?' growled a local as journalists descended from the battle bus. But no need to worry, by the time Cameron left, he had charmed them and genuine warmth and enthusiasm flowed. 'You can do it, Mr Cameron'; 'I'll try!' – they couldn't get enough! Or Blackpool right at the end where two local ladies could be overheard cooing: 'Oh look – he looks tired'; 'He will be tired now'; 'Lovely complexion though'; 'Lovely'. So there were times when Cameron would have dared to dream. And the dream would have been of Crewe and Nantwich writ large.

There was not much dreaming to be done on the Labour side. There was one man within the party who thought they could win, the joke went. But for anyone that was not the current Prime Minister, it felt like damage limitation was all they could aspire to. No one was under any illusions that 'Five more years of Gordon Brown' would light the voters' fires. But the party was where it was. Not out of sight in the polls in spite of it all, and with a leader whose dogged refusal to countenance his own demise had become the stuff of legend.

Gordon Brown's friends knew he was poorly equipped for a television election. Not just the debates (though his failure to master the vocabulary of the medium was cruelly exposed there); but the round-the-clock enveloping throng. How often did we see the furrowed browed concern of his wife Sarah at her husband's shoulder, watching him hedged in with cameras, microphones, pestering journalists and, worst of all, 'real people'. It was an arena that ill suited a man who, for all his years in the public eye, was fundamentally uncomfortable with anyone he did not know.

In addition, Brown railed at being, in his view, excluded from the action – by which he meant the bunker. Labour HQ in Victoria Street where ideas-men schemed, argued and conspired over the Tory demise. That was Gordon Brown's natural environment, his vantage point during three previous successful Labour campaigns. But he had wanted the job of Prime Minister: 'Tell him he's our front man now,' Peter Mandelson would advise those dealing with the Prime Minister's frequent complaints. 'He needs to forget about being a strategist.' Easier said than done.

It was not as though things were much easier back at base. Labour apparatchiks had learned to expect tantrums and clashing egos at the heart of their operation. There was a certain gallows humour with which people would recount, days into the campaign, 'Peter and Douglas haven't spoken for a week.' (And this is only the party's dual election coordinators we are talking about; Mandelson and Alexander, supposedly hand in glove, shared hands at the tiller.)

What made the gallows humour still blacker this time around was that Labour was broke. Running on empty. This was a party with a collective instant recall of the glories of 1997 (and remember the key players of the New Labour generation – Mandelson, Campbell, Gould – were all back in the mix now), a party that had grown accustomed to the patronage of high-rollers and city-slickers. Apart from the very few that had not, in one manifestation or another, been in the trenches of a Labour campaign before, party workers found the whole thing quite a comedown. The cash disparity with the Conservatives manifested itself in complaints from candidates who feared being overrun by Ashcroft-funded opponents. But it was shown up equally in the constant television shots of Cameron or even (the humiliation!) Clegg out and about, up and down the country, ash cloud or, it seemed, no ash cloud; impeccably photogenic locations, appropriately diverse punters.

Labour's shoestring campaign was no match. Journalists on the leader's battle bus joked about when they would escape the Home Counties. And while David Cameron built to a twenty-four-hour crescendo (north to south, through the night, 'no sleep till Bristol!'), Gordon Brown's tour was, in the final week, cut back again. From the outside, one would hardly have thought such a thing possible.

What kept Labour going was the failure of the Conservative campaign to take flight. As far back as 2008, party strategists argued that if they could keep the Tories below 40 points in the polls, there was hope. (In the event, the Liberal Democrats' post-debate bounce made that scenario a reality, though the simultaneous dent in the Labour rating was not exactly what the doctor ordered.) Ask any Labour worker – ragged, weary and beaten-down – they will tell you there is no more sustaining dish than Tory frailty. All the late-night pizzas delivered to Victoria Street were as nothing compared with the pick-me-up of a single poll showing the Conservatives were not – despite all their effort, despite the cash, the youth, the vigour – over the crest of the hill yet.

Labour and the Liberal Democrats were as one in believing the Conservatives could be got at during the campaign. The view was that the favourites were flaky on detail, inconsistent in advocating austerity on the one hand and a bunch of goodies for favoured sections of the population on the other . . . and Shadow Chancellor George Osborne was a perfect target.

On the economy – the key issue of the election – the Tories' opponents both thought the public would favour a safe pair of hands, and proffered their own 'wise men' – Alistair Darling and Vince Cable – as an antidote to Osborne's supposed callow insubstantiality.

George Osborne is well known to be the Conservatives' key political tactician, but some of his economic initiatives, born out of political expediency or a desire to outflank the Labour government, were ill-suited to a new set of circumstances. A commitment to raise the threshold of inheritance tax was hailed as a masterstroke when revealed at the party conference of 2007. After all, that announcement came in the teeth of a gale of rumours that Gordon Brown was about to call a snap election, and put the government on the back foot on what Osborne termed 'the death tax'. (Labour's feeble imitation of the policy was a precursor to standing down the troops and walking away from a fight the party might, at that point, have won.)

In 2010 though, with a recession to deal with, a tax concession for the wealthier few in society was harder to justify. David Cameron's determination to 'recognise marriage in the tax system' was another example of a policy that was more about middle-class mood music than fiscal rectitude. Both commitments were to bite the dust in the harsher arena of the coalition negotiations.

It is easy to imagine circumstances in which the Conservative message could have been seriously undermined by such policies. Equally, one can see how potent might have been the argument that Tory fiscal policy was reckless and lacking credibility had it been made on another day. After all, remember David Cameron and George Osborne had called for government spending to be cut back not just 'in-year' in 2010–11 as has since happened, not even 'in-year' in 2009–10 but right back in the autumn of 2008, just as every other major world economy was doing the exact opposite, and embarking on a massive project of fiscal stimulus in the wake of the international banking crisis. (David Laws, who worked closely with George Osborne during his short period at the Treasury, believes that particular policy – motivated by the need for a dividing line with 'profligate' Labour – could not have been maintained had it been Osborne, not Darling, holding the reins: 'I suspect the policy of the Conservative Party might not have been so different from that adopted by the Labour government had they been in power, because they would have had no choice but to intervene.')

Part of Labour's problem in making their case stick was that the public felt, all in all, that the way the economic argument was played out during the campaign was phony and unconvincing. Even the most cogent argument would have struggled to cut through when there was a widespread public perception that the whole debate was not credible. Watch again the final televised set-piece focusing on the economy which was broadcast by the BBC (should you be so inclined). The British voter would have learned more about the future economic direction of the country from five minutes in the company of Robert Chote, the Director of the Institute of Fiscal Studies, than from these ninety minutes of detailed argument between the men who aspired to lead the country.

Some sigh, shrug their shoulders and say 'It was inevitable,' and 'No politician could have taken the risk of telling the electorate straight.' After all, the Conservatives tried talking about an 'Age of Austerity' at their party conference the autumn before the election, but backed off when the polls and their focus groups showed voters taking fright at the harsh rhetoric.

Nevertheless, a fundamental curiosity of the election of 2010 was that a campaign during which all parties harped on interminably about the virtues of openness and transparency following the expenses scandal was equally a campaign marred by a conspiracy of silence between Labour, Tory and Lib Dem alike. It is true that the three parties spoke in general terms about the need for deficit reduction. Nevertheless, the IFS, understated as ever, said ten days before the campaign's end that it was 'striking how reticent all three main UK parties have been in explaining how they would confront the task.'

After the election, the Conservatives would claim credit for having been straight with the country, or at least, straighter than the other lot. In terms of rhetoric, they were indeed comfortably towards the scary end of the scale, while Labour and the Liberal Democrats maintained that once growth returned to the economy, paying off the country's debts could be accomplished without excessive upheaval.

Even the Tories' 'honesty', however, was leavened with a heavy dose of pragmatism. On the one hand, George Osborne and David Cameron were united in their conviction that the party would have a serious problem if it was elected on 'a false prospectus'. Hungary and Greece were spoken of as countries where the incoming government had not told the truth about their intentions once in power. The new administrations had struggled when trying to enact austerity measures because the people who elected them said they had not signed up to such a tough programme.

So far, so laudable . . . perhaps. But while strong on rhetoric, the Conservatives were as guilty as anyone else when it came to being weak on specifics. On all sides, a tacit agreement was reached: not a word about the coming pain when it could legitimately be avoided; nothing about the inevitable impact of spending cuts on people's lives.

Members of the Conservative Shadow Cabinet half-jokingly referred to 'Osborne's Law' on spending within their own departments – 'If you don't have to be specific, don't be.' The immediate political justification for staying vague was utterly sound: allowing oneself to be tied to a particular figure (a spending target, a budget cap) opened up the risk of getting bogged down in detail and, critically, gave opponents something to attack and, the argument went, something to distort. The party was seriously spooked during the campaign by Labour hammering away at the prospect of swingeing 'Tory cuts', and determined not to give the governing party more sticks with which to beat them.

It remained the case, that against such a background, not only could voters fairly conclude that politicians were failing to talk to them directly about the key issue of the day, it was always likely that whatever economic arguments were put forward on the stump would be greeted with a pinch, if not a dollop, of salt. So often did Alistair Darling insist that the Conservative position on child tax credits did not stack up that it must have felt to the then Chancellor like he was crying into the wind. In order to raise the money they hoped to, he argued, tax credits would have to be removed from couples with a combined income of £31,000 or above. George Osborne had used a figure of £50,000 in his party conference speech, a stance reiterated by David Cameron during the election campaign. In fact, as Osborne's first budget showed, Darling was entirely correct. There are reasons to believe the Labour attack did make some impact on the electorate at large, but in press conferences such was the level of cynicism at the parties' economic plans, Labour's claims were more often than not greeted by a raising of eyebrows. So? Who are you to talk? What are you going to do, then?

As Nick Clegg got the Liberal Democrats underway, the party's prospects felt even more uncertain than was usually the case in a general election. There is a slightly vertiginous excitement to being on a Liberal Democrat campaign, the sense that a swing of one or two points here or there could mean 'the breakthrough' or, if the other way, meltdown. Though the party has built up strongholds, it cannot rely on a single 'heartland' for reassurance when things get rocky. Political nomads in part, the Lib Dems need to keep finding new pastures, or they die.

Clegg's vision of a forward march was the steady expansion of his party's strength at Westminster. He told his MPs he wanted to see their numbers double over two parliaments. When weighing up how much of that task might be accomplished in May 2010, senior figures within the party tended to feel they were entitled to expect growth in the parliamentary party from 62 MPs to something above 70 or 80, the sort of progress that would, after all, at the very least be necessary if Clegg's ambitious target for the next election was to be attainable. Simon Hughes, now deputy leader of the party, believed his guess was at the cautious end of the scale: 'I thought you can never hang on to every seat you've got and we would lose a few (probably about half a dozen), but my thought was we would compensate for that by winning about 20, and we would end up in the 70–80 range.'

With hindsight, obviously, that was far too optimistic, but even at the outset of the campaign, it was plain that there were a number of big hurdles to be overcome, and key factors stacked against the party. The economy was one. Faced with what could be termed a national crisis, and by anyone's reckoning was a huge economic challenge, voters might be expected to turn to the parties they knew best, and whose qualities were most fully documented. The Liberal Democrats were confident that they had managed to dispel much of the public doubt about their economic competence – Vince Cable took most of the credit for that – but persuading the electorate that theirs was the party to navigate the nation through the troubled sea of deficit reduction was likely to be difficult.

Wise heads in the party cautioned that 2005 had been a good year for them, and that they would need to work hard to replicate that result. Under the leadership of Charles Kennedy, a man who was widely recognised and well-liked in the country, the Lib Dems had positioned themselves steadfastly against the Iraq War, and ended up benefiting from the considerable amount of public ill will towards Tony Blair and Labour. What was not clear was whether those people whose votes had been fuelled by anti-war anger would stay with the Liberal Democrats now that the conflict was fading from memory.

Then there was the leader. Nick Clegg, right? The MP for Sheffield Hallam had only entered parliament in 2005, and as far as national politics was concerned, Clegg was an unknown quantity. Even the party could not be sure how Clegg would perform in the campaign hothouse. His only previous experience of having to scrap for votes – the contest for the leadership with Chris Huhne in 2007 – was not an unalloyed triumph. There were hints of complacency and a lack of application in the way Clegg allowed what should have been a fairly easy ride to become a nerve-racking tussle, at the end of which he scraped home by a margin of 500 votes (out of more than 40,000 cast).

The 2010 campaign, the Liberal Democrats hoped, would be the opportunity to demonstrate how much Clegg had learned from that experience. For all that the party talked up Vince Cable, highlighting his experience and wisdom, his prescience ahead of the banking crisis, this would be Nick Clegg's show. The young man was front and centre now. All the more so because this would be the television election, the first time a Liberal Democrat leader would be given an equal platform with his two big party rivals to debate live on TV. The Lib Dems knew they tended to benefit from the increased exposure they enjoyed during election campaigns. The debates could be a massive plus for the party. Clegg could not wait.

The early stages of the campaign were all about Labour and the Conservatives. An old-fashioned, two-party slugging match. Labour was caught cold. For precious days, Gordon Brown and his team found themselves on the back foot over a policy the party had thought was bedded in and – if not exactly uncontroversial, what tax is? – widely accepted and understood. The increase in National Insurance had been announced in two stages, first with a half-point rise in the Pre-Budget Report in 2008 (effective only from April 2011), then a further half-point in Alistair Darling's December PBR, less than six months before the election. (Again, the start point was at the beginning of the 2011 tax year.) When introduced, the Conservatives had criticised the plan, but that attack had waned. In the days after Gordon Brown had fired the starting gun however, the Tory attack was revived unexpectedly and with lethal effect.

The 'Labour's Jobs Tax' campaign was cooked up by George Osborne in the autumn before the election and then, as he later put it, banked. Unbeknown to the then-Chancellor Alistair Darling, when he came to deliver his pre-election Budget in March, his Shadow was preoccupied by one thing above all others – whether Darling would maintain the increase in NI, thus allowing the Conservatives the opportunity for what they hoped would be a key first strike in the election campaign on Labour's economic platform. As Osborne put it subsequently, 'Labour had gifted us a little opening which we had in our back pocket. We waited . . . and deployed it.'

The Conservatives congratulated themselves as leading figures in business signed up to the party's campaign to reverse the measure. They became quite giddy with excitement as Gordon Brown and Peter Mandelson got drawn into a row with some of the outspoken industrialists, after suggesting the businessmen had been 'misled' by the Conservative policy or were victims of 'a deception' (a charge Sir Stuart Rose of M&S, among others, indignantly denied).

The Tory machine was in full cry. Among Conservative press officers, there was a competition to see who could get their man or woman to say 'jobs tax' the most number of times. (Michael Gove's aide, Henry de Zoete, claimed the prize.) Watching and listening to government spokesmen having to defend the measure at length during every interview and every press conference just three days into the campaign vindicated the Conservative strategy. The Labour heavyweights may have had a point (if not National Insurance, what did George Osborne propose? A tax rise elsewhere? A spending cut here or there?), but the Conservatives were forcing the agenda. 'They say they're making the running, we say they're making it up', was Douglas Alexander's defiant verdict. But there was more conviction to the words of a senior member of the Shadow Cabinet, when he joined the Cameron tour on a flight to Plymouth: 'The more they talk about it, the happier we are.'

Within Gordon Brown's inner circle, it was an uncomfortable few days. If any party needed to come out of the blocks fast, it was Labour. Only by establishing a clear momentum at the outset, surely, could the party hope to claw back the Conservatives? Yet here they were, a few days in and it felt like one–nil to the Tories. 'It was very frustrating,' Ed Balls admits. His view came to be that those fronting the Labour effort were insufficiently aggressive. 'Our response on the National Insurance rise was half-hearted, and that was a problem for us. Had we really established in those first couple of days quite what nonsense they were saying . . . ? That was a problem for us.'

Balls may have had a point. The choice of personnel for the Labour press conferences – Peter Mandelson, deft and entertaining 'master of ceremonies' in the middle, with Alistair Darling and Gordon Brown at his sides – was in part designed to protect the Prime Minister. To protect him from going head to head with the journalists he generally despised – in effect to protect him from himself. With hindsight though, some sort of clunking fist rather than the Mandelsonian velvet glove might have been more effective.

Though the Conservatives had reason to congratulate themselves at the time, some who were among the biggest enthusiasts then have come to doubt whether this first week was really such a triumph. Looking back, Michael Gove wonders whether the tone of the debate did not fuel the already abundant disenchantment with politicians. 'The electorate thought that when the general election was called, we would move from quite a stale period of to-ing and fro-ing to a greater degree of engagement on the part of politicians ... that politicians would speak in a more direct way about the things that mattered to them. They were completely turned off by the first week or so of the election, and they thought, "Is that all there is?"'

Even the architect of the attack can understand why the voters did not feel engaged. George Osborne's view is that this was the attritional part of the campaign. Slugging it out in the trenches. And, even, for all that it represented a tactical masterstroke, quite boring. As Osborne puts it, 'It was quite a classic general election campaign [at that stage]. Morning press conferences, announcements, endorsements, counter-attacks ... policy-driven.' Nevertheless, the unequivocal view at the apex of the Tory party is that the 'Jobs Tax' was a crucial part of the overall strategy. 'I think personally it served a very important purpose, aside from its strong economic merits,' says George Osborne, 'which was for the first time in years for the Tory party to resist the Labour onslaught on economic policy.' David Cameron is in complete agreement. His view is that this week stopped Labour getting into their stride on what they like to do best: 'hammering the Tories on the economy'. A final word from George Osborne: 'We held the line, but I'm not claiming it was particularly exciting for the general public.'

Exciting the general public was nevertheless one of the things the Conservatives set out to do. Tied in with the key theme of 'Time for Change' were the positive vibes designed to project the party as the antidote to arrogant, controlling Labour. This 'touchy feely Conservatism' was not an unmitigated triumph. (At least the 'Jobs Tax' did what it said on the tin.)

From the start, even before the words 'Big Society' had passed David Cameron's lips, the campaign seemed designed to project the idea as unwieldy and confusing. The first taster came with what was billed as the launch of the 'National Citizen Service', a favoured project of the Tory leader announced long before in the *Sun* newspaper, and designed to get young people out and about and doing something positive.

It was at this event that Cameron took great relish in mocking the Brown, Mandelson, Darling triumvirate as 'like three men in a boat' (and the Chancellor's shocking pink hairdo earlier that day owing to a trick of the television lights certainly did not help), but it apparently escaped his notice that his own lavishly appointed press conference in the media suite at Millbank Tower was, not to put too fine a point on it, a dog's dinner.

Journalists who had stocked up at the Tories' 'GWB Café' in the foyer (General Well Being. Smoothies, don't you know?), were then forced to wait forty long minutes during which a group of children described the pilot schemes on which they had been enrolled, interspersed with clunky video testimony. And that was before David Cameron and his special guest, one Sir Michael Caine, even got on stage. (You had to feel sorry for the kids – as they talked under the lights, understandably nervous, they would have seen the backs of dozens of photographers and television camera crews, all of whom were turned away from the stage, lenses trained on the star sitting in the front row. Not David Cameron.) And what were Michael Caine's first words at the lectern on this, the Tories' 'National Citizen Service' day? 'I hated National Service.' Thanks for that.

There were even longueurs at the launch of the Conservative manifesto. Lengthy videos of well-wishers and enthusiastic fellow-passengers on the Tory bandwagon; over-rehearsed, pat speeches from half the Shadow Cabinet (employing Sayeeda Warsi, a peer, to attack 'rotten politics' – whose idea was that?), and a so-so David Cameron admitting people were 'not yet engaged' by the election. The very same complaint Andy Coulson had made six months earlier. Not yet engaged? The Conservatives would have to wait only a couple of days, to the first televised debate, for that longed-for engagement to happen. But the electorate's engagement would not be directed in the way that they had envisaged or hoped.

There are a whole bunch of reasons why the 'Big Society', the centrepiece of the manifesto launch, failed to fly. 'Big Society' is extraordinarily oblique as a political slogan – defined as it is by what it is not. (Imagine it instead as *not* 'Big Government' – now it makes sense.) It was a concept even the party's most gifted communicators struggled to encapsulate in a sentence or two. And while one should not doubt that David Cameron believed in the idea profoundly (and has subsequently managed to win the Liberal Democrats round to its key tenets), he was not sufficiently persuaded of the Big Society's value as a vote-winning tool to put this particular agenda centre stage when he had the opportunity at debate number one. In fact, for all that it was a debate about domestic affairs and the state of the nation, the Big Society did not even get a walk-on role.

Today, at the top echelons of the Conservative party there is something of a tendency to explain away the disappointment that the message of the Big Society failed to break through. Speak to people in leadership circles, and you will hear it argued that those who saw the project as a bit of a damp squib misunderstood its real purpose. The Big Society was not designed as an 'on the doorstep' message in a campaign that everyone knew would be dominated by the economy, they say. Instead, it represented a way of fulfilling the need for a governing philosophy wrapping the whole Tory offer up – the sort of thing that is 'needed by the commentariat'.

There is a touch of rewriting history going on here. Remember the posters? The knowing, Soviet-style graphics and in-your-face lettering? 'We're all in this together'; 'Hope', 'Change', 'By sharing responsibility we help society grow stronger.' They were handed out on dinky little postcards to journalists who attended Conservative press conferences, but the appeal was thought to be wider than that. Someone paid for the whole little lot to adorn telephone boxes up and down the country. Thousands of them, doubtless. You could see them (to take a single example) on the glass BT cubicles that stand outside the benefits office on Brixton Hill in one of the more deprived parts of South London. Something for the claimants to admire as they queued before opening time on Monday morning? One wonders which particular member of the commentariat that was aimed at.

The view of Peter Mandelson, who once knew a thing or two about crafting a clear message, was that the Big Society, 'had it been properly stress-tested, would have been found to be unexplainable and unpersuasive.' Once the Conservatives took over in government and the project started being implemented for real, it took on harder edges and seemed increasingly coherent.

The idea of asking more of people in their communities chimes with the necessities of the age – trying to forge something positive from a rough old situation. Like the coalition itself. Born of necessity, cobbled together from the ruins of individual political ambitions, constructing something that might just last?

If the Conservatives' fervent hope was to set a Tory train running and then steam to victory, the scale of the other parties' aspirations were necessarily more modest. Labour chose to highlight its record of investment in the public services at the party's manifesto launch, which took place in the brand spanking new wing of Birmingham's Queen Elizabeth Hospital, the same hospital David Cameron had visited on day one of the campaign. It was a pointed decision – a direct rebuttal to Conservative charges of economic fecklessness according to Gordon Brown who opened his speech by roaring, 'We didn't just fix the roof, we built the entire hospital!'

The Prime Minister's disdain for journalists' questions was par for the course. (Among other things, the hacks seemed to doubt extravagant claims made for Labour's economic legacy, and were even sceptical as to the legality of the hospital venue – Cabinet Office guidelines advise against the use of NHS premises for election meetings.) On this occasion, not only did Gordon Brown enjoy a full complement of Cabinet cheerleaders – 'Perfect answer, Prime Minister,' from the Home Secretary Alan Johnson pretty much summed it up – there was a noisy crowd of Labour activists whose views of the press pack clearly mirrored Brown's own. Broadcasters' questions were loudly booed, and when Graeme Wilson of the *Sun* had the temerity to mention his newspaper's name, he was subject to a barrage of catcalls. Up on stage, Gordon Brown smiled indulgently. They should have done this more often, he seemed to be thinking.

The Lib Dem manifesto event, at Bloomberg's City of London headquarters, was unfussy and businesslike. It was also as much a showcase for Vince Cable as the party leader. Cable, whose photograph featured alongside Nick Clegg's on the Lib Dem battle bus, was much feted in the early days of the campaign, as a focus on the economy, it was hoped, might favour the third party.

Criticising Labour and the Conservatives for steering clear of the economy during their own manifesto events, Cable ostentatiously vowed he would confront the issue of the deficit – the 'elephant in the room' – head on. 'I guess I am the elephant man,' he joked. (You had to be there.) Pre-figuring the ease with which the Lib Dems would sign up to the Conservative economic analysis in the coalition agreement, he kept his fire on the need to reduce the structural deficit and to rein in public spending.

Nick Clegg showed the deftness that became a trademark in fending off the usual questions about a hung parliament. Asked if he could envisage circumstances in which his party would support David Cameron, Clegg retorted by saying several times, 'I want to be Prime Minister.' There were no slips, no gaffes or own goals, but also no sense or expectation of the phenomenon that would seize the party within days – Cleggmania.

3

EMBED WITH CAMERON by Joey Jones

'There are chickens at the drop!'

Strange things strike you when you are in the midst of covering a month-long election campaign, day in day out, high days and holidays. Yet another sunny Saturday, driving past Clapham Common en route to a Cameron walkabout, I noticed a police forensic team at work. Amid the barbecues, Frisbees and hundreds of people fully determined to enjoy the unexpected bonus of warm April weather to the maximum, the scene was rather surreal, almost dreamlike. Three small vans parked in the middle of the grass, a clutch of individuals, in full white overalls and hooded . . . busily and persistently going about their business. Around them, apparently oblivious, were the weekend hordes, the separation delineated only by fragile lengths of tape.

The analogy that occurred to me then, likening David Cameron's campaign posse to this group of policemen and women, is inexact and (as with many things during that time) most likely in part induced by fatigue. Plainly far more separated than connected the two. It was the people outside the tape; the overwhelming indifference of the surrounding public that was most striking, and that, at that time, felt oddly familiar. Here was a bunch of professionals working in full view and within touching distance of the heaving mass of the British public; a group one might have expected to be the object of attention or general curiosity, and yet they could have been on another planet. Outside the tape the patterns of everyday life flowed on. People stubbornly doing their thing. Unstoppable . . . inscrutable.

Sealed off, as one feels on a political campaign, it is only occasionally possible for a politician, political aide or journalist to persuade themselves that what they are doing, or perhaps the events going on in front of their eyes, definitely matter, that here, right now, this is the story, they are the story. Most of the time, the reverse is true. The normal nagging feeling is that the action is happening elsewhere. (From the journalists' point of view, a single example: on a train back to London, Cameron having managed to go ahead, the media pack gathered around the one or two laptops that seemed to have a signal, watching Gordon Brown's 'Duffygate' meltdown, open-mouthed. Complaint to the Tory press minders: 'Why can't you lay on something like this?') Overall though, 'the story' of the campaign of 2010 was simple, but perpetually elusive – a story of a lot of people making up their minds who would be best suited to govern them. What we got in marginal after marginal visited by David Cameron's battle bus was the froth and spume. The connection between the electorate deciding on the one hand, and thirty days of constant chase, scurry and slog on the other, was frustratingly difficult to pin down.

Over the month, journalists who follow a single individual – as I did David Cameron – become obsessed with detail. Hand movements. The way Samantha watches fixedly, almost mouthing the words with him. The nervous laughter when Boris, sharing the leader's podium, cracks a joke. Was the voice a little hoarse that time? Hair OK? Within a short time it becomes clear that with Cameron, there is remarkably little to be gleaned from such scrutiny. It is as pointless as studying the minute vein-like creases that, close up, can be seen to scar each whiter-than-white shirt, hoping to discern a pattern. He is always better than workmanlike, never dazzling. Impressive in his recollection of a script and his command of detail. Charming? For sure. No sense of imminent disaster. David Cameron on the road is just a very, very consistent performer.

As I was buying drinks at Cameron's Bristol hotel, the barman offered to put them on the tab. 'Are you part of the team?' No, not exactly. It is a curious relationship between journalists and politicians on the road though . . . between the followers and the followed. Inevitably a degree of camaraderie develops amid the cast-off packets of crisps, sandwiches and Haribo (someone in Central Office has a seriously sweet tooth, by the way). Tiredness and travel, airport security and early mornings create a bond. (Rarely late evenings on this campaign – Cameron endeavoured to get back to his family at a reasonable time most nights.)

Sometimes all involved can share the sense of the ridiculousness of the venture – such as when Liz Sugg, who organised the logistics of the leader's tour, marched to the back of the bus where Cameron was being fitted with his radio mic and announced with genuine concern, 'There are chickens at the drop!' (*Daily Mirror* Chickens, a flock of hired hands in chicken suits, and a constant menace. Much to their surprise, Cameron chose to confront them on this occasion.)

There is gentle mischief to be made – Cameron, talking to a man who worked as a wine waiter at the Oxford College where the head of the civil service, Sir Gus O'Donnell, occasionally teaches, said in a moment of levity: 'Now we know why the economy's in such a state – the Cabinet Secretary's been drinking!' The game for the hacks was then to persuade his media handlers the joke was an apocalyptic gaffe. 'Cam Slams Mandarin Soak, Drunk At Wheel Of British Economy!' the headline would run. 'Pie-eyed Sir Gus Wrecked My Economy!' and so on. Press Secretary Gabby Bertin sent a text message to alert Cameron's chief of staff, Ed Llewellyn. Just in case.

In general the objective is to niggle and harry in order to force an error or prompt a news line. It is easier said than done with a politician of David Cameron's skill. (Failing that, the more limited aim is simply not to miss anything important.) Boxing the Tory leader into agreeing he would go further on marriage tax breaks than previously announced (a further spending commitment) was viewed as a minor triumph. A live pursuit when Cameron conveniently 'forgot' to answer questions from journalists, and simply hotfooted it after a speech – cameramen scrambling, wobbly shots; off the shoulder; bumped in the scrum, while DC flees the pack, journalists shouting after him – is the sort of scene of mild chaos that immediately results in phone calls from Central Office to the Tory organisers on the ground: 'What on earth was that all about?'

Some images will not quickly be forgotten. Windswept Cameron and his wife on a spectacular cliff top in Newquay (Samantha, who was quite heavily pregnant during the campaign, was pleased neither by the steep stone-stepped walk down to the venue, nor by the next day's front pages, almost all of which showed her hair being blown vertically). There was Cameron showing remarkable sangfroid as he was handed one really remarkably ugly baby. Or the 'Dave and Boris' act, a little sulky and awkward at the Royal Hospital in Chelsea ('Boris was reasonably well behaved' was the Cameron verdict), but much better, animated and enjoying themselves amid the pearly kings and queens of St George's Day in the heart of the City. Sky presenter Kay Burley wearing vertiginous heels and teetering on the Bristol dockside cobbles. 'You can never accuse Sky News of not being balanced again,' I whispered to a press aide. And one image I am glad I did not witness myself. Cameron in his underpants, sleeping on what must have been a mountain of airline-style pillows (there were almost none left for his staff), in the closed-off section at the back of the bus – the bit they called the 'lovepad'. A vital kip on the gruelling, twenty-four-hour final push across the country.

Wakefield was the undoubted low point of that last day marathon. Nothing wrong with Wakefield. But at around three in the morning, tired and grumpy (it was cold, too), a cavernous Morrison's bakery depot felt like the wrong place at the wrong time. Even for David Cameron, alighting on Ed Balls's home turf for the second occasion during the campaign did not feel like quite such a lark. 'Whose idea was this?' he asked, wiping sleep from his eyes as he walked down the central aisle of the bus. At this point, the whole trip felt desolate and silly. Running short on questioners, Cameron told the bakers who were standing in a wide circle around him, 'And we have journalists from the BBC, Sky and ITV with us too, let's see if they have anything they want to ask me . . . ?' I will be honest. At that point, I had nothing. I walked away. It was left to Quentin Letts of the *Daily Mail* to enquire, 'Why are we here?'

However, the twenty-four-hour last day campaign should be filed away and employed next time as the antidote to all those on-the-road thoughts that the whole thing is futile and pointless. Look at the marginals where Cameron dropped in, and the results a day later: East Renfrewshire, easy Labour hold (bad start); Carlisle, Conservative majority of 850 on a near 8 point swing (that's more like it!); Rossendale and Darwen, Conservative majority of 4,500 on a 9 point swing; Morley and Outwood, Ed Balls hangs on to a majority of just over 1,000 defying a 9 point swing; Great Grimsby, Labour by the skin of their teeth – 700 majority despite a 10.5 point swing; Sherwood, Conservative majority of just 214 – a swing of 8 points; Dudley North, Labour majority of 650 with a 4.7 point swing (must try harder); and to finish, a whopping 13 point swing to oust Lembit Opik in Montgomeryshire by 1,000.

If they had managed similar performances across the country, the Conservatives would have romped home. There was nothing different about any one of the visits paid by David Cameron over those twenty-four hours than the many, many others we witnessed in the four previous weeks or so. But who knows? Maybe the whole thing does matter after all? The various victorious Conservative candidates now sitting in Westminster (particularly Mark Spencer, the one who squeaked home in Sherwood) would not say otherwise. From the inside, while it is going on, you can never tell.

When David Cameron looks back today and considers the Tories' eventual election result, he admits the geographical area where the party really fell short was London, and that may have made the difference. What a thought! I bet he wishes he had tagged another few hours to his trip, freshened himself up, drunk a strong coffee or two and headed gamely back along the M4 to the capital.

4

GAME CHANGER

'How do I deal with this guy?'

David Cameron's eyes were glazed. As the camera eased in, he was looking off and up to one side as though fixated by something in the middle distance. Stock-still, arms rigidly at his sides and with a fierce side-parting; had Cameron slipped a hand inside the lapel of his jacket, he could hardly have struck a more Napoleonic (or awkward) figure. 'Uh-oh,' was the immediate thought of his close team watching backstage. Nerves. They knew then. The moment had got to him.

Unforgiving, this telly business, is it not? Wisely, Nick Clegg and Gordon Brown to camera left and right had steadied themselves on their lecterns for that all-important first standing shot of three party leaders together, ready to debate live in the run-up to a British election. A tentative smile on the lips of the Liberal Democrat leader . . . a frown indifferently moderated from Gordon Brown, fingertips of his left hand splayed, and pressed lightly onto his notes.

This was a new world. It was tough on everyone, mind you. The presenter, Alastair Stewart, had, in rehearsals, agreed to introduce each leader in turn by name for his opening remarks. Now though, when he came to Gordon Brown, Stewart chose merely to point at him, and the Prime Minister began speaking. Thrown by the unanticipated change of choreography, the sound engineers failed to keep up. Brown's first words were lost. Off-mic. Consternation in the gallery. Little things matter.

On the 15th of April 2010, British electoral history entered a new phase. The first debate to be broadcast live between the leaders of the three main political parties cemented 2010 as the television election. There would be a winner – Nick Clegg. But there was no catastrophic loser. David Cameron fought back from his initial disappointment. Gordon Brown muddled through.

The decision to press ahead with televised leaders' debates was the result of a curious alignment of motivations – short-term tactics of course, but maybe also a creeping sense that it was the right thing to do; a dash of desperation; a jolt or two from the broadcasters; a certain chemistry between negotiating teams . . . From now on, debates will seem an inevitable and natural part of our election choreography, but it might not have come off. Right to the last, there were no guarantees.

The big television networks wanted it to happen – of course they did. When Sky News unilaterally kick-started the process with a challenge to the Labour, Conservative and Liberal Democrat leaders to take part in September 2009, there was real anger from rival broadcasters, but those differences were soon set aside in recognition of the high chance of success if ITV, the BBC and Sky could demonstrate their ability to cooperate, and their unity of purpose.

Things moved quickly. Following initial commitments from David Cameron and Nick Clegg to take part, Gordon Brown announced his willingness to debate at the beginning of October, though the Prime Minister's statement on the Labour party website was hedged with caveats about the need to allow time for parallel debates between other senior figures on their respective briefs, and his desire to begin debating (classic Gordon Brown) pretty much right away. As one of his aides put it, Brown's idea of a TV debate would have been a test of endurance. Last man standing. An hour and a half? You're joking. A preamble, at best.

Behind the scenes, a more congenial pace of negotiation was being established. A key discussion took place between Peter Mandelson and David Muir (a senior Downing Street staffer) for Labour, and Andy Coulson (Head of Communications) and Ed Llewellyn, David Cameron's chief of staff, for the Conservatives. Mandelson and Llewellyn ultimately ducked out when the negotiating grind took hold, but this 'secret' meeting undoubtedly established trust on the key principle – that the main parties were ready to make this thing happen, and that they were not simply (or at least, not exclusively) playing games.

The negotiations that followed, between three highly competitive broadcasters and three political parties with still sharper elbows, were a tangled web. The venue initially was away from Westminster – the Royal Institute of British Architects near Oxford Circus. A white office; black metal and leather chairs. A neutral space. Later on in the process the Mothers' Union was the scene for some of the most delicate moments of the negotiations, another nondescript, though somewhat homelier office suite, and this time just a stone's throw from the Palace of Westminster.

The permutations were complicated. There were as many arguments between television executives as between politicians. There were moments when the representative of one party might slide an arm round the shoulder of a broadcaster or two and gently try to stitch up his political opponents . . .

moments when the same politicians who had been at logger-heads over one particular point were suddenly found to be as one, and immovable on another issue. Aside from the main meeting space, frugally serviced with sandwiches and coffees, there were separate 'break-out rooms' for each of the politi-cal teams to do their own thing – ring HQ for clarification perhaps, confer in private or simply sit tight and make the rest sweat through the afternoon.

In the notoriously leaky environment of Westminster, all agreed it was remarkable that so little of the detail of the discus-sions ever saw the light of day. Those stories that made it into the newspapers were almost invariably wide of the mark.

The first 'problem' question was an area that could have been expected to prove a flashpoint: the viability of commercial breaks during the debates, an issue of considerable sensitivity to ITV.

Labour was particularly hostile to ad-breaks. When David Muir, the senior negotiator for the governing party, told the ITV team he was not prepared to see this 'great constitutional innova-tion disrupted by advertisements for Domestos', there was fury on the other side of the table. But with the BBC agnostic, and Sky inclined to forgo advertising during a ninety-minute broad-cast that was a PR dream in itself, the main commercial terrestrial broadcaster was left out on a limb, and had to climb down.

Amid the to-ing and fro-ing, the Liberal Democrats could scarcely believe their luck. It was Christmas come early. The Lib Dems always benefit from the increased airtime electoral law insists they are afforded during an election campaign. But for Nick Clegg to have an equal platform with his rival leaders on primetime TV? Maybe not an unhoped-for opportunity (they hoped for it all right!), but its potential benefit for a party that struggled traditionally to match Labour and the Conservatives in fund-raising and campaign spending was incalculable.

Subsequently we have become used to talk of chemistry between coalition partners the Lib Dems and Tories. During the debate negotiations, however, that connection was not so obviously evident. Andy Coulson for the Tories and David Muir for Labour seemed to the broadcast participants to be more on the same wavelength. After all, the two main parties knew that, together, they were a formidable negotiating force, and were comfortable wielding that power where their interests were shared. In terms of the Tory–Lib Dem dynamic, consider that at the outset, before the first formal meeting had taken place, Coulson did not know who the Lib Dem's chief negotiator, Jonny Oates, was. Things have changed. Within days of the election, the two men found themselves sharing an office in Downing Street.

The main parties were not overtly patronising towards the Lib Dems, but the nature of the negotiations was such that the third party was less involved in the most heated discussions. Oates and Lena Pietsch (Nick Clegg's Press Secretary who accompanied him) had a vital, but limited brief. They were charged with maintaining a single key principle: parity. Parity of airtime, parity of stature, not a hint of being the junior partner – that was what it was all about. When it came to discussions about the make-up of the audience, the themes of questioning, the duration of leaders' answers (all of which detained the negotiators for hours at a time), the Liberal Democrats were pretty much unbothered either way.

In one or two respects, the Lib Dem position on TV debates foreshadowed the approach the party would adopt to the coalition talks, months later. Both times, in the immediate negotiation as long as the party were thought to be playing fair (or fair enough!) and were not caught out being obviously disingenuous, they had little to fear. There were the red lines of course.

For debate parity in November 2009, read the alternative vote (AV) in May 2010. There were risks. But in the case of the debates, they were further down the track. Nick Clegg might have bombed in the debates (he never seemed to think it likely, mind) . . . but far more problematic is the looming possibility that the Lib Dems might one day find themselves blamed for the evils of the coalition.

With less at stake in the short term, and with their eyes for the main prize, the Lib Dems seemed more clear-sighted than their opponents. The detail was all for Labour and the Conservatives, but entwined in the clauses and sub-clauses as they were, the blue and red negotiators committed significant errors. Labour's howler nearly derailed the whole process. It was the middle of February. Things looked to be OK. The BBC, ITV and Sky were scouting for venues. Dates were tentatively set. With the agreement of the political parties, lots were drawn for the order of the debates, and the themes. It would be ITV first, home affairs; then Sky News, foreign affairs; the BBC concluding with the economy (the schedule that we eventually saw play out over three weeks of the campaign).

So far, so good. Only it transpired Gordon Brown had not planned it that way. The Prime Minister had intended to demonstrate his mastery of the economic brief at the outset of the debate process, not the end. The economy. Number one. First up. His negotiators had missed a trick. The broadcasters got wind of Downing Street's displeasure when Labour's man David Muir was forced to admit face to face that he had simply not understood that lots were to be drawn for the themes of the debates. Muir wanted the process to be reopened. The response? No dice.

In the ensuing maelstrom (which spread over weeks, and contributed to not a few sleepless nights for politicians and television executives alike), the three TV partners felt obliged to offer a compromise package. Home affairs coupled with the economy in the first debate (to keep Gordon sweet); foreign affairs next as planned; and a free debate to finish. Labour signed up. But the Conservatives' Andy Coulson would not wear it.

Coulson won that battle – the critical trial of strength – but his touch was not immaculate. In moments of self-deprecation he may confess to a desire to control things too much. But it is not a fault that he tries particularly hard to remedy. In the detailed debate negotiations, it felt like there was not a pie without a Coulson finger embedded in it. A particular preoccupation was the role and make-up of the audience. First he objected to the proposed equal number of Conservative and Labour voters in the rigorously regimented panel of spectators. The Tories felt that their poll lead entitled them to an increased representation. On this, he was beaten back. The Conservatives' general concern was that the responses of the privileged few people in the studio audience should not influence the wider viewing public. This resulted in a battery of tight controls being imposed, including the insistence that the watching public should be silent through-out the main proceedings. This could be interpreted as a safety-first tactic, designed to head off the possibility of an error being magnified by audience reaction or, potentially equally damaging, a barnstorming speech by one of Cameron's opponents sparking enthusiastic applause in the studio.

In the event, the spectators in Manchester, Bristol and Birmingham found themselves more tightly constrained than perhaps any television audience before them. They were permit-ted to clap politely at the outset and the close, but not at any other time. Laughter, or any other type of physical engagement with the event was discouraged. The result, for the participants, was an atmosphere of painful artificiality. The irony was that David Cameron, in particular, hated it.

The Conservative leader's main form of preparation for the event was entirely different. It was misconceived and, as events forced him to recognise, not helpful. 'Cameron Direct' was a town hall-style meeting, an event that he relished so much that it was maintained even once the Conservatives took office. (The title became the grander 'PM Direct'.) The reason David Cameron enjoyed the format was simple – he is a politician who feeds off a good audience. Whether with journalists or the general public throughout the campaign, Cameron relished close interaction, and he managed to express himself with real passion and vehemence (something his advisors had hoped he might replicate in the television studio), only when sparked by an interesting question or remark. The debate audiences were simply not up to the job; through no fault of their own, but because of the conditions and limitations that Cameron's own team had fought to put in place.

By contrast, Nick Clegg's preparation was spot on. The Liberal Democrat leader had known from the start that the first debate would be a make or break moment for him. He was determined not to let the opportunity go to waste. The peculiarities of the debate format were something only the Lib Dems convincingly got to grips with. That was no accident. Theirs was the only party that turned the rehearsal process into a science.

From the moment it had become apparent that the chances of debates actually happening this time were strong, right back during the conference season of 2009, the Lib Dems pressed ahead. Spaces were booked to allow for formal rehearsal at such varied locations as Amnesty International, Birkbeck College and the Mothers' Union (which was quickly to become an old favourite). Cameras were wheeled in to replicate the studio environment, music stands substituted for lecterns. Lena Pietsch's background as a television producer was crucial here. Clegg's press spokeswoman knew the paramount importance of connecting with the TV audience, and trialled an approach whereby the Liberal Democrat leader would spend much of his time looking not at the questioner or the moderator, but straight into the lens of the camera – in effect straight at the television viewer at home. There were discussions as to whether the fixity of the Clegg expression might come across as 'creepy', but on balance it was decided that it worked. Equally, it became clear that moments where their man might have seemed to ham things up excessively in the room in fact translated remarkably successfully when reviewed on tape.

Such forensic preparation was always going to be a problem for the Labour team, because Gordon Brown did not have the patience or the flexibility to accommodate himself to the studio surroundings. At first, despite the fact that the debates went ahead on his say-so, there were problems persuading the Prime Minister of the need to knuckle down and prepare for them.

An intensive schedule of 'debate camps' was eventually agreed, with Alastair Campbell as David Cameron, a young researcher, Theo Bertram, playing Clegg, and one of the two debate negotiators, David Muir, as the moderator. The events, which took place in Downing Street, Labour headquarters, and then successively in hotel suites close to each debate venue itself, were a chastening experience for those involved.

The expectations of many of those who had been at Gordon Brown's side for years were not high from the start. Past experience showed that exhaustive prepping was of little value. Presentational advice usually went out the window the moment he opened his mouth; and with it, spontaneity and personal engagement. 'You can see him, he starts to draw down his answers as though they're on file cards,' a friend confided. From this perspective, it was probably better to concentrate on those elements that could be controlled, like making sure his tie was straight.

Beyond that, there was widespread recognition that blitzing Gordon Brown with help and ideas confused him, and made him forget even those things he could handle adequately. The horrifying 'YouTube Address' recorded in Downing Street at the height of the expenses crisis was a prime example of Gordon Brown really listening, and trying to do what was asked of him – in short, desperately striving to do the 'communication thing'. Of course, car-crash did not do it justice. The strange grin hoisted into place at all the wrong moments ended up as the Conservatives' most effective attack poster during the election campaign.

Remembering the YouTube fiasco, not everyone was over the moon when Michael Sheehan, the ex-Clinton advisor flown in at great expense to make sure it was all right on the night, spent much of his time telling his man to smile. 'Gordon!' he would shout to remind the Labour leader to lighten his demeanour, flicking both his wrists skywards with a flourish to mimic the necessary upturn on the corners of the mouth.

The debate preparation was painful at times. Brown knew as well as anyone that he was out of his depth. His original hope, that this format would allow him to speak unmediated to the British public, freed of the distorting lens of the media, was quickly forgotten. Some said it was like watching a performing bear chained to a post. He would try to morph into 'Primetime Gordon', with results so excruciating that observers did not know whether to laugh or cry. In an effort at connecting with the audience at home, Brown's suggested first opening gambit was to thank the viewers for watching the debate 'rather than *Strictly Come Ballroom*'. (Even if he had got the title right, *Strictly Come Dancing* goes out on Saturdays, not Thursday nights.) And put yourself in the place of the aide who had to explain to the Prime Minister that his favoured idea for a debate slogan, in stentorian tones, to be repeated again and again – 'I have a plan' – made him sound like Baldrick? (Then having to explain at length who Baldrick is?) Tricky.

Not surprisingly, as the first event approached, expectations on the Labour side were low. 'Even if Gordon does brilliantly and the other two are much worse than we expect, he'll still lose,' Peter Mandelson told colleagues. 'Clegg will be the "surprise winner",' another weary supporter predicted. 'Gordon's answers will be too long. He's going to go into too much policy detail, try to cram too much in.'

In the event, neither assessment proved to be far off the mark. The night may have been a particular disappointment for the Conservatives given the high expectations surrounding David Cameron, but for Labour, the debate was a confirmation of all that Brown's colleagues had feared. His discomfort in the artificial surroundings of a TV studio was undisguised; his pre-prepared lines sounded pre-prepared, and even the joke he attempted (thanking David Cameron and Lord Ashcroft, the controversial Tory donor, for plastering smiling images of him across the country) was so awkward that there was laughter only when the moderator abruptly cut him off. Gordon Brown did not have the X-factor.

In contrast, of course, Nick Clegg positively shone. His projection to the television audience was total, with an apparently unwavering (mostly unblinking) focus on the camera when the moment was right. But sensing an opportunity to interact with the people in front of him he would seize it, proving able to flick on the full Clegg charm for the studio audience in a manner that was disarming even for those watching at home. (A key example was at the end, when he thanked and name-checked every questioner, having carefully noted them down as the programme progressed.)

Being able to speak first (they had drawn lots some days earlier) was a major bonus, and the Liberal Democrat leader set the terms with his very first words: 'I believe the way things are is not the way things have to be. You're going to be told tonight by these two that the only choice you can make is between two old parties who've been running things for years. I'm here to persuade you there is an alternative.' Over ninety minutes, neither David Cameron nor Gordon Brown, 'these two', as he put it, managed to escape the pigeonhole into which Nick Clegg had so neatly slotted them.

Given Gordon Brown's dark temperament, he had no difficulty accepting he had lost. As he returned to the room where his closest associates had been watching the broadcast, the Prime Minister sank down, banged his fist on a table and declared, 'That was terrible.'

The Conservative reaction was more upbeat. The realisation of what was about to overtake him only slowly dawned on David Cameron. As late as midnight, when he shared a drink in his Manchester hotel with George Osborne, Andy Coulson and his deputy chief of staff, Kate Fall, Cameron was far from despondent: 'I thought I did pretty well,' he told his friends. 'I didn't screw up, and I hit some of the bells I wanted to hit . . .' It was not good enough, as the next morning's papers would show.

Everyone knew the media reaction to the event would be as important as the broadcast itself, and so Labour, the Tories and the Lib Dems had gone into battle when the transmission was over (in fact they pitched in even before the leaders had finished), in the bear pit they called the 'spin room', the bastard child of the leaders' debates. Live pictures of the parties' various masters of the dark arts weaving their spells over hordes of ravenous hacks, most of whom were hard up against a deadline, were broadcast. It was hard to know which of the two events the political classes were more excited by.

From Mandelson and Campbell onwards, anyone who had ever spun for Labour took to the barricades (except Damian McBride of course). In terms of sheer theatre and panache, George Osborne and Andy Coulson could not compete. Nor could the Liberal Democrats, but then, they did not need to. The irony was the whole festival of briefing was redundant. Right from the start, the realisation that this was Clegg's night was steadily dawning on the press pack. But the release of snap polls as the broadcast concluded removed any scope for doubt.

With hindsight, one can wonder whether one or two of the instant polls were all they were cracked up to be. *The Times* with Clegg on 61 per cent; Cameron 22 per cent and Brown 17 per cent? Come on . . . But their instant publication certainly did a job for the Liberal Democrats. It meant nobody questioned the view that Nick Clegg had, overwhelmingly, claimed victory. The polls fed straight into the front pages, which were unlike anything the Lib Dems have enjoyed before or since. ('Enter the Outsider' from *The Times* was a particular favourite of Nick Clegg's team.)

The Conservatives, having pushed to make the debates happen, and having entered the process with such high hopes, suddenly found themselves confronted with a full-blown crisis. The first debate was always likely to take on particular significance, and this truly was the game-changing moment of the campaign. As Michael Gove puts it, 'The impact in the 24 or 48 hours after the debate was certainly greater than anyone had expected. When the media move as a herd in one direction, the noise is tremendous, and it looks terrifying.'

The party polls were a key contributor to the perception that the campaign had entered a radically different phase. They were startling. The Lib Dem tally leaped at the expense of both their rivals, and did not seem to want to slip back. Initially, Labour reacted with glee that the Conservative leader had come a cropper. Among the party's high command, having failed to dent the Conservative lead in the first week of the campaign, the feeling in the immediate aftermath of the debate was that a new narrative, whatever the new narrative, was all to the good. Only later did the realisation begin to sink in that the third party was doing rather too well for comfort. It did not do a great deal for morale in Victoria Street when the odd poll showed the Liberal Democrats in second place. As the days progressed, voices were increasingly raised questioning whether it was necessarily the case that success for the Liberal Democrats would be sure to hurt the Conservatives more than Labour. There had been polls circulated internally showing that for every vote Labour might lose to the Lib Dems, the Conservatives would lose two. A few days further down the track towards polling day, it did not feel so clear cut.

For Labour candidates who were most obviously in the Liberal Democrat firing line (and who had been thrown into a tailspin by the party's abrupt surge), the reaction from party HQ was nothing short of bewildering. Peter Mandelson instructed his colleagues that they should tell the media they were 'insouciant' following the debate. Quite apart from the fact that some 'do' insouciance better than others (and Mandelson is undoubtedly at the right end of that particular scale), one can easily imagine the sense of betrayal on the ground. Put yourself in the position of Emily Thornberry for example (who managed in the end to protect and actually increase her majority over the Liberal Democrats in Islington South and Finsbury), or Dawn Butler (who went down to Sarah Teather in Brent Central), when they, feeling rather less than insouciant, were treated to a barrage of what sounded very much like complacency from senior figures in the national media.

Cleggmania was taking hold in earnest. The organisers of Nick Clegg's campaign, who had become used to the company of the same dutiful band of hacks, suddenly found there were new faces along for the ride. On the Saturday morning two days after the debate, what had been planned as a routine hospital visit in Kingston-upon-Thames turned into bedlam, with a burgeoning press corps surrounding Nick Clegg and his wife, Miriam, desperate to get their piece of the action. With the polls showing the 'Third Party' in second place, the media narrative had swung their way. The papers were clamouring to get an exclusive with the man of the moment . . . there was sudden international interest (Who is this Nick Clegg?), and unlike the Conservative campaign in particular where the accompanying journalists and cameras were kept to a bare minimum throughout, the Liberal Democrats turned no one away. A second battle bus was hired.

On the same Saturday morning Nick Clegg was battling through the scrum in Kingston, David Cameron cut a solitary figure in early morning sunshine standing next to his own bus ('Vote For Change') in a Travelodge car park on the outskirts of Gloucester. Dressed in weekend casuals, the usual black jeans, slip-ons, black shirt and navy jumper (despite the anticipated heat), the Conservative leader was waiting for the go-ahead to drive to a rally in the centre of the city – a rally at which he would signal a change of tack in the campaign, an assault on the dangers of a hung parliament.

As he stood, a local man and his son happened by – a quick camera-phone shot for the teenager with the man likely to be the next Prime Minister. The hotel receptionist emerged, a young woman, bleach-blonde and with vivid blue eyeliner, and struck up conversation. She was anxious. A single mother, her fear was that the Conservatives planned to take away the tax credits on which she depended. David Cameron spent a few minutes endeavouring to reassure her – earnest and sincere, the sort of thing Cameron does best. It was not clear she was convinced. Boarding the bus, the Tory leader confided, 'I get that all the time', blaming Labour for spreading lies about his party's true intentions. He was a frustrated man.

But external frustration was the least of it. In private, David Cameron was in a serious flap. Getting beaten by Nick Clegg? He felt he had let the party down. Sleepless nights and all – this was a full-blown crisis of conscience. 'What have I done?' Cameron asked himself. Later he would tell friends how he would start from his sleep haunted by the thought of those whose careers he had damned: 'Oh my God! Oliver Letwin . . . ! He's finished!' (Letwin, one of the most trusted and well-liked figures in Cameron's entourage, might be able to laugh at the thought now, but sitting on a paper-thin constituency majority as he was, he would have had just as many 'sweaty nights' as his leader professes to have endured.)

Neither Cameron nor his colleagues had realised the critical importance of laying down a marker in the first debate. As Michael Gove put it, when the Tories prepared, the feeling had been that 'Clegg would do better than expected, but not stunningly better than David'. That judgement proved not to be too far wrong when the performances were evaluated dispassionately. But such was the importance of the first debate in dictating the agenda of the election, that the small amount of ground David Cameron lost on his Liberal Democrat rival over ninety minutes of television seemed to open up into an unbridgeable chasm within a matter of hours.

All involved in the Conservative preparation for the debate came to recognise their focus was skewed fatally towards Labour, and Gordon Brown. It was an attitude that can be traced all the way back to the genesis of the process, when David Cameron and his advisors pushed the case for televised debates partly out of undoubted and deep-seated conviction, and partly intoxicated by the immediate political advantage they could draw. The idea was to contrast David Cameron, upfront and eager to take on all-comers, with 'dithering' and indecisive Gordon Brown, thereby reawakening memories of Brown's darkest moment, the 'election that wasn't' of autumn 2007. 'Bring it on,' was Cameron's clarion cry. 'I can't work out whether he's dithering or bottling.'

As the big day approached, fear of a knockout blow from Brown's 'big clunking fist' was all consuming 'We were so focused on the Labour problem,' admits one of the architects of the campaign. The problem was, how to win the debate against the sitting Prime Minister. 'We thought the only way Labour could get back in the race was with a stellar performance by Gordon Brown in the debate. That was the way we had talked about losing the election.'

But what about the other bloke? From start to finish, the Conservatives had a Nick Clegg-sized blind spot. Peter Mandelson has told friends that when he sat down in private with Andy Coulson and Ed Llewellyn right at the beginning – just the two main parties getting together to agree the ground rules – the Conservatives had no real clue why they wanted the Liberal Democrats involved. Labour were keen to have Clegg on stage because they thought he would be difficult for Cameron to deal with, and there was the likelihood the Conservative leader would, in certain important policy areas, find himself isolated. ('But I didn't expect Nick to over-perform,' Mandelson lamented later.)

The Conservatives' own rehearsals had clearly demonstrated that Nick Clegg would be troublesome for them. Jeremy Hunt, then Shadow Culture Secretary, had a whale of a time impersonating the Liberal Democrat leader – all smarm and sanctimony. The general assessment was that the format gave Clegg an inbuilt advantage, and that he would successfully be able to play the two 'establishment candidates' off against one another. During one run-through, Cameron, exasperated at his inability to land a blow on the leader of the third party, threw down his pen and exclaimed, 'How do I deal with this guy?'

As one of the most senior figures in David Cameron's entourage puts it, 'We identified the Clegg problem in the rehearsals. We kept saying at the end of these rehearsals, "Oh we've got a Nick Clegg problem . . ." but then that it'll be all right on the night.'

There may have been one or two doubts about the strategy in the Tory camp, but they were put aside before the big day dawned. One evening shortly before the whole thing kicked off, David Cameron's Press Secretary Gabby Bertin and the Head of the Tory Press Office Henry Macrory bumped into a couple of Gordon Brown's close advisors, Stewart Wood and Tom Price, in the corridors of the Palace of Westminster. Both had been briefing journalists in the parliamentary press gallery on their respective versions of the days ahead. On such occasions, a certain camaraderie can cross party lines. Bertin jokingly wondered out loud whether they were missing a trick regarding Clegg: 'I'm not sure we're getting this expectation management business right . . . ?' Wood and Price were fatalistic. 'We've had thirteen years of Gordon on the telly to manage expectations for us,' they joked.

But when the Conservative spin doctors came to brief journalists in the hours before the debate, the focus was once again

Brown, all Brown. 'Don't forget he's a formidable opponent,' was the constant refrain. 'Labour has been running an effective underdog strategy.' (Oh right?) There was a reference to the likelihood of David Cameron facing a barrage from both his opponents, but aside from that, Nick Clegg barely got a look-in.

Recriminations are not the style of David Cameron and his team. But miscalculating on such a scale was a serious blow to the confidence of the party. It took a while to recover. The days after the debate were hugely disconcerting for party workers as they looked to their election chiefs for a new lead. The foot soldiers in Millbank Tower could see that the usual suspects were meeting – Osborne, Coulson, Steve Hilton . . . – but there was little evidence of a clear, new direction to take. For a short time the campaign felt rudderless. It was dispiriting. Out on the leader's tour, journalists were informed that, in all likelihood, Nick Clegg would win the debate again the week after, and again the week after that. What might a few days before have sounded like expectation management now carried the whiff of defeatism.

Key figures in the Tory leadership circle admit they were thrown. It was, as one of David Cameron's closest colleagues says, 'A disorienting period . . . It was a shock. The important thing was that in the aftermath we didn't make any mistakes. Yes, obviously it was disorientating, but it wasn't the case that anybody lost their heads.'

David Cameron is commendably protective of his troops, and prefers subsequently (knowing that things turned out all right in the end!) to take much of the blame on himself. He maintains that the campaign team did not miss a beat. It is true that by the Monday after the debate, the Tories had successfully negotiated a major change in strategy without (as Cameron would say) a wheel coming off. Now they concentrated their fire on 'deep Labour marginals' thought to be newly vulnerable in the North of England. Lib Dem policies were targeted, and a whole new poster campaign commissioned, viewed within 'Team Cameron' circles as 'gritty' and 'impactful' – a photograph of him, sleeves rolled up and animated at a recent campaign event. In big bold white lettering were key slogans like 'Let's restore discipline in schools', and 'Let's scrap ID cards'.

But as David Cameron walked up the steps of his battle bus in Gloucester two days after the first debate, all that was still to come. Cameron had been receiving calls from friends and political allies, sensing he needed a lift. 'We all tried to cheer him up,' one explains. 'I rang him the weekend afterwards and said, "You know, you have ups and downs in elections, but it's all still there – you can still do it."'

The Conservative leader's mood was reflective. Of course, those ninety minutes were still dominating his thoughts. 'I wanted to come across with clarity, certainty. Passion . . . ? Yes.' He thought back on his performance. There was an acknowledgement that he had only begun to relax 'about three questions in' (i.e. after around half an hour!) . . . mild irritation too that the moderator Alastair Stewart had cut him off once or twice: 'I was terribly polite and did what I was told', whereas Gordon just ploughed on through regardless. And the Lib Dems? Of course, the debate process gives the third party a boost. 'There's nothing you can do about it.'

This morning, he was preparing to shake things up a bit. With Soccer AM on the televisions inside the battle bus, Cameron studied a single page of handwritten notes and listened obediently as Gabby Bertin took him through the Gloucester basics – the candidate, the majority, and so on and so forth. The idea had come to him in the middle of the night, he said, not to attack the Liberal Democrats head on, but to attack the idea of a hung parliament, calling on people who wanted a decisive victory to turn to the Tories. (It was not startlingly original: for months sections of the Tory press had been urging him to do the very same.)

A stump speech by the red-brick docks was the occasion to showcase his argument. It was one of Cameron's stronger performances. When he strains his voice amid the balloon-carrying faithful (to the point of hoarseness), it loses the reedy, plaintive note that can otherwise afflict his delivery. At least this audience was not mute. 'Is five more years of Gordon Brown going to get things done?' he asked rhetorically. 'Nooooo', they bellowed back. 'Is a hung parliament going to get things done? The hell it will . . .' (and look where he is now!) Less than ten minutes, and it was done. Hands to shake, then back into the Jaguar. David Cameron had signalled a new phase to the Conservative campaign: an attempt to set fresh terms for the remaining weeks before polling day.

As the leader's tour turned across the Cotswolds towards David Cameron's Witney constituency – a school visit and a photo-call of Cameron buying flowers (it being his wife Samantha's birthday) – it occurred to Gabby Bertin that they had forgotten something. The night before she had briefed the media about the Conservatives' 'Public Sector Manifesto' telling them the new proposals would be launched by Cameron in the morning with much Big Society-style fanfare. You could see the whole thing laid out in a few small paragraphs on page 2 of the *Sun* – 'Cameron's Plan For People Power' . . . 'Revolutionary plans to give millions of public sector workers the chance to be their own boss.' It was a revolution that would have to wait. The Public Sector Manifesto had completely slipped David Cameron's mind. He, and his party, had other fish to fry.

5

THE DEBATES by Adam Boulton

'Mr Clegg, you're on the front page of the *Telegraph* today?'

In the late spring of 2009, the Head of Sky News John Ryley sent out an email for discussion. With the general election now imminent and inevitable he wondered what Sky News could do to combat voter apathy. We would be committing a large proportion of our resources to covering the campaign and it's fair to say that John was concerned both as a citizen and a TV boss that fewer people, especially younger ones, seemed to be taking an interest – as reflected in two decades of falling voter turnout.

John wanted to use our resources and power as a TV channel to try to boost public interest in the electoral process and we talked about a number of options, including a celebrity-led 'use your vote' campaign. However, we quickly concluded that it was not our role to be prescriptive; people had a perfect right not to vote and we shouldn't make them feel bad about it. (Since I don't vote myself in an effort to sharpen my professional political impartiality, I strongly agreed with this argument.)

However, we all agreed that TV debates during the campaign would certainly make the best use of our medium to increase interest in the election, without making viewers feel guilty or alienated if they chose not to cast a ballot in the end.

Ryley committed both to writing to the three main party leaders to invite them to participate and to launching what became the 'Sky News Leaders' Debate' campaign when the political year started again in early September. He also decided to write simultaneously to the Welsh and Scottish Nationalists promising to hold debates in Scotland and Wales during the election campaign which would be transmitted to the entire Sky News audience.

But how to bring the debates about? The first Presidential Debate had taken place in America all the way back in 1960. But British broadcasters had failed to get the party leaders to take each other on in any of the dozen general elections in the intervening half-century since then.

Personally I had felt keenly that British broadcasters were letting the public down from before I started working in television as a political journalist in the early eighties. I had been involved in numerous attempts to get debates going since then at a very junior level – and, my word, didn't the BBC and ITV like to make the companies I worked for (TV-am and Sky News) feel junior?

These experiences had taught me that the influential, hard-bitten political advisors would always tell the front runner, 'Don't do it. Why take the risk?' And that the ducker would not take much flak since they could blame the broadcasters for failing to agree amongst themselves on viable rules. Both Michael Dobbs and Tim Bell explained how ITV and the BBC would come through the front door to make a common pitch, retuning later by the back door to bid against each other for an exclusive.

(Given that Margaret Thatcher was for debating and Bell didn't want her to do it, he found it very useful to simply tell her that there was no agreement on how it should happen.)

So we at Sky News decided that we would not approach the other broadcasters in advance about our plans. But we knew from the start that we regarded an election debate as so important that we would share it with our competitors by working with them to establish the debates jointly or by making our programme available to them for simultaneous broadcast, live as it was happening.

Without telling anyone else, the BBC had already put out feelers to the main parties inviting them to take part in test debates on the BBC well before the campaign started. (Apart from rather missing the point, this resulted in the Brown camp's irritating demands during the negotiations: 'Why can't we start right away?' Surely an election debate should be at election time, when parliament is not sitting?) In July ITV and the BBC also belatedly invited Sky News to a meeting scheduled for October to discuss debates, an invitation which was then withdrawn when Ryley went public.

It is possible that this lumbering, bureaucratic and internally competitive process would have brought about the debates in 2010 without Sky's unilateral initiative but I doubt it. The BBC felt constrained by their charter as to how far they would go. They stated that they did not consider it to be their role 'to campaign' for debates, and also refused to 'empty chair' any of the leaders who might decide to not participate. Having steadily run down its news and current affairs content for the past decade (with the abolition of such brands as *World in Action*, *This Week*, *First Tuesday*, *Weekend World*, *Dimbleby* and (temporarily at least) *News at Ten*), ITV was ambivalent about the whole idea of debates. Unlike either the BBC or Sky News, ITV's position was that it would not share debates. To get onto the network in primetime (its peak revenue-earning period), ITV's debate would have to be exclusive to the channel, executives insisted. Somewhat dog in the manger, the message from ITV was that they weren't particularly bothered if the debates didn't happen. But the decaying giant's self-regard demanded that it should have a big slice of the action if they did. (ITV's luck held. They won the drawing of lots between broadcasters, and chose to host the first ever TV debate.)

Sky News was bound by neither self-conscious public service ethics nor selfish commercial considerations. We wanted the debates, were prepared to campaign for them and would share what we brought about.

David Cameron had consistently campaigned for political debates since even before becoming leader: 'I have a general view that you have to have TV debates. I pushed it hard as far back as the debates with David Davis [in 2005 for the Conservative leadership].' He had repeatedly challenged Gordon Brown to debate 'anywhere, any how, any time.'

But by the summer of 2009, Cameron was the runaway favourite to win the next election – would he still commit himself to the Sky News debate campaign or 'not take the risk'?

On a hot July day in St James's Park, Andy Coulson, Cameron's communications director, had lunch with Sky News' executive producer at Westminster, Jonathan Levy, and me. We forewarned him about the campaign we were planning, as we did his Labour and Liberal Democrat opposite numbers around the same time. We had one simple question for Coulson: would Cameron commit himself to the Sky News Leaders' Debate, and take part in it, even if Gordon Brown failed to agree to? In other words, if it came to it, would the Conservative leader debate with the Liberal Democrat leader alone during the election campaign? Coulson agreed . . . with one proviso: only if Sky News would say publicly that Brown had been invited to take part. This was no problem for us because we were already committed to pursuing our campaign with maximum openness.

Of course we always wanted Gordon Brown to take part in the debates but Sky News was prepared to go further than any other TV company to ensure that finally election debates of at least some sort took place. Our intention was to increase the pressure to participate on any leader who was holding back. With the repeal of the Representation of the People Act's provisions on broadcasters, the Labour government had deliberately made it easier to produce election programmes. Provided that the TV company showed the intent to treat candidates fairly, a single candidate could no longer shut down a programme entirely by turning down an invitation to take part in it themselves. We simply decided to take advantage of this new freedom, and apply it right at the top of the political hierarchy. With Cameron and Clegg's agreements, Sky News was able to say that a Leaders' Debate would take place in 2010 whether Brown took part or not. If we had to, we would transmit a debate in primetime featuring two of the three main party leaders, something that both the BBC and ITV would have been most unlikely to undertake.

Given that Cameron replaced Brown as Prime Minister and that Clegg became Deputy Prime Minister in a coalition government, one of the dogs that didn't bark was the inclusion of the third man, Clegg, in the debates.

Based on what had happened in previous elections, Sky News assumed from the outset that a two-man debate excluding the Lib Dems was a non-starter. The Liberal Democrats and their predecessors had been ready and able to go to law before, and would do so again with a strengthening case given their growing representation around the country. It was not practical for the leaders to debate in pairs (Brown/Cameron, Brown/Clegg, Cameron/

Clegg) – because parity of audiences could not be guaranteed for each programme. Although he would have liked to have a debate just between the two potential Prime Ministers, Cameron rapidly decided that such an argument would be a distraction from bringing the debates about. Labour did not make an issue of it either once proper negotiations began – doubtless for similar reasons. To begin with Labour were worried that the two opposition parties might gang up on Brown, but by the time the election was in sight it seemed more likely that the two 'progressive' leaders would in practice form an alliance against Cameron. (After the election both camps admitted that they had expected a 'Clegg factor' but had dramatically underestimated just how big it would be.)

Peter Mandelson claimed subsequently that Gordon Brown decided to take part in debates at around the time that Sky News was planning its initiative. Brown was widely expected to make an announcement on his participation the centrepiece of his 2009 party conference speech – but he didn't. Perhaps he felt that the Sky campaign had deprived him of the initiative. In any case it resulted in a bad-tempered live interview with me the next morning, not helped by the *Sun* newspaper's decision that day to switch its allegiance after twelve years of supporting Labour and instead endorse Cameron at the next election. When I pressed Brown on the debates, he accused me of 'sounding a bit like a political propagandist' myself, which was fair enough as far as the debates were concerned, but I certainly had nothing to do with the decision of the *Sun*, Sky's cousin, to switch sides. Our interview took place in a public space with other reporters looking on – the floor of the conference hall. Once it was over on air, Brown appeared to glower for an uncomfortable interval and then, in spite of my attempting to help, he tried to walk off without first detaching his microphone. The *Evening Standard* splashed with

'Brown in TV meltdown', and versions of the interview rapidly became hits on YouTube. One lesson I have learnt in my career is that every interview is worth the effort because the exchanges that have the most impact are almost always unanticipated.

Three weeks later on a Saturday afternoon, Number 10 put out a statement that the Prime Minister would take part in election debates with Cameron and Clegg. David Muir, one of Brown's special advisors, called me with the news. By now the BBC, ITV and Sky News had patched up their differences and joint negotiating sessions with the three parties began soon afterwards, as we discuss in the previous chapter. Undoubtedly the combined authority of the three main news broadcasters, and the variety of committee room skills which each brought to the talks greatly increased their chances of success.

The talks were left to off-screen executives and I played no part in them. Quite properly, if somewhat to my chagrin, the Sky Team of Jonathan Levy and Chris Birkett didn't even keep me up to speed on how the talks were going. On 21 December 2009, much to my relief, the politicians and the TV producers released a joint statement that they had agreed in principle that the debates would take place.

John Ryley confirmed that I would be the moderator for Sky News, along with David Dimbleby for the BBC and Alastair Stewart for ITV. (Channel 4 had joined the broadcasters' consortium and then decided to withdraw. Instead, Channel 4's Krishnan Guru-Murthy hosted the first election debate of 2010 between the economic spokesmen George Osborne, Alistair Darling and Vince Cable.)

It took several months more before the detailed guidelines were agreed between the parties and the broadcasting teams. Press comment made much of the so-called seventy-six rules, but in fact the four-page document was remarkably brief compared to the guidelines for similar debates abroad. The rules allowed each broadcaster to express its personality. I wasn't surprised that the newspapers were so grudging – in my view securing the debates marked the moment when live television became the dominant medium in British elections, forever relegating the printed press to a secondary role.

In any case, I was amused that none of the key protagonists – debaters or moderators – appeared to have paid much attention to what the guidelines had actually said. Both Alastair Stewart and David Dimbleby gave print interviews in which they called for 'the gloves to come off' in a way that would have been a clear violation of the agreement. More amusingly still, Cameron and Clegg both affected disdain for the rules which their advisors had fought for so long and hard.

Sky News staged our biggest debate rehearsal in HTV's studios in Cardiff. On the train home, we found ourselves by chance in the same, largely empty (second class) carriage as Nick Clegg who had been out on campaign stops. Clegg said that he had been rehearsing as well and that he didn't understand why after a minute each to answer the question, there was a second 'rebuttal round' also of a minute each. Birkett and Levy were amused – it transpired that the Liberal Democrat team had insisted on the rebuttal round, because they wanted the maximum amount of time allocated on an equal basis to avoid their man being squeezed.

Just as the election campaign was getting underway, I recorded an interview with Cameron in a pub in Witney. By this time he was pawing at the ground, and expressed the view that the tight rules and ban on audience participation might make the debates 'boring'. Here again I knew that the greatest sensitivity amongst all the parties was to circumscribe the make-up and the involvement of the audience, on the grounds that while being shown up by a smartypants TV moderator was bad enough, being carpeted by an ordinary member of the public could have been fatal. There was certainly an element of gamesmanship in Cameron's last-minute championing of the audience: rightly or wrongly, his camp reckoned that any live audience would give the incumbent Prime Minister the hardest time.

Gordon Brown did not lend himself so easily to relaxed chats. But I made a point of talking at length to his main debate advisors David Muir, Justin Forsyth and Patricia McLernon (a former BBC *Newsnight*, *Question Time* and Sky News producer brought in by Sue Nye, and the only member of the team who had any recent direct experience of working in TV) about the practicalities because, as moderator, I saw it as my role to facilitate programmes which worked.

In reality the moderator had far less freedom of action than a routine TV interviewer. The main power held by the broadcaster was to select the questions. We devoted a lot of energy to this. Our viewers' editor Paul Bromley went through more than eight thousand questions submitted online, as well as hundreds submitted by the invited audience. And our question panel, as constituted under the agreed guidelines, met regularly to go through them, including on the day of the Sky Leaders' Debate itself.

One of the weaknesses of debate organisation was that the parties had insisted that the TV companies should have no role in selecting the live audience for the debates. They also stipulated that each audience should come from within a thirty-mile radius of the debate venue and be selected by an independent company, ICM, to reflect gender, ethnic, and class balances. Even though the debates were hot tickets and we all had people clamouring to participate, this restriction meant that the audiences which actually took part mostly reckoned that they were doing us a favour by turning up. All broadcasters experienced quite high levels of drop-out. A significant proportion of these selected audiences were also reluctant to ask questions. Fortunately the broadcasters had extracted the concession that up to four questions could come from their own viewers, brought specially to the venue, if necessary, from outside the catchment area. These extra questioners were automatically engaged and turned out to be vital in broadening the range of questions in all three debates.

We were still juggling the questions for the Sky News debate with just minutes to go until live transmission. My producer, Hannah Thomas-Peter, developed a system of handwritten cue-cards with all the information I needed on them to run the debates. She was less than amused when I dropped the whole pile and she found herself scrabbling around on the floor in the dingy wings of the set, to rearrange them in time before I was called on stage.

Even once the transmission was underway, we shuffled one of the questions we had selected, judging that it had already been answered. There was also some scope in the guidelines for me to introduce relevant material in follow-ups of my own. We had deliberately designed an intimate set, and I was sat, with my back to the audience, just a few yards from each leader standing at his podium.

We had decided in advance that I would have more of a presence as moderator than Alastair had been in the first debate. Unlike him, I had the luxury of a camera trained on me, head-on, at all times. Mostly I called the leaders by name and I could make hand gestures. But I also had eye contact with them, which meant that while one was speaking, I could check if the others were unhappy or wanted to come in.

We had selected the questions carefully; most of them had 'edge'. There were ample openings for each leader to make direct personal attacks on the others if they so chose. But as I listened to the early minutes of the debate, I soon noticed that each leader was passing up the chance to get personal, as if by agreement. Checking with the participants afterwards confirmed that there had been no discussion between them about mutual rules of engagement. Instead it seems that each camp concluded independently that getting nasty with opponents was too risky. It could backfire either by casting the attacker in an unpleasant light or by provoking a more powerful counter-attack. Unlike PMQs in which formalised abuse is part of the sport, the leaders seem to have concluded that the extended, open and balanced format left each participant too exposed to try to stick the knife in.

If the leaders weren't going to mix it I had a problem. The last thing we wanted was an hour and a half of high-minded waffle. Upholding the rules as moderator was one duty, but there was also my responsibility as a professional TV presenter to make sure that it was a topical, sharp, informative and entertaining show.

In the aftermath of the first debate, there was also intensified interest in one of the leaders – Nick Clegg. Coinciding with our debate in Bristol, both of Britain's leading right of centre papers had had a go at Clegg on their front pages. The *Daily Mail* combed through Clegg's comments during his time in Brussels, highlighting an old article by him from 2002 to produce the headline, 'Nick Clegg in Nazi Slur On Britain'. The *Daily Telegraph* went back through files it had acquired on MPs' expenses, and declared 'Nick Clegg Under Pressure To Explain Private Account Donations'.

Given the saliency of political corruption to the 2010 campaign, most news organisations that day, including Sky News, followed up the *Telegraph* story in particular. We had already picked a question on political ethics for the debate: 'Given the scandals of the last year it is hard to find a person in my neighbourhood who believes in the power of their vote. How do you plan to restore faith in this political system?' But once Cameron and Brown had given their answer without referring to the latest news story, I felt that it was right for me as the moderator to raise the topical issue concerning him with Clegg directly, both to give him a chance to answer with millions of people watching and to give the others the opportunity to follow up if they chose. It was a brief exchange.

Adam Boulton: 'Mr Clegg, you're on the front page of the *Telegraph* today?'
Nick Clegg: 'I am indeed for a complete nonsense story. But put that aside – complete, complete rubbish . . .'

I was confident that my action was within the guidelines for the debates which permitted the moderator 'to seek factual clarification if necessary'. Some viewers argued that I had broken Rule 63 'it is not the moderator's role to criticise or comment on the leader's answers', but of course I had neither criticised nor commented and had raised the *Telegraph* before Clegg answered, not afterwards.

Under the guidelines, each TV company had a live hotline during its programme, so representatives of each party could raise matters of concern directly with senior editors. Although both the Liberal Democrats and Labour immediately questioned what I had just done, neither party registered a formal complaint or demanded an on-air comment during the debate. I spoke to Clegg after the programme and he did not raise the matter at all.

For viewers who wished to take the matter further there was a further avenue for complaint – going to the TV regulator Ofcom. Ofcom was not responsible for the guidelines agreed between the parties and the broadcasters but its statutory duty is to uphold the general Broadcasting Code on standards. Ofcom received a total of 671 complaints after the Sky News debate, complaining that I had breached the rules on impartiality.

Ofcom, however, did not uphold the complaints in an emphatic ruling: 'The reference to the newspaper story was seen by some as the presenter seeking an answer to a specific question about Nick Clegg's conduct where similar interventions were not made as regards the other participants. However, this one question by Adam Boulton would not – on its own – in Ofcom's view raise issues concerning due impartiality under the Code. Further, this comment by Adam Boulton should be seen in context. His comment was related to a question posed by a member of the audience to which the party leaders were responding: how to restore faith in the British political system after various "scandals". It should also be noted that *The Sky News Leaders' Debate* was a ninety-minute programme in which all the three leaders had numerous opportunities for each of them to make their points on a range of subjects, and to cross examine each other on those subjects. Given this, it is clear that the programme was presented with due impartiality with all the politicians facing questions from each other and from the audience. We also considered the programme was a serious and detailed debate on a number of political and policy matters during the General Election campaign. One brief comment by a presenter during a ninety-minute programme (to which Nick Clegg had an immediate opportunity to respond) could not in itself reasonably cause the programme to breach the due impartiality requirements under the Code. As such, we considered that the broadcaster did not breach Section Five or Section Six of the Code.'

By the standards John Ryley had set, the debates achieved everything we could have hoped for. The programmes had massive on-the-day audiences of around 10 million, 7 million and 9 million respectively, including the largest ever audience for Sky News. Research showed that most of those viewers stuck with the debates all the way through. The debates indisputably gave primetime exposure to more than four hours of policy discussion for the first time ever in Britain. The Leaders' Debates encouraged people to stage their own debates locally and canvassers reported that this was the first election when they had been welcomed after ringing on the doorbell, to continue discussion about issues raised by the debates. Despite acres of newsprint having been devoted to the electorate's supposed disengagement with politics, voter turnout in 2010 was up by 4 per cent on 2005, and I believe the debates contributed to that.

Our debate campaign was to raise public interest in the general election, not to affect its outcome. As TV professionals we could declare the debates to be an unqualified success – they placed our medium in the dominant role in the campaign, overshadowing both print and the upstart media of online and on phone.

But the fascinating question remained – what impact did the debates have on the way the votes were cast?

In the months after the election numerous symposia took place. The Cameron camp took a minimalist view. They claimed that David Cameron had been responsible for making the debates happen and that was 'the right thing to do' in 2010 and for the future. However, they argued that opinion polls before the campaign ended up being broadly similar to the shares of the vote won on polling day. So not much debate effect: although those Conservatives who feel most proprietorial about them argue that they played a crucial role in preventing a fightback by Labour. The debates, they say, meant that the election was fought on a broad range of campaign themes rather than a relentless series of Labour claims about 'Tory cuts'.

Labour have portrayed Gordon Brown's late decision to become the first serving Prime Minister to participate in the debates as a masterstroke. David Muir, their chief debate nego-tiator, argued, 'Quite simply the debates cost David Cameron his overall majority.' According to this argument, the parity with which the three men were shown in the debates held the front-runner back from widening his lead decisively during the campaign. Labour strategists also believe that the exhaustive programme of three debates eventually allowed Brown to estab-lish himself as a man of substance to Clegg's cost.

The Liberal Democrats do not deny that debating on equal terms with Labour and the Conservatives fulfilled one of their long-term strategic ambitions. With a Liberal Democrat Deputy Prime Minister and a score of Lib Dem ministers, the party also ended up afterwards established in national political life in a way that it had not been for seventy years. Nick Clegg certainly seized his moment, and without his success in the debates, it is difficult to see how this young and comparatively unknown politician could have established his viability and fairly rapid acceptance as a successful DPM.

On the other hand, the Lib Dems did not break through in 2010. They did not hold the heady position of number two in the opinion polls which briefly tantalised them after Clegg's first debate performance. They emerged from the 2010 election with marginally fewer MPs than they went in with, albeit with a moderate increase in their share of the votes.

So Cleggmania wasn't everything. But where would the Liberal Democrats have been without it? Especially with the Middle East wars no longer as hot a topic as they had been in 2005? Without the debates would they have been subject to the long-feared squeeze between an entrenched Labour party and a revitalised Conservative party?

The debates also placed topics at the top of the agenda that party leaders in the past have often chosen to avoid. Political ethics was one of those. Immigration was another. It was the only issue raised in questions in all three debates – and the party leaders were forced to rehearse their policies on this topic at length. In the view of some campaigners from all the main parties, this open discussion of what is often claimed to be a toxic subject contributed to the poor performance of fringe parties, which try to exploit this 'hidden problem'.

From the broadcasters' point of view it was no bad thing that the political consequences of the debates remained uncertain. In Britain, television was supposed to be impartial after laying the issues before the public. There would be constant argument about changing the rules and the format of the debates before the next general election. For sure, if this parliament ran to a full term of five years, meaning that the general election would coincide with Scottish and Welsh parliamentary elections on the same day, the case of the nationalists to be included in some way would be much stronger.

But the BBC, ITV and Sky News agreed, if we did it all again in exactly the same way next time, it would be no bad thing.

6

DECISION TIME

'Whose idea was that?'

Two days after the debate, Nick Clegg took his expanded Lib Dem tour to the marginal seat of Sutton and Cheam. It was a constituency that the Liberal Democrat Chief Whip Paul Burstow had taken from the Conservatives in 1997 with a narrow majority, but a constituency that was under threat from the resurgent Tories. Less than 3,000 votes in arrears, this was the sort of constituency Clegg knew his party had to take in order to secure a parliamentary majority. Already highly significant even before the Manchester earthquake, in the debate's aftermath seats like Sutton and Cheam abruptly felt the key battleground of the 2010 campaign.

David Cameron had visited the same seat exactly a week earlier. A Saturday morning, lots of people out and about shopping – perfect for the Conservative leader's first 'impromptu' walkabout since the election had been called. Impromptu means the media get a bit of notice, as do local Tory activists, but you never know who else might turn up. The disadvantages are obvious . . . the benefits are in terms of genuine spontaneity, and the pleasure of (limited) surprise. David Cameron loves them.

This is one of those parts of Greater London that feels miles from the capital. Classic commuter territory with its busy crossroads, and ranks of 1930s semis, their mock-Tudor beams rising above privet hedges. Ahead of the melee of the leader's arrival, walking with the Conservative candidate, Philippa Stroud, on this sunny April morning, one was told all about the Liberal Democrat problem in this seat. Their vote stayed static, you see? . . . while Conservative support historically had gone up and down depending on the national view of the party. The 2005 Michael Howard vintage left the Lib Dems a slim majority, but Philippa Stroud's feeling was that the Lib Dem cup was full in Sutton and Cheam. There were no more stones to turn in this constituency under which Liberal Democrats might be found. In 2010, she was confident, the Cameron effect would swing the seat in her favour.

And on the morning of the Tory leader's visit, what an effect it was! The scrum was impressive, the best of the campaign so far. Let's be honest, we all enjoy that sort of thing. Microphones flailing, cameramen walking backwards . . . oblivious . . . snappers intemperate ('What about that clean shot you promised!'), questions from all sides. In short, a health and safety nightmare. David Cameron, it had been agreed, would walk down Cheam's high street, drop into one or two shops (not 'David Cameron Hair', gents' hairdressers, the most obvious photo-opportunity. It was on the shady side of the road.). Then shake hands with placard-bearing supporters, a few words, thanks and off. In sum, despite the chaos it went to plan, friendly people, nothing untoward. The one vague embarrassment was when a young girl of around ten years old, who was happened upon by the Cameron posse as she was locking her bicycle to her dad's, innocently enquired why he didn't wear his cycle helmet. Cameron had the decency to look sheepish.

Watching the faces of passers-by on the opposite side of the road is often a most amusing pastime. 'Look who it is!'; 'Did you see what happened to that photographer?' 'You go and talk to him . . .'; 'No, you!' Over the crossing went the ragbag procession, quite indifferent to traffic and traffic lights, and up a slight rise. The car was waiting. Leads and cables were getting elaborately tangled by the time the Jaguar door swung open, a final wave, and closed with an armoured clunk. (Inside a car like that Cameron wouldn't have heard the ripe exclamation from the Sky News sound recordist – 'Oi, he's got my fucking radio mic!')

So David Cameron left Sutton and Cheam buoyed by the experience and full of optimism. But when Nick Clegg rolled up, seven days later, the political weather had changed. Clegg headed for the other part of the seat, Sutton. The enthusiasm on the ground was more intense in this period than anything Clegg had previously experienced, and his team were particularly encouraged by the number of young people who turned out on this specific visit – keen to see the Liberal Democrat leader, keen to find a way of registering their support. Much had been talked about in the run-up to the election of a failure to engage the young. Assuming it was not too late (it had been suggested more than half of 18- to 24-year-olds had in any case failed to register to vote), there was just a chance the Liberal Democrats might be winning over this most untapped section of the electorate. The same weekend, the wildly successful Internet campaign, which had succeeded in foiling the usual *X Factor* Christmas Number One coronation through promotion of a 'spoiler' single by 'Rage Against the Machine', threw its potentially powerful weight behind the Lib Dems. The new campaign 'Rage Against the Election' proved not even to be a one hit wonder. But at the time, it had the Lib Dems thinking they were in vogue, and there was a popular groundswell in their favour.

When the dust settled a couple of weeks later, the Liberal Democrats won Sutton and Cheam. The Conservative vote increased, as Philippa Stroud had anticipated, by around 3,500 votes – more than enough to take her above the Lib Dems had her thesis about their vote topping out been correct. However Paul Burstow for the Liberal Democrats increased his own vote by more than 2,000, and held on. No one could say this particular battle did not excite the electorate. The turnout, of 72.8 per cent, was well above the national average of 65.1 per cent. Not typical? Perhaps not, but on a night of unpredictable swings and unexpected results, nothing was. Philippa Stroud is now Iain Duncan Smith's special advisor at the Department for Work and Pensions. Paul Burstow MP is Minister of State at the Department of Health.

The days following the Manchester debate were frustrating for Labour and the Conservatives alike. The media focus had turned immediately to Bristol, and the Sky News debate that would take place a week later. Nothing else seemed to matter. There was a striking symmetry to the way both the main parties would complain that the debate process had 'sucked the air out of the campaign'. Traditionalists longed for an old-style election where all three sides would stage morning press conferences and stand up to have seven bells knocked out of them by Her Majesty's Press Corps. Labour argued the Conservative failure to lay on such formal media events reflected an unwillingness to subject their policies to sustained scrutiny. But Brown, Darling, Mandelson et al. soon found that when they fronted up for the press, their arguments failed to cut through. It felt as if journalists and politicians alike were going through the motions, as if the whole campaign pantomime had become redundant. The reason was that the overwhelming media narrative was taken up by the debates: who had won, who had lost (and how badly), and how things might be different next time round.

The general feeling of a campaign in stasis was intensified by the surreal ash cloud phenomenon. Ash from the Icelandic volcano Eyjafjallajökull forced all UK flights to be grounded for long periods, causing immense frustration to travellers and politicians alike. David Cameron's and Nick Clegg's identical twin-propeller planes sat idle (not being able to fly was hardly an issue for the cash-strapped, earth-bound Labour team). And while some helicopter flights might have been possible, campaign organisers wisely concluded the watching public (particularly those stranded at airports or struggling to get on some other form of transport) might not take kindly to their prospective leaders blithely bypassing travel restrictions in some posh chopper.

An opportunity was perceived for Labour, who remembered how Gordon Brown had previously flourished in the hothouse arena of disasters both natural and man-made. When newly installed as Prime Minister in the summer of 2007, his assured response to a bout of floods was applauded (while Cameron was criticised for leaving his own flood-hit constituency for a trip to Rwanda), and contributed to the Labour bubble that burst only when he chose to walk away from the possibility of a snap election, the 'election that wasn't'. And Brown's finest hour was without doubt in coordinating the response to the international banking crisis, both domestically and with his efforts to drive through a concerted global programme for dealing with the situation.

Stubbornly, the ash cloud resisted attempts to manufacture a further 'Captain Gordon at the Tiller' moment. Viewed with a campaigning politician's hat on, it was an irritatingly ephemeral and unmanageable crisis, a little resistant to political stimuli one might say. In fact, as became clear subsequently, crisis was perhaps putting it a bit strongly. 'Send for the navy!' went up the cry from Downing Street, a result of the need to be seen to be doing something. Commandeering the *Ark Royal*, for a Dunkirk-style evacuation (though with a bigger boat), was vainglorious gesture politics, expressive of government impotence more than anything else. There was some comically petty point-scoring, mainly over who had originally thought up one hare-brained scheme or another. (As a general rule, Conservative Shadow Transport Secretary Theresa Villiers could be expected to make a strong claim.)

For a mercifully short period, it felt as though the *Today* programme was dominated by high-level political debate over whether Labour could be blamed for the whole thing (in general, government spokesmen were not persuaded by this thesis), or whether Gordon Brown could take credit for Mr and Mrs Miggins and the Miggins brood getting home in one piece (the direction of this debate was not unpredictable either). In the event, the whole thing dissipated, as clouds will. What happened to the hundred coaches despatched post haste to Madrid? Someone must know. But the media had moved on. It was Thursday again – debate time.

Stir crazy David Cameron had at least had the opportunity to get his debate shtick sorted. The tempo of campaigning slowed considerably to allow additional time for rehearsal. The Conservative leader took no persuading to admit he had made what he described as a 'very bad technical mistake' in failing to look at the camera. He would not be caught out again. At the same time, knowing his off-the-cuff flair, close aides warned that excessive concentration on the detail could be counter-productive. 'I keep telling him not to over-prepare,' confided Gabby Bertin. 'He's so much better when he's spontaneous.' Asked the day before the debate whether he needed to be more like Nick Clegg in his performance, Cameron only half-jokingly answered, 'I need to be more like me.'

The Bristol location was the most comfortable for all three leaders – the small theatre of the Arnolfini arts centre on the dockside providing for a tight, intimate set. The audience was close in, making questioners easily identifiable. Nick Clegg was first to visit the set in mid-morning. On a glorious day in the West Country, the Liberal Democrat leader's disposition was equally, and understandably sunny. 'Is this the place?' he enquired, sticking his head in the front entrance even as potted plants and furniture were being carried into the makeshift 'green rooms'. Just a few minutes in the studio and then he was off again, back (as he preferred in the run-up to a debate) to a quiet countryside hotel; windows thrown open and a walk to clear his thoughts.

Gordon Brown's eyesight problems were always a factor in the debate choreography. Whereas Nick Clegg and David Cameron swapped positions each week (the central lectern was coveted by both sides), it was agreed that owing to the Prime Minister's blindness in his left eye, he would stay on camera right, enabling him a clear view of his rivals, the moderator, and the clock which showed how much time he was allotted for an answer. When Brown first visited the Bristol studio, the unusual layout of the stage caused him considerable difficulty (the fact is that for some time Brown has not had a clear picture of what is at ground level as he walks, making events like laying a wreath particularly hazardous and nerve-racking for him), and he tripped into a shallow pit which was subsequently filled in by carpenters. Another change was necessary before the broadcast – a white piece of cardboard, placed around the lens of the 'leaders' camera'. Without it, Gordon Brown would not have been able to discern what he knew must be a key focal point of his attention against the generally dark background of the studio.

David Cameron was last on set, and spent much longer ensuring things were just so. The intense level of concentration underscored how much was resting on this event for the Tories. Cameron spoke only a little – the talking was done by aides including Andy Coulson. Instead, for almost half an hour, he paced the stage; stood at the lectern; looked to camera, to the moderator, to camera again. Within himself, his brow furrowed, Cameron did not notice the helicopter overhead as he was driven the short distance to Bristol's Hotel du Vin. The Conservatives had aimed to keep his location a secret – the chopper, which happened to be available that afternoon, was the only way Sky News had of following him.

Ensconced in his hotel suite, Cameron and the usual team of close associates drank tea and chatted. Those who were with him felt reassured. It was different to a week earlier. Then he had been keyed up and edgy. This time, their man would be more relaxed and (as he hoped) more himself.

In the end this debate would prove to be satisfactory for all three parties. Nick Clegg did not miss a beat, maintaining the high standards set a week earlier; David Cameron stepped up as expected (a smile for the first camera-shot . . . stinging in his attack on Labour 'lies': back in the game!); and Gordon Brown had the most resonant single line ('Get real, Nick'). There was relief all round. Only one more left. Steady as she goes . . .

The cheery tones of Jeremy Vine: 'Someone has just handed me the tape. Let's play it and see if we can hear it.' And the blood runs cold. Gordon Brown was about to be put through the most excruciating moments of his entire political career.

The image is unforgettable. The Prime Minister in a small radio studio, microphone dangling down, apparently unaware of the camera that must be no more than three feet in front of him. As the Radio Two man presses play on a tape machine way down the line in Broadcasting House, you can see Brown jolt back in his seat as though having received an electric shock. It is not hard to imagine what is going through his mind. Oh my God. His jaw drops. You are kidding. The reaction is violent and instinctive, but immediately as he begins to hear his own voice in the headphones, hangdog resignation takes hold. The shoulders turn inward, and Brown's big left paw reaches up to his forehead, shrouding his knotted brow and eyes. Huddled up thus, he endures it in its entirety.

Gillian Duffy day was the most memorable of them all. A day of all-too-human frailty, error and pain. A day from which a vivid clutch of faces still stare out. Gordon Brown's own face of course, from the agonising disbelief of the Vine interview to the dead, painted-on smile of the self-professed 'penitent sinner' addressing the hordes outside Mrs Duffy's house in Rochdale. Gillian Duffy herself, eyes suddenly widening with shock and bewilderment when she was told by reporters what exactly the Prime Minister had just said about her. (And her lonely silhouette, walking away from the cameras when no journalist could think of a single further question to ask her; a hundred yards down the road and head still shaking.) Gordon Brown was not the only person hurt that day. Sue Nye, of 'I blame Sue' fame, leading the charge with a basilisk stare from the Radisson Hotel in Manchester en route to Mrs Duffy's place. (She who had stuck with Gordon as his gatekeeper from the beginning right to the death, how angry and hurt must she have been?) The personal protection officers – the same coppers we have seen in the background guarding Gordon Brown on the big days – Afghanistan, Obama, the G20 – and now whose final memories of 'The Boss' will have been of standing outside a modest Rochdale semi, in the headlights, the world's media laying siege, while Brown sipped tea inside and grovelled. And then Gordon again that evening, in the throng of a 'recovery' walkabout at Manchester station. Manic, and with desperation always threatening to break through. 'How are you? Nice to see you. Nice to see you. Are the trains running OK? Good . . . good.' Sarah at his shoulder, features creased with the strain, waiting for her husband's agony to conclude.

The first thought on hearing that Gordon Brown had described a voter (and a Labour voter at that!) as 'just this sort of bigoted woman' was that perhaps he had simply been speaking the truth? Maybe this Mrs Duffy character had said something beyond the pale . . . ? Judgement was suspended until the full picture could be established. At the Conservative and Liberal Democrat head-quarters, as word spread of the story, party workers waited breath-lessly by their televisions for the tape to be played. At the first run-through, there was silence. Ears were pressed to TV speakers to catch each inflection of the soft Brown bass-baritone. The extent of the damage did not take long to sink in. The second time around, there was pandemonium. Some in Conservative Central Office were calling it a 'game-changer'. (A misreading – the game changed only with the first television debate.) Neither opposition party chose to put the boot in. Why bother? It was a spectacular Labour own goal inflicted by their star striker. As Andy Coulson told journalists, Gordon Brown's words spoke for themselves.

The Prime Minister himself initially had no sense of the scale of the problem. His primary preoccupation was the conversa-tion with Mrs Duffy itself, which he thought was bad enough and might dominate the media agenda. Gillian Duffy had been ushered towards him by aides just as he was concluding his visit to Rochdale. First declaring herself a lifelong supporter who was now 'absolutely ashamed of saying I'm Labour' the pensioner, who had only just popped out for some bread in her bright-red collared coat, reeled off a list of grievances:

Duffy: But how are you going to get us out of all this debt, Gordon?

Brown: We've got a deficit reduction plan, cut the debt by half over the next four years, we've got the plans that have been set out to do it – look, I was the person who came in and said—

Duffy: Look, the three main things that I had drummed in when I was a child was education, health service and looking after people who are vulnerable. There are too many people now who aren't vulnerable but they can claim and people who are vulnerable can't get claim – can't get it.

Brown: But they shouldn't be doing that, there is no life for people on the dole any more. If you're unemployed you've got to go back to work. At six months—

Duffy: You can't say anything about the immigrants because you're saying that you're – but all these eastern Europeans what are coming in, where are they flocking from?

Brown: A million people come in from Europe, but a million British people have gone into Europe. You do know there's a lot of British people staying in Europe as well . . . [having stated at length his case] So education, health and helping people, that's what I'm about.

Duffy: Congratulations. And I hope you keep it up.

Brown: It's been very good to meet you. And you're wearing the right colour today!

Driving away, sitting in what he thought was the safety of the back of the prime ministerial Jaguar alongside his aide Justin Forsyth, Brown dropped his mask:

Brown: That was a disaster. Should never have put me with that woman. Whose idea was that?

Forsyth: I don't know, I didn't see.

Brown: Sue's, I think. Just ridiculous.

Forsyth: Not sure if they'll [the broadcast media] go with that one.

Brown: Oh they will go with it.

Forsyth: What did she say?

Brown: Oh everything. She's just this sort of bigoted woman who said she used to be Labour. I mean it's just ridiculous . . .

It was only then that the Prime Minister looked down at his jacket and noticed a microphone still attached to his lapel. Pulling the receiver from his inside pocket, he could see the telltale red LED light. It was then that he knew that Sky News, whose microphone it was, would have heard his words. The one thing Brown could not be sure of is how much would have been recorded before the radio mic went out of range, and his voice became inaudible. His gut feeling was though, this would be bad. Time to ring Peter.

People who knew Gordon Brown well were not particularly surprised at what he said. The general consensus was that it could easily have been worse. By this point of the campaign a degree of fatigue was bound to set in, and mistakes were always likely. In the Duffy case, though, tiredness was merely an aggravating factor. The key problem was Gordon Brown's dark paranoia that so seriously clouded his view of the people he encountered on the road. In his defence, friends of the Prime Minister often pointed out that he had a majority of the written press on his back, broadcasters tended to be viewed as being hostile, and a certain degree of 'bunker mentality' was therefore an inevitability. Though admittedly things had come to a pretty pass when Gordon Brown started imagining that a well-meaning (if plainspoken) pensioner was part of the conspiracy against him. By this point, nobody close to him seemed seriously to be trying to talk him around. (They had basically given up trying.) On the fringes of Downing Street, you would still hear exasperation expressed at Gordon Brown's distorted view of the world: 'He sees everything as a problem . . . as a threat,' was typical. But among the loyalists, exasperation had given way to a world-weary acceptance that nothing was going to change. Experience had taught them to be philosophical. As Peter Mandelson would put it, 'He tends to think things are bad when they are good; and when things are bad, that they are worse.' Given that, on this occasion, things were in fact bad – extremely bad – it is a tribute to Brown's immense resilience, his fabled capacity to soak up punishment, that he did not collapse altogether.

In truth there was not much that the governing party could do about the situation. The apology to Mrs Duffy was essential, but damage limitation was in large part futile. Some seemed to want to persuade themselves the whole nightmare was not really happening – consider this tweet from Twitter addict Ed Balls, sent even as Labour's campaign collapsed around his mentor Gordon Brown's ears: 'On Chesil Beach – windy, sunny and beautiful – with our PPC Jim Knight # labourdoorstep (well beach)' Nice to know some people could get away from it all.

If there was a crumb of comfort, it was that with the final debate the very next day the narrative would inevitably move on. In the meantime, recrimination was rife. There was some pity, anger, and a still further-increased air of fatalism in a party that was already largely resigned to fairly undignified defeat. 'It won't cost us in the polls because we can't get any lower as it is,' was what passed for an optimistic verdict from one aide. The pessimists pointed to the subject matter of Gordon Brown and Gillian Duffy's discussion – immigration. This might be a real problem, they feared.

Of all policy areas apart from the economy, immigration played the most significant role in the campaign. Not only was it at the heart of Gordon Brown's Duffygate meltdown, it seems certain that confusion over the Liberal Democrat immigration policy contributed to the party's slipping back at the last minute. And the Tories, who were wary of turning people off as they had in 2005, failed to concentrate on the issue at the start and never got the bounce that they should have. In sum, when the policy architects of the three main parties come to re-examine the successes and failures of the platforms on which they campaigned, there will be general agreement across the political spectrum that when it came to immigration they fell short.

The irony about the Gillian Duffy episode is that had Gordon Brown not made such an unholy mess of the situation, it would have gone down as one of the most successful expositions of the party's policy up to that point. Back in Labour headquarters, when they saw the tape, the view was that the section before Brown got back into the car and mouthed off was overwhelmingly positive. Mrs Duffy made her point, Gordon Brown listened politely and set out his position. It was calm and measured – a proper conversation. It was just the sort of thing, in fact, that the campaign organisers had been striving to achieve.

The positive vibes were undermined just a touch by what happened next. The car door slammed and the niceties evaporated.

He called her a bigot. Labour candidates in constituencies where immigration was a major doorstep issue (most of them, in fact) were aghast. They knew that people would vote on immigration, and were deeply uneasy with the fact that now some would legitimately complain that in raising the issue you ran the risk of being labelled 'bigoted' by the Labour leader. To say the least, it was not ideal.

It was not as though the Labour leader was unaware of the scale of his error. 'This is my worst day in politics,' he told colleagues. Obama's top pollster and campaign aide Joel Benenson, who had been flown in to help Brown with his debate preparation, had not expected anything like this, and was flummoxed. On the Wednesday evening, in his hotel suite 'debate camp' in Manchester, Gordon Brown was quite unable to focus even for a second on what he had previously hoped would be his big moment in the campaign – the final televised debate on the economy. Labour aides, conscious of the effort their distinguished American guest had made to join their last-minute coaching session, felt increasingly awkward as their boss sank from despondency to desperation. It was pointless.

It so happened that Brown gathered himself the next morning and managed to maintain what passed for focus on the job in hand throughout the day. Managing to dredge a respectable performance from such profound depths of despair was a genuine Gordon Brown triumph, though not (given what had gone before) one that he will look back on with any fondness.

While Gordon Brown put his foot in it – a casual slur of an entire potentially Labour-voting demographic? Why not! – the Liberal Democrat leader was tiptoeing awkwardly around his party's policy on the same subject. A further sign of its centrality to the campaign, immigration was the only subject (apart from the economy again) which came up in each televised debate. The argument was a slow burner, but Nick Clegg's discomfort with the issue was incrementally exposed, and became a real issue for his party in the week running up to polling day.

In debate number one (where immigration was the first question), David Cameron gently quizzed Nick Clegg about his policy of instituting regional quotas on immigration. (The idea being that one could ensure immigrants would be directed only to those regions where there was a need for labour, and sufficient spare capacity in key sectors like housing to accommodate them.) Cameron thought it was unworkable. It was the closest he came to getting under the skin of the Liberal Democrat leader during this initial 'hands off' period of his approach towards Nick Clegg. However, he failed to get to the nub of Lib Dem immigration policy – what the party called 'an earned route to citizenship', and most others would call an amnesty.

Labour and the Conservatives alike identified the area as a weak point in the days that followed Manchester, and were determined not to let Clegg off the hook again. Gordon Brown, given the first opportunity in the Sky News debate, immediately pointed out that, 'When we talked about it last week, Nick didn't tell us that he wants an amnesty for illegal immigrants.' Responding, Clegg said: 'The only person actually in British politics who is advocating a blanket amnesty – I'm not – it's Boris Johnson, the Conservative Mayor of London,' though he admitted the policy he was putting forward was 'controversial'.

The principle of the Lib Dem manifesto proposals (which, by the way, bit the dust once they got into coalition discussions – often a good guide as to how closely cherished any policy is) was that illegal immigrants who had been in the country for ten years, but spoke English, had no criminal record and were prepared to live long-term and pay UK taxes should be entitled to become

British nationals. The key problem with the policy, as even Nick Clegg's closest advisors admit, is that at its heart was an information vacuum. Nobody knows how many illegal immigrants are living in the UK, but anyone can have a guess. Accordingly, the policy was open to infinite mischief-making and distortion. Much as Clegg railed against the newspaper headlines of millions to be admitted into the country by the Lib Dems, he had nothing definite with which to hit back, and was in any case disinclined to get into a media-stoked bidding war on the actual number of illegals.

Simon Hughes was one of the few people advising the Liberal Democrat leader who thought that being more specific would help. 'Where we failed is in not saying, "Look, this isn't millions of people coming in – assuming there are 750,000 [illegals], you're only going to allow to stay people who've been here for 10 years, speak English, are willing to put some money into the kitty and haven't committed offences. That whittles the numbers down probably by about a half, leaving a maximum 500,000. Even if they all had spouses who could come, that would only bring it up to a million . . ." There was a nervousness about getting into that territory, and I regret it.'

One can well see why Nick Clegg might have been disinclined to get into 'only a million' territory in a televised debate. Nevertheless, not only did his vagueness open the party to concerted and damaging attack, it left him looking uncharacteristically uncertain under the TV lights.

There was a wider point. Was the policy an amnesty? The Liberal Democrats did not like the policy to be labelled as such, but it did not stop them employing the very same term when it suited them. On an occasion when the party was trying to whip up a split between Boris Johnson (whose policy has been noted) and his party colleagues, one of Nick Clegg's press team sent a text message: 'Boris Johnson suggests amnesty after five years. We say ten years and are much more specific.' The 'A-word' frequently found its way into Liberal Democrat conversation, though generally accompanied with a rueful smile and an acknowledgement, 'An amnesty or, I should say, an "earned route to citizenship . . ."'

By the final debate, Nick Clegg really should have known what to expect. 'Amnesty', 'amnesty', 'amnesty' echoed through Birmingham University's Great Hall, and each time the Liberal Democrat shook his head vehemently. It was a far cry from the relaxed Nick Clegg of the first debate, hand in pocket, gently mocking the two representatives of the traditional political class. Now in Birmingham, the 'new politics' did not look so different. Most damaging was the sense that, once in the crosshairs, this was just another slippery politician, saddled with an argument he was reluctant to articulate, falling back on semantics to get himself out of jail.

The BBC debate represented an uncomfortable start to a rocky final few days for the Lib Dems. There was a general mood in the written press that having had his week or so in the sun, Nick Clegg's comeuppance was due. In the name of 'scrutiny' of the Liberal Democrat platform, traditional allegiances were coming to the surface. The hand of the former tabloid editor Andy Coulson could be perceived in a clutch of stories critical of Lib Dem policies. The Lib Dem team was struggling to respond effectively. Having coped with an explosion of positive interest in their leader, the small body of press minders were now confronted by a full-scale media barrage.

At last, the newspapers could enjoy themselves. An election campaign dominated by television had represented, in many respects, a frustrating few weeks in the world of newsprint. Stories from the papers that genuinely made the weather were scarce (the *Telegraph*'s 'Jobs Tax' letter from leading business figures was the one obvious exception). Now Fleet Street was off the leash. Remember those complaints (in Labour circles particularly) that a campaign played out on TV lacked the visceral, feral edge of previous elections? It did not feel that way at Lib Dem HQ. The whole procedure of listening, research-ing, rebutting was, Jonny Oates would later acknowledge, 'unbelievably time-consuming'. The paucity of resources at the Liberal Democrats' disposal was showing through. And with all hands to the pump trying to stem the tide of negative stories, there was precious little energy left to try to break through with a positive message – and that despite the fact that the run-in to polling day, if previous elections were anything to go by, was a period during which the party was likely to face a squeeze on its vote.

Some old hands suggest Nick Clegg's team should have seen it coming, and been better prepared for an assault by hostile news-papers. Paddy Ashdown had warned straight after the first debate, 'this is serious stuff now – they are going to go for us, you watch.' And the former leader's verdict on the final days is harsh: 'We didn't fight a very good campaign . . . we didn't have a narrative for the last week. I've always said that if you're going to be fight-ing an election you need a last week campaign. I don't think we had an effective last week campaign which gave us momentum.'

Simon Hughes, another man who had seen it all before, agrees that the party was at fault for letting the media narrative get away from them. Particularly damaging, in Hughes's mind, was that the Lib Dem immigration policy was being only half-heartedly articulated at the very moment the issue came to the fore in the campaign. Beyond that, he agrees, 'We didn't have a campaign strategy for dealing with the last week squeeze as effectively as we needed to – something that allows you to power on, keep on taking the initiative. We just didn't have the ammunition for that.'

In the hours after the final televised debate, Gordon Brown retreated to his hotel room. As one might expect after the forty-eight hours he had been through, he looked spent. This was the Labour leader's lowest ebb. The magnitude of his Gillian Duffy error, his failure to command the television debate arena, the scale of likely defeat at the polls . . . all seemed to crowd in. Amid the usual comings and goings of friends and advisors, scouts returning from the spin room, the next morning's newspapers being delivered, he sat on a sofa with his wife, Sarah. Trying to lift his spirits, she read to him the messages of support that had come in via Twitter. (Sarah Brown was, and remains, an assiduous Twitterer.)

Gordon Brown had justly developed a reputation as a man who could not admit when he had got something wrong. This was different. At this moment there seemed no bottom to the well of self-reproach into which Gordon Brown had plunged. Given how often Brown returned in speech after speech to the values his Presbyterian father had instilled in him, it should not come as a surprise that the Labour leader constantly measured his actions by what his father would have thought. When it came to Mrs Duffy, that offhand insult to an elderly lady, the Reverend John Brown's judgement would have been unforgiving, and son Gordon knew it.

On top of all that was profound disappointment at having failed to dominate the argument with David Cameron and Nick Clegg on his 'specialist subject', the economy. Given that preparation for this final debate had been nothing short of catastrophic, most of the Brown coterie were just relieved that their man had more or less held it together on stage. But Gordon

Brown's expectations for this particular evening had been much higher. Originally, he had hoped to make the debate on the economy the defining moment of the campaign. Labour's intention to put the economy centre stage at the first debate was a demonstration of Brown's belief he could score big. That plan was stymied during the debate negotiations with the other two parties and broadcasters, but right up to transmission on the 29th of April Brown had remained sure that he could make his mastery of the economic brief count; convinced he could land the knockout punch, exposing the Conservatives' economic arguments as unsound and dangerous. It was the last chance and it did not happen. That evening as he stepped back into the green room, Gordon Brown's first words to Sue Nye were, 'I'm so sorry.'

Then, amid the gloom and despondency, for no apparent reason Gordon Brown seemed to perk up. 'Peter, aren't you on *Today* in the morning?' he mused. Ideas began to be kicked around ahead of Mandelson's radio appearance. Some lines for a speech were requested from aides who were no less exhausted than the Prime Minister. Gordon Brown's stamina was coming to the fore again. In a matter of moments he seemed to have recovered his drive and purpose. It was two in the morning. Everyone else wanted to go to bed. If you had told them then that Brown was about to have his best week of the whole election, the response would have been hollow laughter.

On the morning after the debate all three leaders found themselves jostling for media attention in the three-way marginal of Derby North. Generally, the rival campaigns strove to avoid one another on the road, but a degree of crossover was inevitable. (There was much merriment on the Lib Dem battle bus when they spotted the Tory coach on a motorway – 'We're overtaking you!' came the text message from a Clegg aide to the journalists accompanying Team Cameron.)

A momentary rush of elation had surged through David Cameron as he stepped off the stage at the end of the recording the evening before. He felt he had clearly won the final televised confrontation (a judgement that was widely shared), but that was not it. The delight felt by the Conservative leader was because at last the whole ordeal was over. Cameron had never imagined the debates would be such a chore. He, like Nick Clegg, enjoyed the process of campaigning – getting out of Westminster, meeting people, geeing up candidates and activists on the ground – and dealing with the TV debates had been an overwhelming distraction, quite apart from the not inconsiderable pressure and strain that went with them. So much time had been taken up with preparation, whether with his close advisors or on individual policy briefs with Shadow Cabinet colleagues. Analysing, poring over the tapes, making tweaks and readjustments for the next week. It was an all-consuming process. Liberated now, David Cameron relished the prospect of a freewheeling final push to polling day.

Visiting a secondary school, surrounded by and taking questions from eager teenagers, Cameron's mood was evidently still sky-high. The leader's Derby school visit was an example of the sort of event that so infuriated Labour planners when they saw it on the television. Shrewdly, Cameron's aides positioned him right in the middle of the school's main staircase. There were youngsters around him; more on the landing above and the hall below. On site, it looked an awkward arrangement with the Conservative leader having one moment to crane his neck, then to lean over the banister to spot his questioners. But for the cameras, it was perfection. Taller than the children, easy to pick out halfway up the stairs where no one could obscure him, and with what the experts call a 'doughnut' of people listening, natural, engaged. 'Why can't we do it like that?' was the constant complaint from Victoria Street, another cross to bear for the beaten-down band of advisors at Gordon Brown's side.

The Labour mood would not have been lightened by the quips David Cameron was firing off at their expense. Informed that Tony Blair had rejoined the governing party's campaign, he was acid. 'Tony Blair is one of the only people who can afford another Labour government . . .' and an afterthought – that the heavily tanned appearance of the former Prime Minister 'will be very good for sales of Tango'.

Back on the bus, Cameron was at his most gregarious, taking particular pleasure at having put Nick Clegg under real pressure for the first time. As well as the 'amnesty' issue, he felt the Liberal Democrat leader had wobbled on the Euro. ('I am not advocating membership of the Euro,' Clegg had insisted. The Lib Dem manifesto suggested otherwise: 'It is in Britain's long-term interest to be part of the Euro.') Cameron explained that when he gets into difficulty, Nick Clegg has a tendency to move both arms in circles, rotating backwards: 'We call it the helicopter.' The feeling was that as Cameron and Gordon Brown concentrated their fire from both sides, the rotor blades were palpably and repeatedly on the move.

The Liberal Democrats knew they had some problems, but the mood in the Clegg camp was that, provided they could weather the storm, they still had every reason to be confident. Nick Clegg could look back on his performance over three weeks of testing and detailed televised confrontation with pride. It was Clegg who had shown the others how to do it. He had written the book on looking at the camera, naming the questioner, engaging with the audience and staying cool with his opening Manchester master class, and will be remembered as the first British politician to take to the new era of live, televised debates with gusto and assurance. In the constituencies, on the stump, things felt good. They felt right. The sort of swing Lib Dems were experiencing was not about to be derailed by a bunch of scratchy Sunday newspapers, right?

There were hard facts to support the view that this might be a breakthrough election for the Lib Dems. Not just the polls, which continued to show a significantly higher level of support than at previous elections, but actual postal votes that had been cast. Political parties are permitted to see a sample of such votes as they arrive, though they are strictly prohibited from disseminating their findings until after the full results are in. According to Chris Rennard, the Lib Dem campaign guru, 'The indications that all the parties had from votes that were opened from postal voters the week before the election was that the Liberal Democrats were doing very much better'; better than the 23 per cent share of the total vote they eventually achieved.

During the final days of campaigning, neither Nick Clegg nor any member of his staff had realised that the bottom was dropping out of their support. Looking back, it seems that there was a phenomenal shift that was not perceived simply because it happened over such a very short time. Chris Rennard asserts, based on the battery of evidence available to the party, that the Lib Dems 'dropped around 4 per cent in the last two or three days before the poll'.

Only hindsight can give an accurate sense of what happened to the third party in the run-up to polling day, because at the time no one spotted the scale of what was going on. True, the Conservatives and Labour both sensed that there was traction as they got stuck into Liberal Democrat policies. True, the Liberal Democrats felt there was pressure coming their way. But when the big exit poll was published at ten o'clock on

Thursday evening, accurately showing the Lib Dems would actually lose seats in the Commons, disbelief was universal. Liberal Democrat, Tory and Labour alike – all were certain that Nick Clegg's party would do significantly better.

In identifying the reasons for the Lib Dem collapse, there is a general consensus that the biggest factor was an energetic and reinvigorated Labour campaign over the last week. Who would have thought it? At the time of 'Duffygate' there was considerable fear in Labour circles that Gordon Brown had struck a mortal blow against his own party. The final debate just a week from Election Day was not disastrous, but there was little more positive that could be said for the Prime Minister's tired performance. So where did the renewed life come from?

Gordon Brown shared David Cameron's relief at being released from the shackles of the debate process. Like the Conservative leader, he found the cycle of rehearsal and post-mortem unbearably onerous. Unlike Cameron, his mood was darkened further by realising that he was simply not much good at the whole business. The hope that concentrating on 'substance' would see Brown through did not make it from the rubble of his nervy and uncomfortable showing in Manchester. From that point, it was a question of making the best of a bad lot.

But with no further debate clouding the horizon, Brown was free to demonstrate his best qualities. Those travelling with the Prime Minister were struck by the increased vim and vigour with which he addressed himself to the task. Brown's campaign might have been threadbare and amateurish, but a determination to overcome the odds was a longstanding Brown characteristic and that underdog spirit came in part to define the final days for him and his party.

The undoubted highlight was a speech delivered at Methodist Central Hall, the imposing domed edifice across the road from

Westminster Abbey, on the Tuesday two days before Election Day. The occasion was laid on by 'Citizens UK', a body which describes itself as 'The national home of community organising'. Vowing to 'unlock the power of civil society', the organisation is a multi-faith project aimed at alleviating the lot of the poor. It is comprised of more than 160 faith congregations, schools, universities, trade unions and community groups. Each of the three party leaders was invited to speak that afternoon. David Cameron first, then Nick Clegg and lastly Gordon Brown. They would find the forum and in particular the audience one of the most stimulating they had encountered during the whole election period.

The two and a half thousand people that packed the hall could not have been further from the stern waxwork panels of machine-picked members of the public (not their fault, remember – those were the rules!) that populated the television debate studios. The 'faith congregation' element of Citizens UK was particularly well represented. There was a fervour and an engagement that was more than merely political. Speeches were closely scrutinised – the listening was intense and respectful. When warranted, generous applause came quickly and naturally.

David Cameron set out his vision of the Big Society with as much passion and lucidity as he had mustered at any time during the past four weeks or so. His speech was received warmly, though Nick Clegg's appearance a few minutes later raised the temperature in the hall further. The delegates had agreed what they termed a six-point manifesto including a 'living wage' higher than the minimum wage and, tellingly, an 'earned regularisation' for long-term illegal immigrants. The Liberal Democrat leader's policy (which a few days later he would scrap – at least for this parliament) was right up their street.

Gordon Brown's speech was nothing short of electric. Emotion was close to the surface from the moment a young girl, Tiara Sanchez, who spoke ahead of the Prime Minister, dissolved into tears as she described how her mother and grandmother, both cleaners at the Treasury of all places, struggled to make ends meet. Without hesitation (for once!), Gordon Brown, who had been listening seated on a wooden chair at the edge of the stage, stepped forward and put his arm around the fourteen-year-old. People were on their feet applauding, not the sort of thing Gordon Brown had experienced a great deal during the campaign, and the intensity of the crowd sparked something in the 'son of the manse'. Gordon was off the leash. 'If you fight for fairness, you have a friend, a partner and a brother in me,' he bellowed. The Labour leader had not enjoyed himself so much since the campaign had begun:

When Cicero spoke to the crowds in ancient Rome, people turned to each other after hearing the speech and said, 'Great speech!'

But when Demosthenes spoke to the crowds in ancient Greece and people turned to each other, they said, 'Let's march!'

The abrupt arrival on stage of an environmental protestor bearing the slogan 'Nukiller power NO' only heightened the mood of feverish excitement. As the man was wrestled to the floor by organisers, the crowd began booing him despite Gordon Brown saying they should not: 'Now, now,' he chided. 'He'll get his chance to ask his question.' As Brown stepped off the stage a few minutes later, the chanting echoed through the hall: 'Gordon Brown! Gordon Brown!'

Labour workers could not believe their eyes and ears but felt torn. Of course they were thrilled that their leader had found his voice, but then there was the frustration of knowing it had come too late. 'It makes me wild,' Peter Mandelson said, as he gave instructions that the film of Gordon's triumph be emailed to all and sundry. Mandelson, after all, had argued at the outset that given set-piece speeches were Brown's one real strength, the campaign should be built around such formal events. The general view was that a speech-based campaign would be too much work and so the fateful decision was taken to allow 'Gordon the man' to shine in his interactions with real people instead. With mixed results, one might say.

The speech served a purpose in that it gave renewed heart to party activists up and down the country who might otherwise have been at the end of their tether. It pepped them up at the very moment many were ready to throw in the towel. It is hard to quantify the effect of such a shot in the arm on the Labour machine, but those who felt its impact would argue this was an important factor in ensuring the party would not cave in, but would hold the line.

The blunt fact is that for Labour to have had the slightest chance of winning (or, more modestly, of becoming the largest force in the Commons), the party needed a brilliant first week, not a dazzling burst to the line at the last. Supporters of the Prime Minister were rueful. 'If only . . .' they would speculate. 'If only he had found that within himself at the start.' Then there would be a shrug of the shoulders. Oh well. Sensing that defeat was around the corner, knowing that Gordon Brown would be forced from the position he had coveted all his life, all in all there were few in the party to begrudge him his last hurrah.

As Brown threw caution to the wind, the party operation was clicking into gear, or so it seemed to Labour's opponents. The Liberal Democrats and the Conservatives alike were the targets of a toughened rhetoric employed by the governing party that they found hard to counter in the last few days. Paddy Ashdown, for one, is convinced that Labour's last gasp effort saved them seats that the Liberal Democrats would otherwise have won. 'Gordon Brown found his voice in the last week of the campaign and Labour fought a far better campaign in the last days,' Ashdown explains. 'That ate into our vote in the northern cities.' It is also widely acknowledged in Liberal Democrat circles that the party struggled to counter a Labour/Tory pincer movement, with both sides insisting a vote for the Lib Dems would let in by the back door the party people least wanted to govern.

Chris Rennard saw the squeeze at first hand as he toured marginal seats across the country. He describes how in Liverpool Wavertree, where the Lib Dems had high hopes of overturning a Labour majority of just under 3,000, the weekend before the poll one could sense the mood of 'let's give Nick a chance' evaporating. 'There were people saying, "Oh my God, if Cameron gets in it'll mean massive cuts. Surestart will go, tax credits will go, all our schools and hospitals will go; we can't afford a Conservative government . . . Gordon Brown may be no good but we've got to stick with Labour."' The calculation being made by voters in a Tory target seat like Winchester, was no less poisonous to Lib Dem chances. Rennard recounts: 'The electorate suddenly thought, "Oh no, it doesn't look like Gordon Brown is completely out of this. If there's any danger of Gordon Brown staying on that would be a disaster. We'll have to vote Conservative to stop him."'

Paddy Ashdown has a pithy formulation: 'Many people returned to nurse for fear of something worse.' In fact the old hands had seen it all before. 1992 was meant to be ingrained in the Lib Dem collective consciousness – the way John Wakeham and John Major stoked fears that given the chance, nothing would please a Liberal Democrat more than to jump into bed with

Neil Kinnock and ease the Labour leader's route into Downing Street. Voters tentatively attracted to the Lib Dems baulked at the thought, voting the Tories back in. This and other setbacks, it was thought, had served as salutary lessons to the party. Perhaps not salutary enough. Funnily enough, it did not seem seriously to occur to Nick Clegg and his circle, or even to those who had endured successive rebukes from a British electorate so stubbornly wedded to the idea of two party politics, that history might repeat itself. Why not? 2010, the year of Cleggmania, felt like their year.

If fear did indeed play a part in determining the way people voted on the 6th of May, the impact of scenes on the streets of Greece should not be discounted. A wave of fierce riots prompted by the Greek government's package of severe austerity measures represented an ominous accompaniment to the final week's campaigning. For the Conservatives, George Osborne and David Cameron had spoken in near-apocalyptic terms about the consequences of the UK failing to demonstrate its readiness to tackle the deficit. Here, as if on cue, were near-apocalyptic images; to reinforce the point the *Daily Mail* ran the front page headline 'Burning Issue for Britain' above a picture of a Greek riot policeman engulfed in flames. Amid the white noise of the last few days of manic campaigning, it is hard to sustain an argument that a voter interested in politics would have caught more than the odd, violent snatch or two of the Greek situation through the media. Nevertheless, it is plausible to suggest, as do the Liberal Democrats today, that as background noise when people were in the act of weighing up who should govern, the mayhem in Greece may have influenced people not to vote for their party. No time to take a risk. Stability, security – that is what Labour and the Tories were saying only they could represent.

★   ★   ★

In the final days, with his hopes of an overall majority hanging in the balance, there were opportunities for David Cameron to take stock, and reflect on how his weeks on the road had gone. Any political leader spends much of their 'downtime' on the phone or BlackBerry, locked in conversation after conversation. But even when the pace of campaigning hits fever pitch, as was undoubtedly the case for Cameron at the climax, there is a degree of space, and monotony to be endured in between. Long journeys, winding roads, waiting in the back of the car in a lay-by while the coach catches up or (as happened in Sheffield the Friday before polling day) while staff at the next location corral an audience of parents for whom the school run is a more pressing priority.

Though not predisposed to gloominess, particularly not with the prize so near at hand, Cameron would have had to recognise that things had not gone to plan. Despite the public's desire to see the back of an unpopular Prime Minister and his tired administration, they continued stubbornly to resist the Tory embrace. 'Vote For Change' the Conservatives had said, but when the game changed following the first TV debate, it was the other lot, the ones no one had really considered, that benefited.

It had been a campaign of adjustments, some violent – recognising the need to confront the possibility of a hung parliament with the Lib Dems holding the balance of power; some minor – 'Just look at the camera!' David Cameron's adaptability had been tested again and again and he had proven himself. (This quality would once more be demonstrated at the critical juncture the morning after the election.)

It is equally true, as Cameron has argued vehemently in the months after the election, that the campaign organisers showed the same sort of fleet-footedness and willingness to accommodate their operation to unforeseen circumstances as did the leader out on the road. However, much as party workers and activists might have admired the smoothness with which gear changes (and the odd handbrake turn) were accomplished, it is in the nature of the infantry soldier looking for clear direction that they would have preferred not to have had to make all these changes in the first place. A simple, clear message to take forward, no deviation, no distraction – that is what many at the sharp end felt was lacking.

Looking at the last week, even David Cameron now acknowledges on balance that the Labour message (that the Conservatives would aggressively cut spending and raise taxes) was clearer than anything his party had to offer. It was also, he argues in his defence, entirely dishonest, founded on a false assessment of what Labour or any government might hope to protect following the election. George Osborne's view was, and remains, that if the Labour party had managed to stay in government they would have had no mandate for the cuts they had even pencilled into their plans. By being straight with people, the argument runs, the Tories have made it possible to take tough decisions without a clamour going up that, 'We didn't vote for this' – in effect, honesty in the campaign made it possible to govern subsequently. (Tell that to the voters who believed Cameron and Osborne's insistence that they had 'no plans to raise VAT', Labour would retort.)

Being able to say he had been honest and straight with people must have offered David Cameron precious little comfort on those days when a fear began to take hold that Labour was starting to take chunks out of his party in earnest. In the last week of the campaign in particular, Cameron was hearing from colleagues at Central Office that Labour was hitting hard on cuts, and it was working. 'The big problem was cuts, cuts, cuts,' he told aides subsequently. There is little sign that he and his key advisors felt anything other than powerless to respond. Indignant anger was attempted (Cameron's attack on 'Labour lies' in the Sky News debate in Bristol was replicated throughout the campaign), but reassuring people that a Tory government would not be as bad as all that could only work so far. After all, when it came to cuts, cuts there would be.

For all that one can now discern how Labour's vote hardened in the final days, the Liberal Democrats fell away and the Conservatives failed to dispel the 'cutters' label, on polling day the moods of the three parties did not reflect this underlying reality.

As Labour's old guard awoke and trudged wearily back towards the windowless silo of their Victoria Street headquarters, sleep having been the order of the day for those who were not involved in the operation to get out the vote, the air (what air there was in there!) was heavy with frank trepidation. They were shattered, after all. The general sense was that it was going to be ugly.

The Conservatives had learned to be cautious. They knew they had not come as far as they had wanted. David Cameron continued to maintain in private as well as in public they had a mountain to climb, and looking at the electoral map – the constituency after constituency after constituency that had to fall their way – was a sobering experience for any party worker. Nevertheless, the chance of a governing majority was there. It might be hours away. Excitement was bubbling. Why would you not dare to hope?

And the Liberal Democrat leader? At around four o'clock on the afternoon of the 6th of May, as the country went to the polls and with government in abeyance, Nick Clegg and his wife Miriam had a bunch of journalists round to their Sheffield home for tea. It was the result of a joke. When chided over his parliamentary expenses record by Andrew Neil at a press conference, Clegg had come up with one of the more awkward phrases of his generally fluent campaign. Referring to the pebble-dashed semi-detached house listed as his second home, he insisted, 'It's not my home, it's yours – it's the taxpayers'.'

The resultant teasing from journalists who had been at the Liberal Democrat leader's side throughout the campaign culminated with an insistence that Clegg allow them to visit 'their' Sheffield home. The invitation that followed demonstrated the good grace and humour that had become a hallmark of the Clegg campaigning style. It also showed how comfortable he was with the situation the party found itself in. Tea, coffee and abundant cupcakes were served. Clegg and his wife laughed and joked with the hacks they had both come to know well. There was no sign of nerves. This was a man who within hours expected to reap the rewards of the Liberal Democrats' best campaign in years.

PART II

HUNG

7

THE OFFER

'It's what I want to do; my instincts tell me it's the right
thing to do'

'What are you going to do, Mr Cameron?' shouted journalists.
'Over here, David!'; 'This way, Mr Cameron!' Cameras were
penned back in tight banks on either side of the doorway; a further
bellowing mass, mixed in with supporters and passers-by on the
other side of the road (one or two snapping away from windows
above), was beseeching him to turn their way. Emerging from
the back of his silver Jaguar, David Cameron walked up the three
stone steps of the St Stephen's Club in Westminster; under the
ornately carved wooden portico and through the brilliant black
double-door. He did not look back.

The elegant members' club backing onto St James's Park,
whose first patron was Disraeli, had become David Cameron's
favoured venue for press conferences during his time as leader of
the opposition. Now he had returned – the hope was – for just
one last time. This speech, on the afternoon of the 7th of May
2010, was designed to ensure the Conservatives should soon no

longer need to hire such premises to get their message out. The speech had been shaped to map out David Cameron's route to another nearby listed townhouse: Number 10 Downing Street.

The room in which journalists awaited the Conservative leader was a fever of speculation. The level of expectation – already intense – had been heightened still further by the unusual restrictions imposed by the party machine. A single reporter was permitted to attend from each news organisation. The lobby's finest. As they had filed in one by one, most had endeavoured to glean precious intelligence from Cameron's aides. 'Just wait to hear what he has to say,' was the response from Andy Coulson and Gabby Bertin. 'He won't be long.' Fatigue and uncertainty made the competitive press pack even pricklier than usual. What were they about to witness? What cards did Cameron have to play?

Normally, the smart money would have been on David Cameron to claim full victory. In the aftermath of an indecisive election, the Tories could have chosen to fill a room with cheering supporters and bright banners, and to shout down any journalist brave enough to suggest the outcome had not been a total triumph. Why not? The Conservatives were the largest party, Labour had surely had their day, and the Liberal Democrats, the only viable partners in government, were licking their wounds after a shocking election night.

But David Cameron had chosen to take a different path. After steeling himself in an adjacent room, the white side door opened and he strode, unsmiling, to the small plain wood lectern, its usual party slogan removed, that had been positioned in the centre of the room. The television pictures would show the trees of the park, sunlit in the wide window at Cameron's back. There were no frills, and no excitable party fans. A baleful, poor reproduction portrait of Winston Churchill that hung on the wall to his right was the room's most striking decoration. The whole thing might have been designed to give the impression that this was a proposal to the country as a whole, not just as an ambitious party politician chancing his arm. Andy Coulson, standing at the back of the room, must have been well satisfied. As usual, the front seats had been reserved for the broadcasting stars. This time, though, David Cameron would not be taking questions.

As Cameron began to speak, Gordon Brown and his advisors inside Number 10 stopped what they were doing. The Prime Minister had delineated his own position, out in front of that famous front door just fifty-two minutes earlier. Now Gordon Brown had to listen. Phones were silenced for once. He put his feet on the desk and turned his back to the television screen.

Nick Clegg was in the party's headquarters in Cowley Street with advisors including members of the negotiating team that would swing into action later that afternoon. As in Downing Street, a hush fell on the room. On a whiteboard were scrawled the latest figures for parliamentary seats, Labour (256), Conservative (302), Liberal Democrats (56), the Unionists, Nationalists and the rest (27 – with 9 left to declare). It had only taken a cursory glance to see that the numbers with the Tories would work, and the numbers with Labour were 'extremely difficult'. What had David Cameron and the Tories computed?

In fact, David Cameron was about to put the Liberal Democrats firmly on the spot. Having watched the third party shout from the fringes of Westminster politics for so long, Cameron had chosen this moment and this setting to find out what the Lib Dems were made of.

In the small hours of that Friday morning, David Cameron real-ised that if he was going to become Prime Minister of Great Britain and Northern Ireland, he would have to wait a little longer than anticipated. The results were not stacking up quite as hoped. An overall majority was out of reach. Cameron and his entourage had chosen not to watch the televisions that had been set up in the bar of the Windrush Leisure Centre in his constituency of Witney in Oxfordshire. Instead they retreated to the manager's office, set up a laptop and followed the election night programmes as well as an indifferent Internet connection allowed. They would have heard the one loud cheer of the night go up at a quarter to two, from four Labour activists who were sitting, lonely but defiant, around a table of empty glasses. 'Yes!' they shouted at the TV as the returning officer in Tooting, South London, announced that Sadiq Khan had maintained his grip on the seat, a key Conservative target.

Cameron had spent the day keeping up the bravado of a leader in waiting. There was an evocation of Lincoln as the media were informed that he had spent some hours chopping logs at his constituency home Dean Farm, a relatively modest country place, quiet and isolated in a tiny hamlet some ten miles from the centre of Witney. (What a contrast to Gordon Brown, who according to an inexplicably demeaning briefing to the Press Association had 'lamb stew for supper' followed by 'a nap'. Samantha Cameron served up chilli con carne, less retro more metrosexual.)

Cameron had also used several of the politically neutral hours of polling day to plan privately for government and a new Cabinet over lunch with his closest advisors Ed Llewellyn, Andy Coulson, deputy chief of staff Kate Fall and George Osborne at the nearby Oxfordshire farmhouse in the village of Asthall Leigh owned by Steve Hilton, Cameron's highly paid guru, and his wife Rachel Whetstone, a Google high-flyer and former aide to Michael Howard. Patrick McLoughlin, the ex-coal miner and Chief Whip of the parliamentary party, was also asked to join the discussions. He was sufficiently confident of re-election to desert his Derbyshire Dales constituency on polling day – just as Osborne left it to party workers to get out his vote in Tatton, his footballers' wives corner of Cheshire.

By the evening 'Team Cameron' was back home in front of the TV. As night fell, the hum of satellite truck generators could be heard in Dean's single narrow lane. A small number of journalists gathered outside the gate, lights illuminating the stone side wall. Would Mr Cameron say anything as he left home? He would not. Too much was up in the air. The exit poll for Sky News, ITV and the BBC released at 10 p.m. suggested the Conservatives were on course to be the single largest party but they would fall short of an overall majority. (Conservatives 307; Labour 255; Liberal Democrats 59; Others 29 were the figures.)

Like most observers, David Cameron was sceptical. It did not feel right – a feeling of unease heightened when he had to deal with a rather premature telephone call of congratulations from the Governor of California, Arnold 'The Terminator' Schwarzenegger. Cameron, along with on-screen anchors and their political guests alike, felt that the Liberal Democrats, who had enjoyed such an eventful and apparently successful campaign, would score higher, probably at the expense of the Labour party and certainly not lose four seats as predicted. (Labour and Liberal Democrats shared the Conservative view – according to Chris Rennard of the Lib Dems, a senior though rival pollster told him, 'It was an absolutely ridiculous poll. He thought we were probably winning every single seat in Newcastle and we won no seats in Newcastle!')

When, just after midnight, the time came to make their way to the count, the Camerons' 'shire yeoman' theme continued. David and Samantha Cameron halted their motorcade on its way to the counting centre for a drink with supporters at the

New Inn, a local pub, conveniently owned by a Conservative party activist. (Extended drinking hours on polling day are one of the treasured perks of British electoral law.) Initially barred from the cramped and sweaty snug owing to legitimate fears of overcrowding, those journalists who managed to make their way through the scrum found Cameron nervously sipping on a Coke at a long table in the front window, his mind clearly elsewhere.

For the Conservatives the high point of election night came at 1 a.m. on the edge of Bristol when Chris Skidmore overturned an 8,000 majority to take Kingswood. This was 135th on the Tories' target list and gave off the palpable whiff of outright victory. However the fuller picture of early results mulled over in the New Inn was positive but not ecstatic. It began to seem that the professors and pollsters might have got it right after all.

To reach that overall majority of 326 seats, the Conservatives needed around 19 gains in the north-east of England, but it looked as if they were on course for a mere 10. In the Midlands battleground totemic seat of Birmingham Edgbaston, a smiling Gisela Stuart foretold a Labour-hold (although two partial recounts and a deal of nail-biting were still yet to come). Then after Tooting, with the clock ticking on to 2:30 a.m., the Tories failed in the target seats of Gedling and Bolton North East. Things were looking particularly bad for some of Cameron's hand-picked stars on the A-list. None of the so-called *Tatler* Cameronistas, bright young things who had been featured flatteringly in the glossy snobs' magazine, would be elected – including Shaun Bailey, the black candidate in Hammersmith, and Joanne Cash, the flighty Notting Hillbilly, who was re-imposed by the leader personally after she fell out with her local party.

As he stood on stage listening to the returning officer just after 3 a.m., David William Donald Cameron no longer cut the bouncy, confident figure he had been for much of the campaign.

A massive personal vote of 33,973 votes (well over half the total cast) was quite beside the point. There was a weary smile as the Monster Raving Loony Party's veteran candidate Alan 'Howling Laud' Hope in his trademark white suit and Stetson, celebrating a rather more modest 234 votes, was first to shake his hand in congratulation.

Knowing that candidates, activists and supporters all over the country were relying on him to show a lead, David Cameron endeavoured to stay as upbeat as possible. Following generous praise for those who had stood against him, and the local debates they had staged together in the constituency (as if he did not have enough debates to contend with), Cameron declared that 'the Labour government has lost its mandate to govern our country'. These were carefully chosen words. He did not claim the crown.

It was a notably more cautious speech than that of his closest colleague George Osborne who even before midnight had insisted: 'It is pretty clear that Labour cannot continue in government. Labour ministers need to get real.' Osborne, the man who had run the Conservative campaign, was understandably letting off steam a little. The pressure on him had been enormous, and while Cameron succumbed to profound, though short-lived disappointment, the overwhelming feeling for George Osborne, sat on a metal folding chair in Macclesfield Leisure Centre watching the results alongside three TV reporters, was of relief. Osborne thought the key point to be taken from the night was that the Conservatives had decisively won the popular vote. The nightmare scenario that had dogged him and close colleagues had been of a situation in which the Tories won around 280 seats, Labour the same, which would leave things distinctly sticky. With the result as it was, the Shadow Chancellor concluded that one way or another, he was on his way into government.

Having made his acceptance speech in Witney, David Cameron and his entourage swept past the waiting reporters. With news helicopters clattering overhead, the Cameron motorcade headed down the M40, and into London. Their destination was the Conservative Campaign Headquarters (CCHQ) in Millbank Tower, overlooking the Thames.

The party had flogged Maggie's fabled CCO – Conservative Central Office – three years before in part to wipe away the memory of successive defeats by Tony Blair and in part as a speculative property deal on the advice of Lords Saatchi and Ashcroft. Neither goal was entirely achieved when the European Union's combined representatives in London bought the lease and renamed it 'Europe House'. Since then, like Labour who abandoned John Smith House, south of the river under Tony Blair, the Conservative party had led a peripatetic existence, expanding and contracting into nondescript suites of offices around SW1 according to the funds available and the demands of the political cycle. There was more than a nod to Blair the Conqueror when Cameron chose as his launch pad for the general election the same offices and media theatre that New Labour occupied for its landslide victories in 1997 and 2001.

Blair had always stopped for a victory party – the new dawn outside the Festival Hall, on the lawn outside Millbank and in the County Hall Hotel, and at the National Portrait Gallery – but there was no such triumph for Cameron. Yet instead of retreating into the private room he shared with George Osborne, the ever-gregarious party leader sought comfort in company watching the results come in with his staff, and candidates returning to HQ, congratulating them and modestly celebrating what success there had genuinely been.

The question now, with the result unclear but leaning strongly towards a hung parliament, was what would Nick Clegg have to say? Gordon Brown's acceptance speech, as MP for Kirkcaldy and Cowdenbeath, was largely immaterial. As expected, Brown gave no hostages to fortune, committing himself only to playing his part in the formation of 'a strong, stable and principled government'. Brown and Cameron alike knew that the man who would take the first step in shaping that process was the Liberal Democrat leader. The near-silence on the Brown charter heading back to London (punctured only by the contortions of the press who tried out a range of gizmos to broadcast live from the plane) was partly born of disappointment at the result, but was mainly because the Labour leader's entourage knew that now, all they could do was wait. The next move was Clegg's. News received at 3.40 a.m., as his plane waited on the tarmac, reinforced Gordon Brown's sense that there was a lot still to play for. Rochdale, home to Gillian Duffy, had gone Labour's way. Nothing should be taken for granted, he might have thought.

The Liberal Democrat leader had waved journalists off following their polling day tea party chez Clegg, but he was now holed up in his Sheffield home, and somewhat less desirous of the attentions of the press. It had been a brutal evening, and Clegg had been brought to earth with a bump.

While it was widely recognised that he had turned in his weakest performance in the third and final debate, hopes for Clegg and his party had remained stratospherically high right up until the moment of the publication of the TV exit poll. That poll, suggesting that the Lib Dems would lose seats, was the object of a mixture of bewilderment and derision in the early parts of the evening. Clegg's chief of staff Danny Alexander, speaking on the radio, made clear he simply did not believe the numbers. At the top of the party, there was an acceptance that they might have been pushed back in the last week, but not that their Commons representation would be reduced. As result after result trickled in, the realisation steadily dawned. It became clear that the poll was basically spot-on.

Poor Nick Clegg's frustration was only intensified as he found himself at the heart of a distracting row, caused when some voters were unable to cast their ballots. A little local Cleggmania had ensured that in his constituency of Sheffield Hallam (as in some other parts of the country), enthusiastic, if possibly inexperienced, voters had thronged to polling stations in the final hours they were open, only to have the doors shut in their faces by law at 10 p.m. Instead of being able to concentrate his energies on the electoral picture as it emerged, as he would have desired, Clegg had a bunch of frustrated, involuntary non-voters on his hands – some of whom had come straight to his home from the polling station. He spent the first hours of the night denouncing those who had conducted the ballot.

Then, at the very moment the Liberal Democrat leader was most anxious to return to Westminster, to consult with colleagues and gauge the next step, he became bogged down in an interminable count. Hours later than he had hoped, at just before 4 a.m., Nick Clegg's car backed right up his short driveway to the door, with reporters corralled down on the pavement. It was raining hard. On every similar occasion during the election campaign, there had been a cheery word or a wave from the Liberal Democrat leader. Not tonight. Head down, he and his wife Miriam headed to the count, where they would, once again, be made to wait.

It was not until after 6.30 a.m. that the nation first heard from the man who might now hold the balance of power in parliament. Nick Clegg looked wan and battered. 'We simply haven't achieved what we had hoped,' he admitted. He maintained the casual, straight-talking manner that had become his trademark, and had been thought so popular. 'As to what happens next, clearly the final election result is still a little unpredictable. People have voted but no one appears to have won emphatically.' Caution seemed to have shaded into uncertainty, even a degree of punch-drunk detachment. 'Firstly, and I think this applies to all political parties, I don't think anyone should rush into making claims or taking decisions which don't stand the test of time. And I think it would be best if everybody were just to take a little time so that people get the good government that they deserve in these very difficult and very uncertain times.'

The one nod to the negotiations that would follow was at the close: 'Whatever happens in the next few days, weeks, months, I will be guided, and the Liberal Democrats will be guided by the values and the principles on which we fought this election. A fairness in our society, a responsibility in providing stability and growth to our economy at a time particularly of growing uncertainty as we've seen in recent hours and days in the economy and in the world around us. And real change to the way we do politics.' A few minutes later, he was on the train back to London, to assess the damage.

What were the watching Conservatives to make of it? For Cameron it wasn't bad – no doors had been shut – but it wasn't good either, and it certainly wasn't enough. Nobody would have been surprised that Clegg was pointedly ready, perhaps even eager, for the drawn-out period of negotiations that the Cabinet Secretary and his friends had so lovingly prepared for. Equally, principles of fairness and economic rectitude set up no new barriers. The disappointment was twofold. On the one hand the Lib Dem leader had not even commented on the relative performances of the parties – government down, Tories up – let alone acknowledged that the Conservatives had come first, although they had not won. But, above all, the Tories were waiting for a reiteration of the position Clegg had set out again and again throughout the campaign on who should form a government in the event of a hung parliament. His words in the *Sunday Times* on 25th April were typical: 'I tie my hands in the following sense: that the party that has more votes and seats, but doesn't get an absolute majority – I support them.'

In Sheffield, there was not a hint of all that. Might Clegg be keeping his options open? Might he even be considering a change of tactic? These were the concerns that would keep the Tories on tenterhooks over the coming hours, until the Liberal Democrat leader came to speak again later in the morning.

In fact, Nick Clegg had every intention of sticking to his word. He had been thrown by the unexpectedly poor result, but the opportunities afforded his party by a hung parliament were now starting to come into focus, and Clegg knew that the manner in which he might now force the agenda was critical. It was determined that his throw of the dice would be all the more effective were it to be played not in rainy Sheffield at the fag-end of a miserable night for his party, but on a new day at the Liberal Democrat headquarters in Cowley Street.

4 Cowley Street is one of many gifts to politics from David Sainsbury, who acquired the property originally for the SDP, only for the Liberals to inherit it on the merger of the two parties. The Liberal Democrats occupy a solid Edwardian building in what is almost a cul-de-sac of Queen Anne houses, which make popular pied-à-terres for the more successful members of Westminster's political elite. One former Labour Home Secretary could spit from his front doorstep to the Lib Dems if he so chose or if his close protection officer allowed him. A former occupant of his house, Sir David English, the *Daily Mail* supremo, died there. Just up the street plaques commemorate such famous old inhabitants as Lord Reith of the BBC and Lawrence of Arabia.

As their leader made his way back to the capital, the inhab-itants of the building were weary and disconsolate. One man bucked the trend, at least as far as weariness was concerned. The party's Head of Communications, Jonny Oates, had slept through the Liberal Democrats' most traumatic night. Convinced that no party would emerge with an overall majority, his view was it would be as well in a hung parliament situation if at least someone did not have their mind befuddled by fatigue. At eight o'clock on the evening of election day Oates went to his bed and, contrary to colleagues' predictions, was asleep until four the next morning, thereby missing out on the drip, drip agony, but getting something of a shock when he turned on the television.

Over the next few days, Jonny Oates would play a key part in coordinating the dissemination of the Liberal Democrats' posi-tion in the media, and shoring up his notoriously leaky party to maintain strict secrecy around the coalition negotiations. There had been a great deal of discussion in leadership circles before the election about the importance of using the media not just to argue the Lib Dem case should a hung parliament arise, but also to maintain a constant reassuring commentary on events from figures beloved of the grassroots such as Simon Hughes. This, it was hoped, would ensure the party membership understood what was going on, and did not feel cut off from events at the centre.

By the time of Oates's first conversation with Nick Clegg shortly before dawn on the post-election morning, all that was to come. The Liberal Democrat leader was still deep in recrimination mode, asking himself why this had happened? Paddy Ashdown, the former leader to whom Clegg was closest, confirms he went through a very dark period. When the two men spoke, with Clegg still at his count in Sheffield, his mood was a combina-tion of disappointment and exhaustion, Ashdown recounts. He himself 'was in grit my teeth mode because I'd seen it happen to us time and again.' There was a slight element of 'I told you so': 'I remember saying to him earlier, "Look out for the last week!" . . . He was low at the count because we were falling short of our expectations.'

Speaking to advisors and confidants, Clegg soon bounced back. Chief of staff Danny Alexander was among those who helped shift the leader's state of mind. The two men had talked repeatedly about how they would deal with a hung parliament situation over past months, and found it was not such a stretch to move the focus from 'what might have been', to 'what might be'. On the train, when Paddy Ashdown spoke to Clegg for a second time, his mood had decisively shifted. 'Nick had picked himself up and was thinking about the next move. In politics you think about not the last thing but the next story. We agreed it was important we change the story from "Lib Dems do badly" to "Lib Dems initiate coalition talks".'

The articulation of the Lib Dem position undoubtedly mattered to David Cameron, and was a significant preoccupation. However, the Conservative leader had determined he would not allow his own stance to be dictated by Nick Clegg, and was ready to seize the initiative. All in good time. Having heard the Sheffield acceptance speech, Cameron determined the best thing was to have a couple of hours' sleep, and ready himself for a critical day. He and his wife were driven the short journey across Westminster Bridge to the Park Plaza Hotel. Finding herself unable to sleep, Samantha went home to North Kensington at around 8 a.m., just as her husband was stirring.

As Samantha Cameron was driven back home to get some rest, she would have heard the familiar voices of Peter Mandelson and Theresa May on the car radio playing for time and trying (as everyone else was) to sound like they had a clear sense of what was going on. The instructions that had come down from on high for anyone representing the main parties in the media were clear: they should not give ground or make unnecessary concessions. Just hold steady and wait for the party leaders to make their play.

Anyone looking at the polls over previous months would have had to acknowledge there was a strong chance of a hung parliament. But you would think from the song and dance people were making that some had never quite believed it would happen. Now British politics were careering into the unknown both as to what the outcome in terms of the next government of the UK would be and as to the process by which it would be reached. On the airwaves, overnight results programmes were extended into the breakfast slot in the hope things might become clearer. That would take a while.

The forum of British politics shifted as well, smashing the established pattern – of settled results followed by trips to the palace and assumptions of power and admissions of defeat from party headquarters. Everything was still up for grabs and in the digital era, of multi-channel rolling news every lunge for power over the next five frantic, frustrating and sometimes farcical days, would be played out live on 24/7 TV.

With no government, there was no parliamentary business. MPs flooding back into Westminster found that the theatre for debate had shifted from the Chambers of the Commons and Lords to the other side of the road running alongside the Houses of Parliament – the ad hoc televised talking shop on Abingdon Green. The media village consisted of hastily constructed studios, platforms erected on scaffolding, gazebos galore and a mass of journalists and assorted helpers, all aiming to get the most insightful interviewees onto their channel first. All interested participants would race to get their viewpoint to the waiting cameras and microphones. This was as much a battle within parties to determine what was acceptable to its 'grassroots', as it was between them. An obscure MP (or even ex-MPs such as the defeated Evan Harris and Lembit Opik) could transform themselves into the stars of the hour simply by wandering over and giving a comment.

Then there were those who couldn't or wouldn't go public. Influential but unattached figures such as David Davis or Jon Cruddas, say, who had opinions which mattered but who were not in the negotiations. Privately such people and their surrogates – their known sympathisers and workers – would trade intelligence with broadcast journalists safe in the knowledge that one way or another thanks to on-air comment, blog or Twitter their views would soon be out in the open.

Meanwhile, the real action was out of sight. The secrecy that would surround the negotiations of the coming days was guarded with great success by all three parties. The detail of what was discussed was not disclosed. The very fact some meetings took place only became public knowledge months after it was all over. The 'spin' offered by the usual media sources was almost non-existent: talks were invariably 'positive' or 'constructive' (even 'positive and constructive').

Everyone – anchors, reporters, producers, fixers, technicians – worked their contacts and their phones and BlackBerrys for nuggets of information and speculation which were immediately fed into the cauldron of the round-the-clock media.

With no secure new government in place, there was a breakdown in authority around Westminster. Parliamentary ushers and police allowed cameras to roam more freely around the precincts – there was no power structure to say that they could not. So a politician of interest had to take great care if he or she did not want to be cornered by a camera team and harried reporter in search of an exclusive.

This was new politics without rules. It was politics where nobody would get everything they wanted. Over the next five days, any party and any individual that attempted to dictate terms would only look foolish. Compromise, accommodation and give and take were all in the air. From the leaders of the three main parties, some fancy footwork was required.

Around nine o'clock in the morning, the Tory leader's suite in the Park Plaza was buzzing. The hotel had opened less than two months before, and it had become the base for the senior team over-nighting in London during the campaign. Built at the south end of Westminster Bridge and occupying every inch of the roundabout which separates the old County Hall from Waterloo Station, its better rooms command tantalising views across the Thames to parliament – a modern, progressive building yearningly close to power.

Cameron, freshly shaven and in a clean shirt, was doggedly chewing through a full English cooked breakfast – a traditional culinary habit which he seems determined to make a trademark.

Coulson, Osborne, Llewellyn, Hilton, 'the chief' Patrick McLoughlin, Gabby Bertin and Liz Sugg had all been invited to join the levee from 9 a.m. Not all the gang knew about the hideout. 'You'd better come here' McLoughlin was told over the phone, only to have to ask just where exactly 'here' was.

No one was quite sure what to expect. This was not how it had been supposed to happen. The clear Conservative majority they had been fighting for would have seen Cameron through the gates of Downing Street and into office that very morning. Instead, uncertainty reigned, an air of suspension. All of those present knew that somebody needed to take charge.

If there was disappointment among Cameron's top team at finding themselves on the wrong side of the river, it was less than seasoned observers might have expected. By the close of the campaign, though they hoped for more, the most senior Conservatives had begun to recognise the likelihood of overall victory was diminishing. The day before, as they had sat around Steve Hilton's farmhouse table and joked about what Friday might bring, all present had a go at predicting the result. David Cameron and George Osborne both said they would win between 300 and 310 seats. Pretty much on the money, as it turned out.

What nobody had considered was the extent of the Liberal Democrat collapse, which had a determining impact on the decisions that would be made on the Conservative, and indeed the Labour side, during the subsequent hours. The expectation for the Tories had been that if the Lib Dems did as well as the polls showed, the big loser on the night would be unequivocally the Labour party. That would leave the Conservatives, as the dominant and victorious force, free to claim the keys to Downing Street, and govern as a minority, even if they did not achieve the crucial 326 seats needed for majority control. Almost the identical calculation had been made by Gordon Brown. The day of the poll, Brown met with his immediate team, and it was agreed that if the Tories got over 300 seats, Labour should acknowledge their right to govern.

That would have been the classic Westminster way of doing things, the old-fashioned route. But on the morning of 7th May things no longer felt so straightforward. Naked political calculation showed Labour had done better than Gordon Brown's party had feared they would, and the Prime Minister would therefore not readily accept that he was out of the game. Beyond that, there was a general sense that the message from the electorate was confused, but also (and importantly) a little truculent. What was the voice of people? Perhaps, simply, that they did not want any one party to 'win' the election. That was David Cameron's sense. He awoke with an idea in his mind. There was a chance, he thought, that the country might be ready for something different.

Cameron has since claimed that he had not previously thought about the detail and wording of the coalition proposal for more than a minute. He describes it as a 'fairly epiphanous moment'. The electoral picture was clearer now. 'This is what we've got to do,' he thought. 'I'm going to make a big offer,' Cameron told his colleagues. 'It's what I want to do; my instincts tell me it's the right thing to do.'

There was no dissent, Osborne immediately thought it was 'a brilliant throw of the dice'. And for those who might baulk at the idea of soon sharing power with the Liberal Democrats there was the consolation that Cameron's ploy smacked a little of a Godfather style 'offer you can't refuse'. Many within the party thought the Lib Dems would not be able to swallow a pact with their Conservative rivals. If they proved not to be equal to the challenge, Cameron was unequivocal. He would 'nail them in opposition' for failing to provide the country with a stable and enduring government.

Cameron's friend, neighbour and church co-communicant Michael Gove MP, reckoned it was one of his finest hours: 'He's just a natural born politician. He can read the currents and eddies in politics supremely well. And he knew two things. First, that while rejecting Labour, the electorate had not endorsed the Conservatives one hundred per cent and, second, he knew that a governing opportunity was there for anybody who could get the Conservatives and the Liberal Democrats to work together.'

If there was a chip on the Tory shoulder that morning, it was over the constituency make-up, something they are now pledged to alter through far-reaching boundary changes. It is widely recognised that population changes have left the Conservative party an uphill task in their desire to attain an overall majority. Among the top echelon of Tories, more than one ruefully concluded that had the vote been more equally distributed between constituencies, they would have won outright.

Michael Gove's view is that Cameron put such considerations out of his mind. 'In the period after a general election in which he'd fought his guts out, didn't get the result he'd hoped for – that we'd all hoped for, and which, if the electoral system had been fairer, he would have richly deserved – instead of simply cursing his fate he thinks, "OK what does this tell us? Right, these are the facts, I'll deal with them."'

There was an immediate need to ensure the party would buy into such a radical, and unexpected course of action. Cameron spoke to all the previous Tory leaders still active in politics – John Major, Michael Howard, William Hague and Iain Duncan Smith. (There was little point, alas, in contacting the ailing Margaret Thatcher. She would be kept for a ceremonial tea marking the True Blue recapture of Number 10.) Howard, the present leader's mentor and predecessor, who had cleverly contrived his own exit to deliver the leadership to either Cameron or Osborne, now warned jokingly that Gordon Brown was trying to cling on to power by 'what remains of his finger nails'.

Through the morning Cameron had further conversations with senior figures on all wings of the party from the designated Leader of the House Sir George Young and Kenneth Clarke on the left, to Liam Fox, then Shadow Defence Secretary, on the right. Even the maverick David Davis, a once and (who knows?) perhaps future leadership challenger, was brought into the loop. The net was cast wide, but word of what David Cameron intended to do did not leak from the inner circle, nor the Tory parliamentary party.

As the Conservatives were preparing the ground for their next step, Nick Clegg finally made it back to London. By the time his car drew into Cowley Street, having picked him up from St Pancras Station, declared results from constituencies around the country made it a mathematical certainty that there would be a hung parliament.

Anyone wanting to drive along Cowley Street that morning would have found their route blocked by the most immense throng of reporters, camera crews and satellite trucks. Looking back, Friday the 7th has come to be seen as David Cameron's day, but given the shocks he had endured overnight and his complete lack of sleep, Nick Clegg deserves a degree of credit for simply holding it together for his own big moment. Stepping from his car just after 10.30 a.m. he was immediately mobbed, the first real indication of the chaos that would take hold in Westminster over subsequent days. This was not the time to adlib. On the big occasion he stuck closely to the script. David Cameron and his colleagues would have loved it: 'Whichever party gets the most votes and the most seats, if not an absolute majority, has the first right to seek to govern, either on its own or by reaching out to other parties.' Then he explicitly added, 'It seems this morning that it is the Conservative party that has more votes and more seats . . . it is for the Conservative party to prove that it is capable of seeking to govern in the national interest.'

There was plenty for the Labour party to cling to in Clegg's statement; plainly enough wriggle room had been built in to allow for the Lib Dems to come their way if negotiations with the Tories failed. But for David Cameron, it was enough to confirm him in his chosen course of action. Steve Hilton was sent off to work on the speech for that afternoon, Andy Coulson booked the St Stephen's Club (he ended up reserving the room for the entire afternoon, uncertain when the leader would be ready), and

Cameron's chief of staff Ed Llewellyn was authorised to make the first tentative overtures to the Liberal Democrats. Llewellyn, a former career diplomat, had one or two Lib Dem contacts owing to his time working for the then High Representative in Bosnia Herzegovina, Paddy Ashdown. He texted Danny Alexander, explaining that David Cameron would make a statement later in the afternoon, and indicating it was something they 'might want to pay close attention to'. Knowing Llewellyn's reputation as a man of unerring courtesy and boundless understatement, the Liberal Democrats' top team, in turn, took their cue to get some much-needed sleep.

For all that the Conservatives and Liberal Democrats were making the running, there was still only one Prime Minister – Gordon Brown. From Scotland, Brown had made it back to Labour HQ before seven o'clock in the morning. After addressing the party workers there he went over the emerging electoral arithmetic with his closest advisors. Brown was bullish. He told Peter Mandelson and Andrew Adonis that in the new House of Commons now taking shape, he saw the possibility of forming a government with 'the Liberals'. Assuming the SDLP, the Scottish and the Welsh Nationalists would vote with Labour along with the independent Sylvia Hermon from Northern Ireland and the Green leader Caroline Lucas (the party's first ever MP), and assuming that the DUP would abstain, he calculated wildly that he would have a '20 plus' majority for a Queen's speech. Immediately Brown ordered that contact should be made with the Lib Dems.

Andrew Adonis phoned Danny Alexander a few minutes later. Over the coming days the unelected peer and Transport Secretary, once regarded as an ultra Blairite, would become Brown's key agent in the coalition talks. The son of a Greek Cypriot immigrant waiter, Adonis had transformed himself via

Oxford University into one of the centre left's leading intellectu-
als, obsessed equally with state education and railways. Crucially
Adonis had cut his political teeth as a Liberal Democrat, serving as an Oxford City councillor between 1987 and 1991, and
had even been chosen as a prospective parliamentary candidate
in Westbury, before he resigned and joined Labour in 1995.
Nonetheless he still maintained many personal friendships and
contacts in his former party.

Adonis had volunteered himself as a go-between by penning
an appeal in the *Independent* during the first week of the election
campaign – 'It's madness to split the centre-left vote'. Ostensibly
this was an appeal for tactical voting – at any rate for Labour in
Labour/Lib Dem marginals but Adonis's past as an Oxbridge don
shone through as he lectured his readers on policy and political history. Adonis's political hero and mentor was the late Roy
Jenkins. He had even abandoned work on a biography of the
great man to become a Blair minister and there were shades of
'Woy's' besetting sin, arrogance, as Adonis asserted: 'The truth is
that the Lib Dems, for all their local opportunism, have national
policy that is similar to Labour's. The difference is that Labour
can implement its programme. The Lib Dems have no realistic chance to implement theirs without a Labour government.'
Taking in Gladstone, Asquith and Lloyd George who had 'fought
the Tories relentlessly', Adonis warned that a 'similar fate' would
befall Clegg if he followed Lloyd George in 1918 and went with
the Conservatives; he would 'split his party' and 'destroy his
political authority'.

Adonis ticked off his view of the areas of policy agreement –
investment in public services, fair taxes, constitutional reform,
action on the environment and in the manifestos, notably for
the National Insurance rise and against the £6 billion of cuts.
He admitted there were some differences on criminal justice and

proportional representation but rounded off by flagging Labour's commitment to hold a referendum on the alternative vote.

A month before the election, therefore, Adonis had effectively laid out Labour's agenda for coalition negotiations with the Liberal Democrats. Now perhaps he would have the chance to put it to the test.

So, contrary to what both Labour and Lib Dems claimed at the time and subsequently, the first contacts on coalition were between them and not with the Conservatives. At 7 a.m. the Prime Minister shouldered his way back into Number 10 ignoring the question shouted by reporters: 'Are you going to resign, Mr Brown?' From there, sustained by a heap of bacon, he called such friends as he had who he thought might have influence with the Lib Dem leadership including Paddy Ashdown, Ming Campbell and Vince Cable. Given Clegg's public commitment to speak first to the largest party, both sides agreed that the Lib–Lab dealings would be kept private for the time being from both their wider parties and the media and, of course, the electorate.

The Liberal Democrats were not the only party Labour needed to woo. A stop-the-Tories rainbow coalition would require the support of just about every other MP in the Commons. On the face of it, the obstacles to convincing Northern Irish parties of the need to unite in this way across the sectarian divide were particularly intimidating.

Brown said he had reservations of principle about dealing with the DUP in particular – and rued the price they would be bound to exact from the Treasury. But these were overcome. By the end of the day the Northern Ireland Secretary Shaun Woodward, a defector from the Tories and a Mandelson trusty, was heavily involved in a courtship effort. In spite of subsequent denials from Labour's campaign chief Douglas Alexander (and very likely without his knowledge) Woodward also reached out

to the Scottish Nationalists, well known to him from the British
Irish Council, and asked the SNP to use their contacts to bring
over the DUP, with whom the Nats are surprisingly friendly.
Such was the level of distrust, however, that Angus Robertson
MP, the SNP's leader at Westminster, made a point of collect-
ing and storing voicemail messages from Labour to prove that
contacts had taken place.

But New Labour did not stop at private negotiations to form
a government. True to form, a spin operation was launched, as if
by instinct, to manipulate public expectations. Essentially Labour
attempted to morph the newly re-minted consensus view that
it was Gordon Brown's constitutional duty to stay in office as a
caretaker until a new government could be formed, into the self-
serving perception that the constitution said it was his duty to try
to form a new government.

Lord Mandelson took to the airwaves to explain to anyone
worried, that Gordon Brown was there for them – yea unto the
highest in the land: 'He is the Prime Minister. I don't think it
would help matters if he were suddenly to stand aside. He just
can't resign and leave a vacuum for the Queen to deal with.'

Deputy Leader Harriet Harman went still further as she
outlined her interpretation of Brown's onerous responsibilities
going forward: 'It is his obligation to carry on to see whether he
can form a majority and take that forward. That is his obligation.
He can't throw in the towel.'

Over the next few days Gordon Brown would rely mainly
on this coterie of unelected advisors. Some of the MPs closest
to him were in their constituencies recovering from the election
campaign, including Brown's protégé, Ed Balls. Balls confirms
that 'the people round Gordon in those days were fundamentally
Alastair Campbell, Peter Mandelson, Andrew Adonis and, to
some extent, David Muir, Justin Forsyth, those sorts of people.'

(Muir and Forsyth were both special advisors. Forsyth was an expert on development, who had successfully made the transition from working for Blair to become a highly partisan operative for Brown. After the election he became CEO of Save the Children.)

What was the objective? Some have since suggested that from the outset it was recognised that Gordon Brown would have to step down, and the key task was to manage his departure in a manner that would offer him dignity, and secure the party maximum advantage. Ed Balls is scornful of what he views as a self-serving rewriting of history. '[They] were attempting to prepare for the next government with Gordon as Prime Minister, that was what was going on. I don't think there was any doubt in Gordon's mind that that was what he was planning to do. And I think that they fundamentally didn't believe that for historic reasons, the Liberal Democrats could choose the Conservatives.'

Balls's final point is worth dwelling on, for it was a perception shared by many within the two main parties, and the media. In fact, on the Friday, many Liberal Democrats would have said the very same thing. The Lib Dems? And the Tories? No chance. On the Conservative side, some who in the evening would be sitting down and negotiating a deal with the Lib Dems were in the very same morning profoundly sceptical at the idea of the Liberal Democrats taking up David Cameron's offer.

But while Gordon Brown might not have doubted the viability of his continuing premiership, only now leading a 'progressive coalition' instead of just the Labour party against the Conservatives, others very close to him were apparently contemplating a change at the top. According to the Lib Dems, on Friday afternoon Peter Mandelson texted Danny Alexander (Alexander was a man in demand!), asking 'Is GB a problem?' Nick Clegg's closest advisor was cautious, responding that policy was the most important thing for his party. Nevertheless, Alexander pointed out, 'We'll have to discuss the matter when we come to it.' His view was shared by the Lib Dem leader. The top team in Cowley Street could not believe that given the defeat the party had suffered under Gordon Brown's leadership, a 'very, very substantial defeat' in their view, Labour was seriously contemplating allowing him to stay on.

According to some readings of the events following the 6th of May, Gordon Brown's persistence did the coalition partners-to-be a favour. A month or so after Cameron took power, his Chief Whip speculated on what would have happened if Brown had decided to resign that very morning, having lost the election. Patrick McLoughlin's view was that the Lib Dems would have been deprived of the space to negotiate with both sides and that a weak minority Conservative government would have been the inevitable, though not desirable outcome.

The moment the nation learned of Gordon Brown's intention to keep going (for the time being at least) was when technicians arrived in Downing Street to set up a lectern and speakers. The Prime Minister himself emerged shortly before 2 p.m. It was no coincidence that Gordon Brown's statement came less than an hour before David Cameron was due to speak. The Labour leader, true to form, was not about to let his opponent get in first. The words were artful and calculating. Little wonder. Alastair Campbell had been working on the draft inside Number 10 since late morning.

Brown offered what he modestly called his 'assessment of where we are', saying he did so not as leader of the Labour party (of course not!), but 'as Prime Minister with a constitutional duty to seek to resolve the situation for the good of the country.' Milking the authority of the office for all it was worth, he went on to set out with statesmanlike aplomb the steps that he and Chancellor Alistair Darling were taking, with international partners, to confront the deteriorating situation in the Eurozone. (This was the sort of flourish so long coveted by David Cameron and his colleagues, but afforded only to the man at the helm of the nation.)

The meat of the speech was an offer to the Lib Dems; an offer that was of necessity coy given that another suitor had been given precedence, but an offer nonetheless. 'Clearly should the discussions between Mr Cameron and Mr Clegg come to nothing, then I would of course be prepared to discuss with Mr Clegg the areas where there may be some measure of agreement between our two parties.'

Gordon Brown well knew the centrality of electoral reform to Lib Dem thinking. Doubting that the Conservatives could offer anything close to what the Lib Dems might require, he played what he thought might be the trump card, when he spoke of his 'plan to carry through far-reaching political reforms, including changes to the voting system.' Showing even more leg, the Prime Minister even allowed Lib Dems to dream that proportional representation might not be off the agenda – 'I believe that you the British people should be able to decide in a referendum what the system should be,' a studiously unspecific formulation. Labour's manifesto had already backed the alternative vote, viewed by the Lib Dems as a halfway house to PR. Might they go the whole hog if the public supported it?

There was no mention of Labour's setback, losing seats and vote share while the Conservatives had overtaken them. Olympian magnanimity jostled awkwardly within his short speech with steely-eyed, down and dirty horse-trading. What a poker face it was! As the door closed again behind Gordon Brown, there was applause from the staff who had been watching inside. The Prime Minister was not dictating terms, but he was in the game.

Gordon Brown hit the phones as Westminster, and the nation, waited to see how David Cameron would respond.

When he spoke at the St Stephen's Club, David Cameron did not once use the word 'coalition'. It had featured in earlier drafts of the statement, but was taken out, owing to general agreement among Cameron and his colleagues that 'you didn't need to say it', it was obvious in the terms and the scope of what was proposed.

Instead, the Conservative leader spoke of his belief that: 'There is a case for going further than an arrangement which simply keeps a minority Conservative government in office.' He barely paid lip service to the idea of a minority Tory administration, constructed on the basis of 'confidence and supply' (where a smaller party agrees to support the larger on its budget – the supply – as well as during any votes of no confidence used by other parties to try to bring the government down), an arrangement which many observers had expected to be the core substance of the speech. 'It's been done before, and yes we can try to do it again,' Cameron acknowledged. 'But I am prepared to consider alternative options. It may be possible to have stronger, more stable, more collaborative government than that.'

The heart of the speech was a 'big, open and comprehensive offer' to the Lib Dems. This was David Cameron's own formulation, and it is a phrase as resonant as it is, today, misremembered. The entire senior Conservative staff (from the top man down!) seem to have convinced themselves Cameron said 'generous' – 'big and generous'; 'big, open and generous' or some similar formulation. Even Liberal Democrat colleagues in Downing Street have now come to share the misconception. 'Generous' never once passed from David Cameron's mouth. It was the other word that 'you didn't need to say'.

What made the speech more than words was Cameron's willingness to put flesh on the bones. It was plain that he was completely up to speed with the Lib Dem manifesto, and Lib Dem priorities generally. On a 'pupil premium', designed to give additional funding to children from poorer backgrounds: 'We agree with this idea, it is in our manifesto too, and I am sure we can develop a common approach.' On the environment: 'The Liberal Democrats in their manifesto have made the achievement of a low-carbon economy an absolute priority and we support this aim.' On the Lib Dems' manifesto commitment to raise the basic rate tax threshold to £10,000: 'It has always been an aspiration for the Conservative party to reduce taxes, especially on those who earn the least, and we are happy to give this aim a much higher priority, and to work together to determine how it can be afforded.' A shared perspective on civil liberties and scrapping ID cards was skipped over, and Cameron signalled his willingness to do business on the key area of electoral reform. 'On our political system we agree with the Liberal Democrats that reform is urgently needed to help restore trust – and that reform must include the electoral system.' As to what shape that reform might mean, Cameron was vague, perhaps too vague for Liberal Democrats' comfort, perhaps necessarily so given the central importance this issue would take in the impending negotiations. All he would offer at this stage was 'an all-party committee of inquiry on political and electoral reform.'

Cameron set out the Tory red lines too. This, he knew, was important in order to reassure his party, but also facilitated the coalition talks, because the Lib Dems could now be in no doubt about which areas the Conservatives viewed as 'non-negotiable'. A commitment not to cede further powers to the European Union, a 'strong' policy on defence and an assertion that 'I do not believe that any government can be weak or soft on the issue of immigration which needs to be controlled properly' featured here. On the economy, Cameron made clear that they would not be diverted from their favoured course of action, in making immediate cuts to public spending. 'No government will be in the national interest unless it deals with the biggest threat to our national interest – and that is the deficit,' David Cameron warned. 'We remain completely convinced that starting to deal with the deficit this year is essential.'

Cameron ended his speech by setting out the reasoning behind his bold step and explaining why, in his view, those within Tory ranks who might be caught off guard would quickly come round to the idea. 'The Conservative party has always been a party that puts the national interest first,' Cameron insisted, but his point was that a coalition was right not because he wanted it, but because the country demanded it. 'And the best thing, the national interest thing, the best thing for Britain now is a new government that works together in that national interest, and I hope with all my heart that is something that we can achieve.'

There were no questions to the Conservative leader. As he stepped from the room, it was left to George Osborne to deal with a barrage of journalists' enquiries. In the melee, the word 'coalition' was repeated again and again. 'Was this a coalition proposal?' 'Wait and see,' Osborne teased. In politics a non denial should more often than not be taken as a confirmation but many of the press reporters present appeared to have difficulty computing the enormity of what had just been proposed, scarcely able to credit that a partisan politician could even consider sharing power with another party.

It was a leap of faith that marked a new political generation – as two Tory veterans concurred when they talked it over later that month. They may both be Welsh but on the Conservative spectrum Michael Howard and Michael Heseltine are far apart. The first was the Eurosceptic, 'prison works', former leader who created the conditions for Cameron to come to power, the latter was the anti-Thatcherite, Europhile ex-Deputy Prime Minister. Yet given Cameron's hand to play, they both admitted that they would have gone for minority government – and that they would have been wrong.

To Nick Clegg and his team, Cameron's statement felt like the real deal; 'very positive and generous'. As Danny Alexander puts it, 'He had gone further in addressing the four key themes than we'd expected and that left us feeling that there really was a serious discussion to be had.' Other Lib Dems admit to having been taken aback at the breadth of Cameron's vision. A group of MPs who watched Cameron in the outer office of Nick Clegg's Commons suite included one of the negotiating team, Andrew Stunell. For him, the offer was unexpectedly bold. 'We all looked at each other. We had been waiting for this moment for so long, we could hardly believe it was happening.' Paddy Ashdown was impressed: 'The really surprising thing was the speed, and states-manlike nature of the response from Cameron. He was clearly up for something substantial, and I thought he grasped his moment very well.'

Nevertheless, a coalition offer from the Tories did not come completely out of the blue for those Liberal Democrats who had been involved in analysing hung parliament scenarios over the past months. For David Laws, 'It felt like exactly what we had expected, which was that if there was no overall Tory majority then we expected that the Conservatives would open up talks on a very all-embracing basis with full coalition on offer. It would make sense for them to do so both because that would then provide a stable government, but also because it would put us on the spot.'

Not everyone was impressed by Cameron's statement though. In Downing Street Gordon Brown told his aides that Cameron had shown weakness – he should have demanded the keys to Number 10 immediately. Brown did not believe that a Con–Lib Dem pact could ever happen because of the ideological and personal differences between the parties. Instead, ever the tactician rather than the strategist, he calculated that the offer would strengthen the Lib Dems' negotiating position by playing the two suitor parties off against each other. The Prime Minister's analysis prevailed and no one dissented, although Mandelson subsequently wrote of his private feelings that Cameron had at last acted boldly: 'I was almost alone in our ranks in being impressed . . . to me, it sounded like the new politics, and I thought the public might welcome the idea of the Tories being willing to moderate their manifesto and make common cause with Nick Clegg.'

The Labour team with the Prime Minister at least acknowledged that Cameron had regained the initiative, however imprecisely, and the general mood flagged. Mandelson was soon stretched out asleep on a sofa but Gordon Brown hit the phones again. He called Ed Balls, tried to win over newspaper editors and scarcely paid attention as Jack Straw hedged his position with reservations at the other end of the line. The Labour wooing of Liberal Democrats continued apace.

David Cameron spoke to Nick Clegg on the telephone shortly after his speech, establishing the parallel leaders' channel that, over coming days, would be vital in resolving problems that were too tricky for the negotiating teams to deal with alone.

And now that they were 'on the spot', the Conservatives were not about to let the Liberal Democrats walk away. There was talk on the Lib Dem side about waiting for the next morning to begin formal negotiations, but George Osborne and his colleagues were having none of it: 'We were like, "Let's get this process underway!"' one recalls. The Cabinet Office was chosen, and soon afterwards rival four-man teams (Osborne, Hague, Letwin and Llewellyn v Alexander, Laws, Stunell and Huhne) sat down for the first time.

8

STRANGE DAYS

'. . . that was when the world changed for me'

The circus that enveloped Westminster and captivated the country on the days between Friday 7th May and the following Tuesday, when David Cameron became Prime Minister, was unprecedented and surreal. They were days of wild speculation, brinkmanship, whispering in dark corners, Le Carré-style subterfuge, media scrums, agony, dignity and triumph. And the whole lot revolving around a bunch of middle-aged men (this is perhaps doing the then thirty-eight-year-old George Osborne a disservice!) in a nondescript room poring over policy documents.

Two bodies were entirely prepared for the situation: the civil service who under the stewardship of Sir Gus O'Donnell had readied themselves minutely for a hung parliament; and the Liberal Democrat party for whom this had always been the only viable route to power. The Conservatives were much more prepared than they looked, and Labour (who were only apparently left on the sidelines) rather less so.

When the Conservative and Lib Dem negotiating teams entered the Cabinet Office on Friday evening, Sir Gus showed them into the conference room he had set aside for proceedings. A narrow table stood in the centre with seats along each side, and other officials waiting to greet the parties. It was very, very warm. It was not only the lack of adequate air-conditioning that the politicians found stifling, though. The whole rigmarole of civil service involvement in the process was to the taste neither of the Conservatives, nor the Lib Dems. They had eyes only for each other. As David Laws recalls: 'The civil servants were there obviously expecting to facilitate [the talks]. I think the Queen's Private Secretary was there when we turned up as well. Gus O'Donnell offered to have the civil servants service the meeting and look after us all and we said we didn't need any help. So there was this rather sad "Sir Humphrey-type" scene where he kind of disappeared round the door, hoping that we would change our minds, right up to the final minute.'

Andrew Stunell recalls that the rejection of official assistance ('These are the civil servants that are going to help you,' he remembers being told) was in effect a first bonding moment for the negotiating teams. It was the moment that 'We realised that we were going to do this thing on our own.'

The ice broken, they were free to get on with the job. The first meeting was principally about process, and how a deal (whether full coalition or confidence and supply) might be ratified by the two parties. William Hague explained that if the negotiators could agree, he would check with David Cameron and with the 1922 Committee and that would be pretty much that. On the Liberal Democrat side, Danny Alexander launched into what he describes as a five or ten minute spiel about Lib Dem internal processes – the triple lock, the federal executive, conference, the works. There was amusement on both sides of the table at the parties' contrasting ways of doing business.

There was one key realisation for both sets of negotiating teams. Coalition was viewed unanimously as the best way forward. The Lib Dems had gathered as much from David Cameron's 'big offer' but were not completely certain it was for real. On the Conservative side, it came as a real surprise. William Hague explains, 'From the moment when they sat down there that Friday night, that was when the world changed for me. Their enthusiasm for a coalition, and the fact that we proved to be able to get on with them so well in a personal way . . . It was all a bit of a shock.'

There was a certain amount of having to pinch themselves going on with the Conservatives, as it began to occur to them that they might have misjudged the Lib Dems. At no stage had they anticipated that the Lib Dems would be as prepared to enter a coalition. Now though, the team were forced to recognise that immediately and very clearly the four men opposite were much more interested in a coalition than they were in supporting a minority government.

The Lib Dem strategy was not a spur of the moment decision. It had deep roots. As the party with most to gain from a hung parliament, their deliberations had been carried out over many months, and with considerable thoroughness. The full negotiating team had been formally appointed by Nick Clegg in December of the previous year so they were ready to go the moment it was necessary. They met regularly, shared out policy briefs (the economy for David Laws, the environment and constitutional reform for Chris Huhne and so on . . .). They came together during the election campaign when it was clear a hung parliament was an increasing likelihood. Their last meeting before polling day was on the final Sunday, when they agreed, that if it came to it, they would all be in Cowley Street by eleven o'clock the morning after the election, ready to pick up the pieces – wherever they lay.

Danny Alexander, MP for Inverness, Nairn, Badenoch and Strathspey, led them. He was closest to Clegg as his chief of staff, and had worked on the manifesto. As an Oxford PPE (Politics, Philosophy and Economics) graduate and former communications director for both Britain in Europe and European Movement his political connections belied his relative youth at thirty-seven, with only five years at Westminster behind him. They stretch the full spectrum from Peter Mandelson on the left to the Tory columnist Peter Oborne on the right, for whose 'White City All Stars' cricket team he is the demon opening fast bowler.

The former architect and Baptist lay preacher Andrew Stunell, sixty-seven, MP for Hazel Grove, Greater Manchester since 1997, was no better known – except to Liberal Democrat activists. Stunell had more than thirty years' experience working for the party from being leader of Cheshire Council to Chief Whip in the Commons. He knew what the party would swallow and his job was to be the team's conscience, as well as to apply his intimate knowledge of local government.

The other two Lib Dem negotiators, Chris Huhne, fifty-five, and David Laws, forty-four, supplied what passed for glamour. Both had experience of deal-making in the City and both now had a convenient cushion of 'a bit of money'. After Westminster (the same school as Clegg but much earlier), business and financial journalism for the *Guardian* and flirtations with Labour and the SDP, Huhne had become a Lib Dem MEP, then MP for Eastleigh in 2005, a highly marginal seat where he increased his majority in 2010. As a freshman MP he had stood twice for the party leadership, against Ming Campbell and then, in a close contest, against Clegg. Huhne was charged with the Lib Dems' number one priority – reforming the electoral system in their favour. David Laws, Ashdown's successor as MP for Yeovil, led in economic discussions, to nobody's surprise. After Cambridge he had forged a stellar career in banking, becoming a vice president of JP Morgan while still in his twenties, before being elected in 2001, having worked in the Lib Dem back office alongside Clegg.

The process of readying the party for a hung parliament was not left only to the negotiators. At the apex of the party, the ramifications of a result which left no single party with overall control were a constant subject of discussion, particularly between the leader and Danny Alexander.

During this period, the party 'wargamed' the entire range of possible scenarios. What became clear to them was that the process could not be imagined in a vacuum, simply by evaluating the various arithmetical outcomes; weighing up the potential policy offers from each side and so on. The more they looked into it, the more one factor loomed over proceedings – the economy and, specifically, the budget deficit. Dealing with the deficit – imposing spending cuts and tax increases – was going to put immense strain on whatever make-up of government emerged. Under the scenarios that were developed, however, a 'confidence and supply'-style administration did not look to have a chance of making it through a year, let alone a parliament. If the governing partners were not locked into the process of deficit reduction – if they were not genuinely 'hung together' – then it became almost inevitable that when the going got tough, the arrangement would collapse. As Danny Alexander puts it, 'It became clear that it was difficult to establish confidence in the government if it could fall apart at any moment.'

This was not an appetising prospect for the Lib Dems. 'Strong, stable government' was a formulation employed by all three parties in this period, but for the Lib Dems, 'stability' was of particular importance. Firstly there was the instinct for self-preservation. If a minority government collapsed in the months after May, that would mean another general election. At that election voters would likely seek to manufacture a more decisive result, and turn back to the traditional governing parties – Labour and Conservative. But on top of that, only a stable government could hope to deliver the Lib Dems the long-term prizes they have fought so long for, in particular electoral reform. What the Lib Dems were looking for – what they needed – was an agreement that was sustainable for the full term of a parliament. In the impending pressure-cooker of cuts, job losses and uncertainty, they concluded only a coalition genuinely fitted the bill.

If the pleasant surprise for the Conservative team was the level of enthusiasm from the Lib Dems for coalition, the Lib Dems were no less heartened by the detail and coherence of the Conservative proposal. What the Tory team put forward did not feel like a 'back of a fag packet' plan, cooked up that morning to deal with the unexpected situation of finding themselves not in government. And it wasn't. The Conservatives were far more prepared for the eventuality than was publicly recognised at the time, or indeed has become clear subsequently.

The prime mover of the Tory preparations for a hung parliament was George Osborne. Several weeks before polling day, he raised the issue of a hung parliament in private with David Cameron. 'We really must prepare for the possibility of having to talk to the Liberal Democrats,' he told him. Cameron agreed, but did not want to get involved himself. With the challenge of the television debates claiming almost all of his energy, the Tory leader felt he could not spare the time for so delicate a process. Given that Cameron's key task was precisely to ensure that a hung parliament did not come about, it was agreed that he keep his mind uncluttered by speculation about what might happen if the Tories fell short.

It was settled. Osborne would take on responsibility for looking into the issue. William Hague, Oliver Letwin and Ed Llewellyn were co-opted to help. Thus the Conservative negotiating team was conceived in embryo. In the midst of the electoral fray, it was a project of the utmost sensitivity. No one was told who did not have to be. Even some of David Cameron's most intimate aides were kept entirely in the dark. Over successive weekends during the campaign, the four men met at George Osborne's Notting Hill villa for supper. Each with a copy of the Liberal Democrat manifesto (with its sparsely functional cover and blue lettering), they sat down to work out where in its hundred pages there might be an overlap with their own policies. In effect, the team felt, the best approach was to take the Lib Dems at their word. They would assume Nick Clegg's assertion, that he would first turn to the party with the strongest mandate, to be true; and they would work on the basis that the policies the party had made central to their platform during the campaign were indeed the ones they would strive to see enacted.

Gratifyingly, the Lib Dem prospectus was viewed by the Tories as a clear and useful guide. When drawing up the manifesto, Danny Alexander had seen his principal responsibility as ensuring that it was financially credible. (It was within this context that the Lib Dems committed to phasing out tuition fees over several years rather than scrapping them outright.) Financial pressures concentrated minds, forcing the party to decide what it really wanted, and what was expendable. When coupled with the knowledge that in any future negotiation to enter government clarity and simplicity would be helpful, the party settled on a core platform. There were four pillars: fairer taxation (including the basic rate tax threshold at £10,000);

innovative education (including the pupil premium); a greener economy; and cleaner politics (electoral reform, principally). All four were to find a mention in David Cameron's 'big, open and comprehensive offer' speech.

The Conservative team discovered that looking for overlap between the two parties' policies was a less arduous process than they had feared. Around the dinner table, there was a rueful acknowledgement that because they had been so preoccupied with Labour and Gordon Brown, the Tories had not realised how far their party and the Liberal Democrats had travelled towards one another. As one negotiator puts it, 'We hadn't quite seen that the more socially liberal Conservative party had a lot of overlap with the fiscally conservative Liberal Democrat party.' If you could place one party's plan on top of the other like architects' transparencies, the feeling among the Tories was, you would find that about three quarters of it fitted. All the civil liberties, climate change, and taxation policies overlapped a lot once you had accepted getting rid of George Osborne's plan to raise the threshold of inheritance tax, perhaps surprisingly something neither he nor his three colleagues had great difficulty with. The work that Osborne, Hague, Letwin and Llewellyn completed became the basis for the eventual coalition agreement. A few days before the country went to the polls, it was shown to David Cameron. Though he had played no part in the process, Cameron signed off on the document.

The policy principles that the four negotiators set out clearly informed David Cameron's St Stephen's Club address, and played an important part in persuading the Lib Dems that the Tories would take their ideas seriously. There was, nevertheless, a big difference between the principle underlying what Cameron set out the day after the election, and what Osborne and Co had been secretly working on. Their presumption had been that a minority

Conservative government propped up by the Liberal Democrats was the way ahead. He went for full coalition, unequivocally.

There were two reasons why a coalition was not fully considered by the negotiators. First was the generally held presumption that the Lib Dems could not stomach it. The other was the expectation that if the Tories ended up short of an overall majority, they would be only just short. William Hague's best guess during the campaign was that the party would end up on 315, not 307. Only a few seats' difference, but it would most likely have changed everything. Take away the Sinn Féin members, add a couple of Ulster Unionists and, the thinking was, you would more or less have a majority. On that basis, and according to the many other permutations that ran through high-ranking Conservatives' brains during that period, scraping around for a coalition partner was the last thing they would be thinking about.

However, two Tories had allowed themselves to muse about the potential benefits of a full coalition government even during the election campaign. They were David Cameron and George Osborne. The Conservative leader and his closest political friend and advisor had set aside precious time during the weeks before polling day to sit down, have dinner and unwind, and chew the fat. While the meetings were ostensibly designed to talk about the debates process and how the campaign was going, once Osborne and Cameron were alone, the issue of a hung parliament was discussed. One way or another, the possibility of a coalition cropped up. Whoever it was who first mentioned the idea (and through the haze of several hectic months, recollections came to vary), both men essentially set their thoughts to one side – Cameron in order to pursue a campaign he intended to win; Osborne to complete his and his colleagues' work on the Lib Dem manifesto – work that was posited on the greater likelihood of a Conservative minority administration.

The ideas that David Cameron and George Osborne rumi-nated on over two dinners in the run-up to the second and third debates were ultimately to find their voice (and their 'big, open and comprehensive' formulation) only after polling day. The conclusion towards which both men, in varying ways, felt their way was the selfsame conclusion that the Lib Dems had reached through an entirely different process: namely that governing as a minority would be very difficult in practice. A coalition, Cameron and Osborne speculated, might be a much more stable form of government.

It was a tentative discussion, the sort of thing that in the heat of an election campaign and with so much to play for, David Cameron could permit himself only in private, and with his most trusted collaborator. There was also, at this point, an opportun-istic dimension to what they explored. Making a full coalition offer might be the right thing all round. Even if the Lib Dems did not accept the deal, they calculated, it would be a good thing for the Conservatives to be seen to have put on the table.

So when, a couple of weeks later, the opportunity presented itself, Cameron was ready, and able to seize the moment. Focused on the immediate task at hand, the Tory leader had shut out any thought of a hung parliament, minority government, coalition or whatever else from his mind as he embarked on the final push for victory.

But on that morning of 7th May at the Park Plaza Hotel, in his first waking moment Cameron's thoughts returned to the territory he and Osborne had warily explored together. Things fell into place. It seemed preferable. This was a government that might actually do something; a government that could last. 'Aim high,' David Cameron told himself. 'If you fall short, at least you tried.'

A few hours after David Cameron's epiphanic moment, the negotiating teams assembled to see if they could make the whole speculative adventure happen. The wiliest political operator on the team was George Osborne. Just thirty-eight, the Shadow Chancellor had been intimate with Cameron ever since they had worked together as party aides before both entering parliament at the 2001 election. The son of a hippyish baronet and wallpaper tycoon, Osborne was educated at St Paul's not Eton. Like Cameron he went to Oxford and was a member of the Bullingdon Club, but being five years younger he did not overlap there with his friend.

William Hague, Cameron's 'deputy in all but name', was the obvious choice as captain and spokesman of the Tory team. Still only forty-nine, the MP for Richmond Yorks already had more than twenty years in parliament under his belt, as well as four years as Conservative leader. In seeking to unite the party, Cameron had made a point of cherishing its previous, mostly unsuccessful leaders and had already confirmed Hague as Foreign Secretary in any Tory government to come.

Oliver Letwin, MP for the highly vulnerable Dorset West constituency, was the oldest member of the team at fifty-three. The only one to have gone to Cambridge (where he was a member of the University Liberal Club), the others all having gone to Oxford. Letwin had an unfortunate career as a front bench spokesman largely because he was too outspoken and too nice. Gaffes included having to go into hiding after being frank about Tory plans for cuts during the 2001 election, and letting a burglar into his own home because he asked to use the toilet at 5 a.m. in the morning. However, the professorially brainy Letwin, with a PhD from the London Business School, had found his métier in the boiler room of progressive Conservative policymaking: 'Ask Oliver to compare 16 manifestos and he'll come up with a document of spellbinding brilliance,' Cameron explained. In the case in question he'd only had to compare three manifestos.

Ed Llewellyn, Cameron's chief of staff, was the fourth Tory negotiator. An unelected official he had overlapped with Cameron both at Eton and Brasenose, Oxford. A diplomat and civil servant by training he had useful links both to the Liberal Democrats and the wet wing of the Conservative party, having served as an aide both to Chris Patten during his governorship of Hong Kong as well as his time spent with Ashdown in Bosnia.

For neither side, Conservative nor Liberal Democrat, was there the slightest doubt that their interlocutors were credible and united. Both valued the importance of having the party leaders stand back from the coalface of discussion, leaving them able to take a longer view; but there was never a hint that what was on offer was not with the full authority of both David Cameron on the one side and Nick Clegg on the other.

Sir Gus O'Donnell was delighted that such discussions were taking place. Unfortunately, although Sir Gus and his civil service colleagues had been the midwife to the coalition process, the politicians were ultimately unhappy to have him in the room while the baby was born.

As the polls and projections solidified from the end of 2008 on, interested academics and civil servants could see just as well as many politicians that a hung parliament was a real possibility and they started to prepare for it. One motive was common sense – as O'Donnell pointed out to MPs on the Justice Committee in February 2010, he was the most senior civil servant after twenty-eight years' service but even he had not been around in 1974, the last time it had happened.

O'Donnell, and his predecessors, including some who had been directly involved in 1974 such as Lord Butler, and academics and journalists, notably Professor Robert Hazell of the Constitution Unit at University College London and Peter Riddell, then of *The Times*, also began to argue that things had not gone terribly well that year. The Liberal leader Jeremy Thorpe had had to make his escape from the media over a ploughed field; outgoing Prime Minister Ted Heath had not been able to contact the people he needed; senior mandarins had been left sorting out the constitutional proprieties in gentlemen's clubs and Mayfair restaurants; there had had to be a second general election that year anyway; and everybody still said, wrongly in their view, that it was up to the Queen to choose the new Prime Minister. On top of that, nowadays, Riddell warned, 'There is both ignorance and danger in the world of 24-hour news, of sovereign funds potentially dumping sterling and things like that'.

This free association of the great and good then took it upon themselves to re-educate the politicians, the civil servants, the media and the public about what could or should happen if there were another hung parliament. Outside official channels the benefactor David Sainsbury endowed a new Institute for Government to the tune of some £15 million, from the fortune derived from his family's grocery chain. As well as his early bank-rolling of the SDP and Liberal Alliance, Lord Sainsbury (Eton and Cambridge) had made multimillion-pound donations to New Labour, serving in the Blair administration as minister for science. He had formed the impression that there was considerable room for improvement in the workings of government: 'It's like a Rolls-Royce which was made 60 years ago but isn't really appropriate for racing today. It was once a good machine but now it's frustrating ministers and civil servants.'

The new institute produced two highly influential reports in late 2009: 'Transitions: preparing for changes of government', followed by 'Making Minority Government Work: Hung parliaments and the challenges for Westminster and Whitehall'.

The 'Transitions' document, co-authored by Riddell, directly addressed the concern of civil servants that a change of government between political parties looked likely at the general election and that the last two changes (Callaghan/Thatcher in 1979 and Major/Blair in 1997) had not gone particularly well. It was not until several years after Mrs Thatcher had come to power that the civil service realised how radical her plans were; they had neither understood nor expedited her manifesto. Likewise the civil service had never really gelled with Blair, his small coterie of advisors in opposition had simply become 'sofa government' in office, while Blair looked to outside agents to implement the changes he wanted. If they got the coming transition right, the civil service might hope to regain some of the influence lost to 'the sofa'.

In parallel with the Institute for Government's work and with the authorisation of Prime Minister Gordon Brown, Sir Gus O'Donnell set about codifying procedure on these questions by compiling a new 'Cabinet Manual'. O'Donnell was a meritocratic figure, having attended the Roman Catholic Salesian College in Battersea and then Warwick University before an inevitable postgraduate stint at Nuffield College, Oxford. He knew the interfaces between politicians, civil servants and the media better than most having been Press Secretary to John Major both at the Treasury and Number 10, Permanent Secretary at the Treasury, Britain's representative at the World Bank/IMF in Washington and Cabinet Secretary to both Blair and Brown.

O'Donnell's work culminated in early 2010. By the time that Gordon Brown announced that the manual was being prepared, O'Donnell had begun to hold meetings with his officials about possible outcomes at the election. There were two big sessions in January and April bringing together staff from Number 10, Buckingham Palace, the Cabinet Office and other government departments. At the later meeting, in April with the election upon them, officials gamed 'one scenario (No. 4) which, as it turned out, was very close to the actual result.'

The Cabinet Secretary also consulted academics over a sandwich lunch in the Cabinet Office – the professors invited were Robert Hazell, Peter Hennessy of Queen Mary, University of London, and author of a number of genre-crossing books about government process, Vernon Bogdanor of Brasenose, Oxford, and coincidentally David Cameron's former tutor; Rodney Brazier, Professor of Constitutional Law at Manchester University; joined by Peter Riddell of the Institute for Government and *The Times*. But O'Donnell bridles at Hennessy's comment that 'it was all sorted out then'.

Instead O'Donnell looked closely at what went on in the UK's sister democracies of Canada, Australia and New Zealand – all with the Queen as Constitutional Head of State. New Zealand was particularly fruitful because a shift there to proportional representation had made 'hung parliaments' just about inevitable. (If Britain were ever to adopt PR, O'Donnell is sure to be commended for thinking ahead once again.)

The New Zealanders had already codified much of what Britain was now trying to do. O'Donnell freely admits that New Zealand provided him with his model for the Cabinet manual. However New Zealand also caused him some problems when he went there in April 2010 for the annual meeting of British, Canadian, and antipodean Cabinet Secretaries – ash in the atmosphere from Iceland's Eyjafjallajökull volcano delayed his flight home by a week (although O'Donnell insisted he was able at all times to monitor the developing political situation back in Britain).

In late February O'Donnell published his Cabinet manual draft 'Chapter 6: Elections and Government Formation' and he appeared before the Commons Justice Select Committee, although his constitutional work was largely overlooked because he was also questioned about new allegations in a book by Andrew Rawnsley that Gordon Brown had bullied staff. 'You go from the sublime to the ridiculous!', the Cabinet Secretary expostulated to the MPs.

The Institute for Government and the Cabinet Office also made efforts to ensure that journalists were up to speed with their views. They targeted rolling news organisations such as Sky News in particular because they judged (correctly as it turned out) that at times of political uncertainty viewers would turn to live coverage of developments. 'We want to make sure you get it right', one team of briefers explained to the surprise of Adam Boulton and Jon Craig.

The combined wisdom of the institute and the Cabinet Office could be summarised simply:

1. In the event of a hung parliament, there would be no power vacuum – the incumbent Prime Minister remained in office, with executive power, until he or she resigned. (Unfortunately this was perverted in two ways in 2010 – some newspapers accusing Brown of squatting in Number 10 – while some of his advisors tried to suggest it was his 'duty' to form a new government.)

2. It was up to the politicians to negotiate between themselves to see who could form a government which would command parliamentary support. Government resources would be made available to assist this process, which would take several days at minimum. Talk of a continental style forty day hiatus never seemed credible.

   (On the recommendation of the House of Commons Modernisation Committee, Gordon Brown doubled the time allowed by precedent between election day and the assembly of the new parliament, and between the election and the Queen's speech to twelve and twenty-four days respectively. Simon Hughes pointed out in advance that twelve days would be quite enough time for the Liberal Democrats to approve any deal under their 'triple lock' procedure – MPs, federal executive and party membership.)

3. The Queen would not be involved in discussions. She would only ask a new Prime Minister to form a government once the old one had resigned and once she had been informed that a new government was viable by a 'golden triangle' of advisors from the civil service: the Cabinet Secretary, the Queen's Private Secretary (Christopher Geidt in May 2010) and the Prime Minister's Principal Private Secretary (Jeremy Heywood).

   (This was obviously designed to protect the monarch from any suspicion of political partisanship. Professor Robert Blackburn of King's College London went further with the controversial suggestion that the establishment might be attempting to insulate the political process in advance from the consequences of the 'meddling Prince' Charles becoming King. O'Donnell and his colleagues dismissed this theory.)

4. The Queen would not be minded to grant an early dissolution for an early general election. If the incumbent Prime Minister (Gordon Brown) formed a new government which collapsed, he or she would be denied a general election – the opposition would be invited to try to form a government first. Even if the opposition took power first, there would be reluctance to hold

another election until a considerable time had passed, most likely more than a year. In other words 1974 would not be allowed to happen again.

(This finding was the most controversial since it militated against the traditional power of the Prime Minister to call an early general election. The experts argued that the voters had collectively given their opinion in the general election and that they should not be troubled again, it was the job of the politicians to make the will of the people, as expressed, work.)

As it turned out both sides in the new coalition government adopted this mode of thinking by taking up the idea of fixed-term parliaments and proposing to remove the Prime Minister's power to dissolve parliament early.

O'Donnell briefed the party leaders on his recommendations around the time that he published his chapter. And even though it remained in draft, he spoke again to the Prime Minister about it the morning after the general election. Brown then 'confirmed his permission for the civil service to provide support to political parties as set out in the guidance'.

If constitutional coup it was, it was a very British coup bringing together the worlds of Chris Mullin and Sir Humphrey Appleby. Certainly, as Sir Humphrey might have said, the transition all went according to Sir Gus's plan. Countering accusations that he had effected a coup, O'Donnell insisted: 'It is very clear to me that this was not a power grab. The overwhelming view of expert commentators is that the civil service prepared well, that the guidance we published helped to clarify how things should work, and that the actual process worked extremely well.'

The one thing the Cabinet Secretary and his colleagues wisely did not attempt to quantify was the level of hysteria that would accompany proceedings. Never can the sight of four men walking across a road clutching ring binders have prompted such excitement. 'Here comes Danny Alexander with Andrew Stunell, and now we can see Chris Huhne making his way through the crowd and yes . . . it's David Laws!' (Clad in his Barbour jacket, Laws seemed to take some perverse pleasure in gently ambling amid the frenzy. Ed Miliband has not forgiven him for being late for the first Lib–Lab meeting.) Never can statements of the banality of William Hague's 'Well, we've had an initial meeting. That's all there is to say at the moment' (on Friday night) have been subjected to such forensic and exhaustive journalistic analysis.

Those who were, in one way or another, 'in the loop' scoffed at the ill-informed media comment one moment, while doing all they could to ensure the batteries of reporters scouring Westminster remained in the dark the next.

Occasionally though, a snippet might emerge that was not entirely divorced from the true state of affairs. On Saturday lunchtime, as David Cameron, Nick Clegg and Gordon Brown were all three preparing to attend VE Day commemorations in Whitehall, it was reported that Clegg and Brown had spoken the day before, and the conversation had descended into a 'diatribe' and a 'rant' from the Labour leader. Labour and Liberal Democrat media managers both went into overdrive to bury a story that would not do the mood music between the parties any good. Harriet Harman indignantly insisted that, 'Any suggestion that it was in any way angry would be wrong.' An official Lib Dem statement was just as convincing: 'Any suggestion that it was in any way angry or hostile would be wrong.'

While 'rant' may have overstated it, what is clear is that no bridges were built during this critical first contact between the Labour and Lib Dem leaders. Without even a nod to the relative performances of the parties, Brown had opened up by reducing the election outcome to maths: 'Nick, the only issue is a majority of seats in the Commons', and proceeded to lecture Clegg down the line on why he should see things his way, why they should form a partnership and, effectively, how much of Brown's manifesto Clegg could help him save. Gordon was 'Gordonish' according to Mandelson who was listening in. Coming off the phone, the Prime Minister told aides who had implored him to 'be charming' that he had done his job.

The truth was that a personal connection between Nick Clegg and Gordon Brown was non-existent. In the period since Clegg's election as leader of the Liberal Democrats, neither man had made the slightest effort to get to know the other. The frostiness was only intensified by the contact into which circumstances now forced them. Despite that, frustration later developed in the Lib Dem camp that an assumption had gained ground that Nick Clegg wanted Gordon Brown gone simply because he did not like the man. The key issue for those in the Lib Dem leader's intimate circle was Gordon Brown's failure as Prime Minister. Given his party's defeat, in their view he could not credibly stay on. In addition, the imperative that any incoming government should be seen to be fresh and new could hardly be accomplished with Gordon Brown at the helm.

The issue of Gordon Brown's future would be dealt with through increasingly tortuous and uncomfortable meetings over the coming days. On Saturday morning, Nick Clegg had his own party to think about. In preparing the ground for coalition negotiations, those heading up the Lib Dems had recognised the paramount importance of consulting the party, and bringing delegates with them. In the period after Britain went to the polls, not a day went by without a meeting of the Lib Dem Federal Executive, the parliamentary party or both. (It was entirely predictable that even as David Cameron drove up Downing Street and into office

– what were the Liberal Democrats doing? Of course, preparing for yet another internal consultation.)

Clegg duly arrived in Westminster to meet with his Shadow Cabinet at 10.30 a.m. on Saturday morning, and by lunchtime, the Liberal Democrat Parliamentary Party were assembling for their first full meeting since the election. In other circumstances, the gathering would have been intended above all to welcome new Lib Dem members to the House. Given the way the result turned out, such pleasantries were all but redundant. The chosen venue was Transport House in Smith Square, a historic bastion of Labour. Once the headquarters of the mighty Transport and General Workers Union, then later the Labour party, rather more prosaically the building now accommodated the Local Government Association (being at least officially renamed Local Government House). The Liberal Democrats had co-opted it as their election HQ during the Kennedy years, but Clegg had abandoned it for the Work Foundation's light and distinctive round tower behind New Scotland Yard. He could hardly be blamed if Transport House's windowless inner conference hall held bad memories for both parties – in 1983 Jim Mortimer had publicly announced Labour's qualified support for Michael Foot there and in 2005 Kennedy had experienced his sweaty, shaky news conference meltdown the morning after the birth of his son.

On this occasion a sense of drama was provided vicariously because Transport House was besieged by a 'fair votes now!' demonstration that had opportunistically extended a march to parliament further on to Smith Square. Simon Hughes and then Clegg himself came out to pacify the crowd with impromptu speeches in which they promised not to back down on their shared quest for electoral reform. 'Reforming politics is one of the reasons I went into politics', Clegg shouted through the bullhorn handed to him. The colourful Portsmouth South MP Mike Hancock enjoyed a less romantic fate when he left the meeting to relieve himself – tweets and blogs immediately reported that he had stormed out in protest.

The party's media operation issued a series of unhelpful, even misleading statements. Less than a quarter of an hour after confirming that no further talks were scheduled with either the Tories or Labour, the Liberal Democrats announced that their negotiating team would meet their Conservative counterparts for further discussions at 11 a.m. on Sunday at the Cabinet Office.

Clegg obtained the permission he needed to engage with the Tories but most of those at the meeting were much more sceptical than he was, and even hostile to a lasting deal with the Conservatives. The sceptics' main worry was that any agreement would be short lived and that the Tories would be bound to cut and run for an early election within a matter of months. 'There was no point in us negotiating the entire Lib Dem manifesto,' according to Lord (Chris) Rennard, the party's former chief strategist, 'if it was only going to be a government that lasted four months. We also felt that we did need to make progress on constitutional reform and we weren't getting that initially.' From this came two of the key Liberal Democrat demands in the coalition talks that followed: progress on electoral reform, and fixed-term parliaments to ensure that neither party could ambush the other by forcing an early election.

Even the Lib Dem negotiating team, though impressed by their Conservative opposite numbers, knew they must remain alert to the possibility of the wool being pulled over their eyes. According to Andrew Stunell, it was not just the grassroots that were wondering, 'Was this for real?' Nick Clegg's designated four-man team knew that sometimes, for all the other side's apparent good intentions, a negotiation can be designed to fail. That wariness took a little while to wear off. They were determined not to be the fall guys if things went wrong.

There were many more who simply recoiled instinctively at the idea of partnership with the Tories. As so often before, a clear division was opening between right of centre Lib Dems, such as David Laws, and veterans, including most who had passed through the SDP and Labour, who believed that their party was far from equidistant between the two main parties and instead much closer to Labour.

Laws acknowledges that at this point, the Lib Dem mood was more positive towards Labour than in the immediate aftermath of the vote, when he, Nick Clegg, Danny Alexander and others had been wielding their whiteboard markers and computing the possibilities. On the Friday morning he says, 'I think there were a few people who just felt as an instinctive reaction to the results coming in that the mechanics of delivering anything other than a Tory deal was going to be very difficult just because of the pure arithmetic.'

Getting a sense of grassroots' feeling undoubtedly played a part in persuading the leadership to bring Labour more seriously into the equation. 'Sentiment . . . may have changed a little bit over the next forty-eight hours,' Laws conceded. There were 'Some people thinking, well actually not only is it sensible for us to keep both parties in play, but also maybe the arithmetic isn't quite so impossible.' Danny Alexander concluded, grudgingly, 'Looking at the numbers, it was always going to be very difficult, but it was a conversation worth having.'

Those who set to work exploring the 'Lib–Lab option' were the true believers. As Paddy Ashdown, a key conduit in the coming hours, puts it, 'I was emotionally committed to that at the time.' Ashdown buoyed up his hopes after the meeting by consulting Chris Rennard, nationally renowned as the Lib Dem grandee who understood political maths.

Rennard argued that Labour and Liberal Democrats combined would outnumber the Conservatives and that the remaining smorgasbord of minor parties would be inclined to give a fair wind to a minority 'progressive government' (subject of course to a few financial and policy sops thrown in their direction). He told Ashdown: 'You could have had potentially a minority Labour/Lib Dem administration if all the MPs in those parties wanted to go along with it, if the 10 MPs who were nationalist or green wanted basically to support it or abstain in a motion of confidence and hope to get proportional representation at the end of it, there were 10 people who could be sympathetic [6 SNP, 3 Plaid, 1 Green]. You had 3 SDLP and an Alliance party who'd probably be pro the government, 5 Sinn Féin who wouldn't attend and wouldn't be part of the calculation, and 8 DUP. You had no idea what they would do on individual issues but who would nod more to the Conservative party. So potentially you had *just* something of an alternative.'

The view that there was a possibly viable alternative to a Conservative/Liberal Democrat deal was reinforced that lunchtime by Alex Salmond. Scotland's First Minister told Sky News that his party was ready to join a 'Rainbow coalition' with Labour and the Liberal Democrats that would have enough votes in the House of Commons to carry a Queen's speech and a budget. Salmond presented this as his own initiative but ensconced in their 'ain hame' at the weekends is usually when the cross-party lines linking Scotland's political leaders hum most loudly.

However, significantly, neither the Lib Dems in the know at the heart of the dealing, nor the Lib Dems on the fringes were ever confident that a 'Rainbow coalition' would command anything like Brown's putative 'twenty plus' parliamentary majority. Far from forming a stable bloc behind their Labour partners, they envisioned a much cruder bargain. Active or passive support would allow Labour to enact a budget and to stagger on for about eighteen months or so when another election would be held. By the time the new vote took place the other parties would have extracted their side of the deal: AV or, even better, PR would already be in place, and, in the case of the Scottish Nationalists, a new permanent funding settlement by which the government in Edinburgh would collect its own taxes, balancing the books with a single 'cheque' from Westminster.

As the Liberal Democrats' meeting dragged on, Cameron and Brown were briefly on the sidelines. The only time they had found themselves in the media spotlight that Saturday was during the ceremonial appearance at the Cenotaph, an experience that threatened to be acutely uncomfortable.

At midday the three men who would decide who would run Britain had no alternative but to be photographed side by side. In their official capacity as national leaders, all three attended the ceremony commemorating the sixty-fifth anniversary of VE Day. In 2010 they had had the debates, but such moments of national solemnity are often the only chance for the leaders of rival political parties to mix with each other, not so much during the service, as when they gather together privately in a side room before proceedings get underway. It was on just such an occasion that Cameron had first spoken to Clegg a few years before. Now he looked on in astonishment as, just a couple of yards in front of him, Brown was trying to engage Clegg in serious conversation while they waited. The Tory leader couldn't quite believe his eyes, considering any serious bargaining to be wholly inappropriate in the circumstances. As they came out of the Foreign Office he asked Clegg what Brown had been saying: 'Oh my God, he's still having a go at me,' the Lib Dem leader replied.

Once out in the open air in the full glare of the cameras, the event went more smoothly, even though it witnessed a unique simultaneous triple wreath-laying by the three leaders.

Prime Minister Brown had expected that he would lay his wreath first on his own, a task he found difficult because of his poor eyesight. But, the true pecking order was now up for grabs, so the Ministry of Defence had decided at the last moment that all three men should step forward simultaneously to lay their tributes. This they all managed, though none had military training, with relative precision. The cameras were trained on the trio throughout the ceremony but failed to catch any of them in a revealing visual gaffe.

From Whitehall, Nick Clegg had hotfooted it to the meeting of his Liberal Democrats, and no sooner were those talks concluded – with senior MPs exiting by a back door to avoid commenting – than Clegg had to rush off again to a gathering of the Lib Dem Federal Executive, this time at his Work Foundation HQ. The Federal Executive was one of the Lib Dems' 'triple locks' on entering into any coalition. So it was good news for Clegg that, having earlier pacified his MPs (another lock), he could leave the second meeting claiming that it had endorsed his strategy 'of focusing on the national interest'.

As the leader went about the complex dance of internal party consultation, talks with Labour took a step forward. The buzzing of telephone contacts between the parties had continued unabated since Friday morning (Brown with Cable, Mandelson with Alexander, Adonis with Alexander, Laws and others, Alastair Campbell with Ashdown, Ed Miliband with Simon Hughes and much, much more), but now the parties' designated negotiators were to meet for the first time.

Given that the public gaze was trained on the formal discussions with the Tories, it was time for a little sleight of hand

and misdirection on the part of senior members of the Liberal Democrat party. At 4.20 p.m. David Laws told the TV cameras that formal negotiations would begin with the Conservatives tomorrow, after the previous night's preliminary talks. He did not tell them that in fact his next move that afternoon would be to go directly on to face-to-face negotiations with Labour. These were held in secret at the Liberal Democrats' request. As Laws explained later: 'We didn't want to be going in and out of the Cabinet Office with different people because it would have looked a bit tart-ish.'

Peter Mandelson and Danny Alexander had fixed their date over the phone that morning. Gordon Brown had then called Ed Balls out of the blue to say he needed him to be one of the Labour team. 'I said to him "Look, I've only just got home [to Yorkshire]. I'm not going to come back again. In any case my very strong advice to you is to get out. Because I think the appearance of you sitting in Downing Street while the Conservatives and Liberal Democrats have discussions looks very strange. Most people should be in their constituencies, this is what you should do." He then went off the phone in a slightly grumpy way.' An hour later Brown rang back to say he would go to Scotland but only if Balls attended the meeting in London. The Education Secretary complied, but in his haste to escape without speaking to the journalists staking him out, he left to drive south without his jacket: something he realised when he found he had no wallet with which to pay for a petrol fill-up during the 190-mile journey. (His wife Yvette sorted out payment over the phone.)

The two teams met in Portcullis House, the near quarter of a billion pounds modern block above Westminster tube station which has rapidly become parliament's more salubrius hub. The chosen room 319 on the third floor was at the disposal of the Lib Dems and overlooked Big Ben. The Lib Dems fielded the same team that had met the Tories the night before, four MPs who would all end up with jobs in the new government: David Laws, Chris Huhne, Andrew Stunell and Danny Alexander.

Labour were represented by four members of the outgoing government: two MPs, Ed Balls and Ed Miliband, and two Lords, Andrew Adonis and Peter Mandelson. Harriet Harman MP, the deputy leader, had been added to the Labour team but was not present, according to everyone except Mandelson who subsequently wrote that she was there – his failure to notice her absence perhaps an indication of the openly low esteem in which he holds her. Harman had replaced the Chancellor Alistair Darling, who by now was headed to Europe to discuss the economic bailout of Greece, and who in the remaining days of talks would do no more than go through the motions of supporting Brown's position.

Like the first negotiations with the Conservatives in the Cabinet Office, these initial Labour–Lib Dem talks proved inconclusive. Balls reckoned that the Lib Dems were 'surprised, positively' that he had made the effort to dash back to Westminster, pleased because his presence showed Brown was in earnest.

During an hour and a half of talks, there was no attempt to address policy questions in detail. It was perhaps just as well, because unlike the Tories who had turned up fully armed with a detailed document – headings for discussion and so on – the Labour team arrived with no agenda and seemed content to wing it. The negotiating team, which was drawn up in the immediate aftermath of the election result (whereas the Lib Dems and Tories had known their roles for some time), had not had time to sit down and organise a coordinated front, and it showed. There were doubts about the viability of the process from the start. As one member of the negotiating team put it, 'Everyone had gone into it thinking it was worth a try, but there were quite big obstacles. Our sense was that the talks with the Tories were not going very well [wrong, as it turned out!]. So we thought maybe this has more chance than might appear at first glance.'

The complaints of 'arrogance' and 'bad body language' that became public knowledge after the talks between the two parties broke down the following Tuesday are not fully representative of the Lib Dem perception of this first meeting. While rancour and a degree of personal dislike ended up poisoning the process, when the two sides were feeling one another out on Saturday afternoon, the problem from the Lib Dem perspective was mainly that they found Labour's position confusing – it was not clear where Peter Mandelson and his friends were coming from.

Not only did the lack of preparation on the Labour side seem to betray a degree of half-heartedness, the schizophrenic nature of the Labour team perplexed their Lib Dem counterparts. Peter Mandelson and Andrew Adonis were openly positive about the endeavour, while Ed Balls and Ed Miliband (and later Harriet Harman) seemed cool. While the Labour team dismiss the more lurid accusations later laid at their door as 'rubbish' (Ed Balls says this first meeting was 'very friendly and very positive'), it is more widely acknowledged that the last-minute way in which the party engaged in the process contributed to a sense of mixed messages.

The Lib Dems mostly took the opportunity during the hour and a half the two sides spoke to reprise key points of their manifesto, testing the water to get a sense of Labour's appetite to move. This was viewed by the Lib Dem negotiators as a 'listening' session, mindful as they were not to give away too much of the substantive detail of their negotiations with the Tories while they were at such a sensitive stage. This was not the forum for aggressive demands for the head of the Prime Minister, or tub-thumping speeches about PR. Nevertheless, the issue of electoral reform was discussed, and the question of whether the alternative vote system could be attained without a referendum (which would become such a touchy subject as the days wore on) was among the points raised. The tenor of the debate was such as to lead the Lib Dems to believe that Labour might prove a tough nut to crack.

There was always a high chance these negotiations would be prickly. As a general rule, Lib Dems are particularly sensitive about being patronised by Labour. (Labour people would say they have a chip on their shoulder about it.) The view within Nick Clegg's inner circle is that senior Labour figures have tended to view their party as like a rather naïve, idealistic younger brother, with no sense of what real politics is about . . . no grasp of the compromises that are necessary in order to govern. The issue on this occasion was that having spent time just hours before with a Conservative team that was willing, indeed at times eager to compromise and to make common cause where possible, the Labour team in comparison appeared inflexible and intransigent.

David Laws says the advantage of talking with the Tories was that 'They felt like discussions between equal partners, because neither of us had been in government – we didn't come with the arrogance of power or feeling, as I think some of the Labour party people did . . . that they were having to negotiate with a third party having lost power.' For Paddy Ashdown, who was getting a running commentary on the rival talks at this point, it was all about baggage: Labour, after thirteen years in government, 'were not constitutionally or emotionally able to ditch all the work that they had done and come light-footed to the negotiations. They were weighed down by two kinds of baggage – one was the baggage of the policies they'd already got in train, with all the huge momentum of government machinery behind it, and the other was the emotional baggage – "We've been masters of the universe for 13 years, who the hell are these upstarts telling us what to do?'"

With no real progress made, nor any great catastrophe to threaten the course of the negotiations, both sides left Portcullis House in the full expectation that they would be meeting again, and again in secret. Knowledge of the Lib–Lab meeting was not widely disseminated at the top of either party – two days after his brother had taken part in it, an ill-informed David Miliband advised Gordon Brown on the Monday that it was time to start discussions with the Lib Dems.

That same Saturday evening, another secret meeting was held, this time between David Cameron and Nick Clegg. With journalists, and the public under the impression that the Tory Lib Dem process was pretty much the only game in town, escaping the focus of the media was a problem for the two leaders. With the outcome of events uncertain and both technically remaining potential prime ministers, Clegg and Cameron retained the Scotland Yard close protection teams assigned to them during the election. Through an elaborate game of back doors, side doors and car switches, they arrived at Admiralty House on Whitehall, a stone's throw from Trafalgar Square, without the media getting wind – no mean feat at that time given the concentration of cameras in Westminster.

Leaving the officials in an outer dining room, the two men retreated into an ugly inner parlour (nasty cotton print curtains and mismatched furniture) and spent the best part of seventy minutes talking alone, their longest meeting together yet. It was a meeting of two leaders each of whom believed power was within their grasp after their first test at the ballot box. For once it seems that the official version later revealed to the press of 'constructive and amicable' talks was on the money.

Cameron returned home feeling he might soon be walking into Number 10. The meeting of Tory and Lib Dem negotiators scheduled for the next morning would clear the way to a comprehensive agreement, he hoped. But David Cameron did not know the full picture then. Cameron was entirely unaware of the talks with Labour that had been going on down at the other end of Whitehall almost at the same time as he sat and chatted with the Liberal Democrat leader.

9

IN THE BALANCE

'We've had the heavy petting, now can we get full consummation?'

The eleven o'clock meeting of the Conservative and Liberal Democrat negotiating teams on Sunday felt like a big one. In the full live glare of the media, the negotiators walked from parliament, across Whitehall and into the Cabinet Office dodging questions and microphones equally adroitly. Expectation mixed with pressure. From their first-floor room, the four Liberal Democrats and four Conservatives could see their goal, Number 10.

The two teams met for a total of six and a half hours facing each other across the thin conference table. With relatively few MPs around Westminster on a Sunday afternoon, it was a chance to explore what sort of an agreement might be possible before the consultations with the wider party which would have to take place the next day.

There was an extra element of urgency because the financial markets would start to open around the world within hours. If they were not already sufficiently aware of the interest in the

City, the Cabinet Secretary was always on hand to gently apprise them of the situation. According to one negotiator, 'Every time we would walk into the Cabinet Office, Gus O'Donnell would say "You do realise that if you don't have a government, there could be a real problem with the markets?"' The volatile situation in Greece and the Eurozone helped to further concentrate minds. Pictures were coming in all weekend of riots in Athens, while in Brussels EU finance ministers continued to prevaricate over the proposed bailout for the ailing Greek economy.

The theory that the UK might be tested by speculators in the same way Greece had been was one of the key planks of Conservative economic thinking. George Osborne had long talked of the possibility that because of the Labour government's supposed reluctance to tackle the deficit, sterling might come under pressure, the government would be forced to pay more to service its debts and interest rates would rise. The theory was, to say the least, the focus of fierce political contention. Now, with the uncertainty of a hung parliament to add into the mix, those at the top of the civil service seemed to share the view that had been most intensively articulated by the Conservatives over recent months – that market volatility was indeed a real and imminent danger. The former Cabinet Secretary, Lord Andrew Turnbull, complained to the media that the markets would be negative in the case of talks 'dragging on and becoming acrimonious and contentious'.

In addition to his own frequently stated concern about the markets, Gus O'Donnell had at the outset of the negotiations offered to bring in two 'wise men' to brief the negotiators on the pressing nature of the UK's economic concerns. According to David Laws, O'Donnell 'made clear he had Mervyn King and someone else on standby to come in and tell us how dire the situation was.' The second individual, apart from the Governor of the Bank of England, was in fact the Permanent Secretary to the Treasury, Sir Nicholas Macpherson.

The proposal presented the Lib Dems with something of a conundrum. While no one passes up the offer of a chat with such senior figures lightly, they instinctively bridled at outside involvement. David Laws explains the negotiators' position: 'We said we don't think we really need that, partly because we knew there would be sensitivities in the markets, partly because we felt a little on the Lib Dem side that this was designed to push us a bit, and we felt it risked being an intrusion into the negotiations.'

The Liberal Democrat team stressed that any such discussions would be better dealt with by their Treasury Spokesman, and so telephoned Vince Cable and handed the matter over to him. There was no further talk of such outside assistance in the following days of negotiation, but Laws retains the sense that the proposal was not as helpful as Gus O'Donnell evidently intended it to be. 'We felt that there was a risk that it was trying to give us a political steer,' he says.

What neither David Laws nor his negotiating colleagues was then aware of was that the suggestion the Governor and the head civil servant at the Treasury might be involved had come from one of the men on the other side of the table, George Osborne. The Shadow Chancellor had discussed the framing of the negotiations with Gus O'Donnell not long before they got underway. The Cabinet Office venue was Osborne's call. Given the options of Admiralty House, Portcullis House, and other government buildings, Osborne chose the building on 70 Whitehall because it was right at the heart of government (designed to focus the minds of the negotiating teams); and it was right next to Gordon Brown, putting pressure on him to go. At the same time, Osborne proposed that briefings from Mervyn King and Nicholas Macpherson might be useful for both sides.

Gus O'Donnell took up his suggestion, and the 'wise men' were put on standby.

The 'political steer' David Laws refers to would have been, from the Conservative Shadow Chancellor's point of view, self-evident. Going into the talks, it was clear that the most likely bone of contention with the Liberal Democrats on the economy was the timing of spending cuts. The Tories were adamant that given the size of the deficit, cuts could not be put off – they would have to be made straight away. The Lib Dems had consistently argued that such a course of action would be reckless given the fragile state of the economy. How to change their minds? The Conservative leadership believed the Governor of the Bank of England was onside with their analysis – as early as March, David Cameron had said 'We've had very fruitful and productive discussions with Mervyn King about this issue . . . about the need to get to grips with the deficit.' Osborne knew that King's testimony, coupled with the opinions of Nicholas Macpherson, might help bring the Lib Dems round to the wisdom of in-year cuts.

The Governor was certainly up for it, but King got his chance only belatedly the day after the coalition was formed, when he used his monthly news conference on inflation to endorse the coalition's commitment to an immediate start on cutting the deficit (something he had spoken against a few months earlier). Mervyn King noticeably switched his emphasis from the broad cover he had given Gordon Brown and Alistair Darling in their policy of maintaining the stimulus to an apparently more emphatic endorsement of the coalition's in-year cuts.

The Conservatives had expected it would be much harder work to get the Lib Dems to agree to the proposed £6 billion of in-year cuts than proved to be the case. For the Tories, it was a vital and totemic concession. In order to get their side of the bargain, they were ready to provide a good deal in exchange, especially on the Lib Dems' fairness agenda of protecting the less well off who they believed would be hit hardest by greater austerity. Osborne dumped his inheritance tax cut (which the Lib Dems considered to be a 'millstone' for him anyway). Few figures were attached to commitments by agreement but assurances were given: movement towards the key Lib Dem pledge of a £10,000 threshold for income tax; restoration of the earnings link to state pensions accelerated; more money for a pupil premium.

In the event, the Lib Dems might have come round to immediate cuts even without such a raft of concessions. Nick Clegg, who described the policy not long before the election as 'economic masochism', has subsequently explained that in fact he had 'changed his mind' even before polling day. The Greek crisis (a 'complete belly-up implosion' as he put it) and the febrile mood of the markets had convinced him of the need to send out a signal: a change of heart brought about by the 'financial earthquake . . . on our European doorstep.'

It is not clear, however, that when the Liberal Democrat negotiating team went into the Cabinet Office, they had made it all the way to the end of the Road to Damascus travelled by their leader. David Laws, who led on the economy for the Lib Dems, says that two factors had caused the party to shift: the Greek situation and the test that the markets would put on any coalition government in the UK. 'We were of the view ourselves that speeding up deficit reduction would be necessary and there would need to be some form of emergency budget.' But as to in-year cuts? 'Obviously our natural position was that the speeded-up deficit reduction should start in April 2011 when the economy was likely to be better grounded in terms of recovery which had always been our view as to when most of the deficit reduction should start.'

The reason Laws and his team felt able to change their view, and agree to begin making cuts a year earlier, was essentially pragmatic. 'Six billion pounds wasn't going to cause the economy to implode,' they felt. They knew it meant a lot to the Tories, and recognised that on the fundamental economic issues they would have to give ground somewhere. 'We felt that to the extent that it was a signal that the coalition was going to be quite serious about deficit reduction, and in our view was unlikely to make much difference to the state of the economy, that it was something that we could quite happily live with.'

With hindsight, Laws says the Liberal Democrats were as guilty as anyone else for the overheated rhetoric with which the proposed timing of spending cuts was discussed. 'The six billion of in-year cuts had been rather hyped up by both sides during the election. It suited Labour, and us to some extent, to argue that this was going to torpedo recovery, and it suited the Tories to present this as some dramatic move to restore financial stability.' The true picture was more prosaic in his view: 'It was only 6 billion pounds out of an economy that's massively bigger than that. Nobody could argue for a minute that that was going to topple the economy over into recession.'

It was not exactly the position the Conservatives had steeled themselves for. After all, this was the party whose economic spokesman Vince Cable had written not long before of the UK economy under the headline: 'The patient's on a dripfeed. Cuts now will kill us.' In the event, the economy detained the negotiators for far less time than might have been anticipated.

It meant the talks were free to range into other areas. 'The process was very policy-orientated,' one negotiator recalled. 'We dealt with education, income tax, the budget, the fiscal situation, the green economy . . .' On areas like civil liberties there was almost complete agreement. The Lib Dems felt they had pleasantly surprised the Tories by being willing to be tough and put fiscal responsibility at the forefront of the discussions. The Conservatives, they could tell, had clearly expected that the third party would be populist and flaky about having to make budget economies.

Together, the Greek crisis and the coalition negotiations gave the Lib Dems the cover to shift their position, and reverse their rhetoric. Truth to tell, Clegg, Cable, Laws, and subsequently Alexander have all looked more comfortable being economically tough than they did during the campaign, trying to deploy dividing lines with the Conservatives.

There was, however, a sticking point to the negotiations. The two sides could not agree on the issue of electoral reform. Any well-informed commentator would have predicted the problem. On one side, you had a Conservative party fundamentally wedded to the system of first past the post; on the other the Lib Dems for whom proportional representation is the holy grail.

When it came up at an early stage in the discussions, PR was knocked back by the Tory negotiators without a second thought. As the Lib Dems would have understood, they said there was no way they could accept it, and no way they could sell it to the party even if they wanted to accept it. Chris Huhne tentatively proposed a way forward. Huhne's idea was that his party could accept the Conservative plans for reform of the House of Commons that included a fast-track boundary review process to equalise constituencies, and also a reduction in the number of MPs. 'In exchange,' he suggested, 'we'd like you to support a referendum on a reformed first past the post system.' George Osborne smelled a rat. 'That's very interesting. What do you mean by reformed?' he enquired. Huhne speculated that you might do first past the post, but instead of just a cross against a candidate, you could rank them in order of preference . . . ? It did not take the Conservative side more than two seconds to spot that this was the very definition of the alternative vote system. 'Oh no,' Osborne insisted according to David Laws. 'There's no Tory support for any of these things.'

David Laws told the Tory team that unless they gave ground, it was hard to see a way forward, explaining to them, 'My long-standing view is that the Lib Dems will never go into a coalition with anyone unless there's some form of electoral reform. So this is going to be quite a difficult issue.'

At this stage, the discussion did not get much further. It was agreed mutually that the issue should be 'parked', and referred to the two leaders to try to find common ground. The Conservatives gave the impression that significant movement on the point was unlikely.

A variety of convoluted methods were employed over the coming days to try to skirt around the issue. The Conservatives, despite their inbuilt hostility to AV, offered a free vote in the House of Commons on whether to have an AV referendum. Knowing that the votes would not stack up, the Lib Dems knocked them back. The Tories then promised that the party leadership – David Cameron, George Osborne and William Hague – would publicly state their intention to vote for the referendum, thus giving a lead to Tory backbenchers. The Lib Dems were not satisfied.

Meanwhile, parallel discussions between Nick Clegg and David Cameron were no more successful in finding a compromise. So with the AV blockage unresolved, the two teams agreed to rein in their hopes for a coalition, and sketch out instead the outline of what a 'confidence and supply' agreement would be. By the time the Sunday meeting ended after 5 p.m. the deal was pretty firmly pencilled in. It looked as if both party leaders would have something, albeit an anticlimax, to put to their parties the following day.

The reality was that both sides knew there was bound to be a considerable degree of brinkmanship over an issue this important. As one of the Tory team put it, 'They had it in mind to get it out of us in the end, a referendum . . . and we had it in mind that if we were going to concede that, we were only going to do it at a late stage . . . at a critical moment.' The Liberal Democrats, meanwhile, hoped a referendum commitment would come; sensed it might, but could not be sure.

Not surprisingly, the comments to the media camped at the Cabinet Office doorstep were downbeat and noncommittal, though Hague said the two sides planned to meet again 'in the next 24 hours'. He explained that a 'positive and useful' session had ranged across political reform, economic issues, deficit reduction, banking reform, civil liberties. Danny Alexander (as was his wont) said any new agreement would have deficit reduction at its heart.

(Actually these remarks were not delivered 'on the doorstep'. The three steps leading to the door of 70 Whitehall were deemed to be government property. And, since they were not in government yet, Conservatives and Liberal Democrats were politely instructed by the Cabinet Office to address the media only once they'd stepped onto the pavement.)

With discussions stalled between the Liberal Democrats and the Conservatives, the parallel process with Labour assumed still greater importance. For the Lib Dems, there was another iron in the fire. The central fact that gave them hope that Labour might be able to provide what the Tories had not was that the Labour party had already given a manifesto commitment to introduce, and campaign for a referendum vote on AV.

On Sunday morning, back in Scotland, Gordon Brown was busy on the phone to his Liberal Democrat allies. He rang Ming Campbell four times and he called Vince Cable to tell him that he was ready to step down as Prime Minister as part of an agreement. Cable replied that a vague promise was not enough – the Lib Dems would require a categorical deal.

It was a deal that the Prime Minister could only make in person, and he therefore returned to Downing Street as soon as he decently could to pitch into the fray. Around 2 p.m. TV cameras on helicopters circling above Westminster captured live pictures of a tieless Prime Minister, briefcase in one hand, a son's hand in the other, leading his boys in through the back door of Number 10 just off Horse Guards Parade. The pictures inevitably included his two sons John and Fraser, so Downing Street contacted the broadcasters asking them not to use them again because of a long-standing agreement not to show politicians' children.

Brown consulted Mandelson, Alastair Campbell, Ed Miliband, and Harriet Harman but his real purpose was to hold a face-to-face meeting with Clegg in secret. The Cabinet Office had been asked to arrange this and Sir Peter Ricketts, the Permanent Secretary at the Foreign and Commonwealth Office had agreed to put his office at their disposal (interestingly the Foreign Secretary, David Miliband, who has an even grander suite, had not been approached). The two men met alone for an hour and a quarter in the oak-panelled room while Ricketts paced up and down outside, joking with passers-by 'Don't mind me. I'm only renting my room. I am of no importance.' (A few days later Cameron would appoint Ricketts Britain's first ever National Security Advisor.)

Reportedly at one point laughter was heard through the door. Sources close to Brown have subsequently claimed that the Prime Minister offered to step down in the autumn once the electoral reform bill had been secured, but there were only two people in the room and Liberal Democrats did not appear to feel that 'the personnel issue' – Brown's desire to stay on as Prime Minister

– had been resolved so fully. Mandelson also felt that the issue was still open after the meeting, since Brown had only told him that Clegg had raised 'the legitimacy and saleability of a coalition with Labour'. Brown briefed colleagues that he had told Clegg it would be a mistake to ally himself with people who were 'anti-Keynesians, anti-Europeans, anti-growth'.

As luck would have it, Gordon Brown was caught on camera making the short journey on foot between the back doors of Number 10 and the Foreign Office. Downing Street was forced to confirm to the media that a meeting had taken place: 'Gordon Brown phoned Nick Clegg last night. Following the discussion they met at the Foreign Office to update each other.'

But by now there was growing speculation about Brown's own future as Prime Minister, even within Labour ranks. In Manchester, heavyweight MP Graham Stringer claimed to have canvassed at least a dozen colleagues: 'Not one thinks he should stay,' he said. Some ex-ministers had followed David Blunkett in going even further. Malcolm Wicks took to the airwaves to advise Brown to take defeat 'on the chin' and not seek a 'ridiculous' coalition with a 'ragbag' of nationalists. George Howarth argued that Cameron should be given his chance.

Now, having met Clegg, Brown was at least prepared to discuss the option of quitting with his advisors, including Sue Nye – his long-time aide, and perhaps the closest thing to a decent, well-balanced and disinterested human in his retinue. Brown told Mandelson: 'I have been humiliated enough.' If he was to go he wanted it to be with dignity and in a way that his 'sacrifice' would benefit the Labour party. According to Mandelson, there was still no conclusion on 'the how and the when', the manner or the timing of such a démarche.

As if to underline his determination to stick around, Brown had a defiant email sent to all Labour party workers in which he expressed his determination to fight on to secure economic recovery. So Brown was now giving two justifications for staying put. To the wider public he presented himself as essential to the economy, but to Clegg he was suggesting that his continued presence as Prime Minister would guarantee that Labour delivered on AV.

A further sign that his future had not been resolved at the Foreign Office meeting was that Clegg and Brown agreed to meet in person again, for the second time that day. This time the two men were backed up by lieutenants, Peter Mandelson and Danny Alexander, and this time even greater pains were taken to keep the meeting from the public gaze. Brown and Mandelson took a circuitous route to the House of Commons. First they walked down a secret underground tunnel from Downing Street to the Ministry of Defence. These tunnels were part of 'Pindar', a bunker system or 'citadel' under Whitehall designed for military coordination in times of crisis. (Pindar was named after the ancient Greek lyric poet, whose house survived when Thebes was razed. You are never far from a classical allusion when British mandarins are around.) From the MoD the two took an unmarked car for the short journey to the House of Commons. Night had fallen.

The two sides' accounts of this encounter vary – it took place in the prime ministerial suite in the long corridor behind the Speaker's chair, which overlooks Parliament Square and New Palace Yard. Mandelson 'found their exchanges impressive: firm, but with sensitivity on both sides'. However he conceded that the meeting was inconclusive regarding Brown's fate: 'Nick saying that Gordon's early departure was essential . . . and Gordon recognising that they would have to talk it through further.'

But the Liberal Democrats felt betrayed. If Brown had ever given any commitment about going, they judged that he had now backed away from it. Ashdown summed it up in a private conversation to his protégé Clegg: 'Here is this man – old and at the end of his career – he's had nothing in his mind all his life but remaining in Downing Street and being Prime Minister. This has been his whole life's ambition, and suddenly you bound into his office taking away the prize that his whole life's been about. The emotional problem with that is very great.'

Privately Ashdown felt: 'Gordon (a) didn't want to leave Downing Street, (b) didn't feel he had to, (c) thought he'd done rather a good job and (d) was faced with this guy of not yet forty-four who comes in to tell him "You've got to go, mate".'

Clegg, 'the guy of not yet forty-four', was left with a dilemma, which left the possibility of an agreement with Labour either much closer or further away depending on how you looked at it. On the one hand Brown was now talking about paying the ultimate price in political terms, which Clegg had set as the condition during the campaign; but on the other his refusal to be specific further crushed any hope that there could ever be trust between Labour and Liberal Democrats. Clegg did not know for sure what Brown was offering him, but he had not been flatly rejected. Whatever his distrust of Brown, and his scepticism that the numbers needed were actually there, the Lib Dems would demand that he keep Labour in play – at least this might help 'squeeze' a better deal from the Conservatives.

Not so far away, David Cameron suffered through a desultory evening based in the leader of the opposition's suite of offices overlooking the Thames in 'Norman Shaw South', just downriver from Westminster Bridge and Portcullis House. George Osborne had called him after the session with the Liberal Democrats and repeated to him what he had been telling him all along – never mind about all these negotiations, for a Lib Dem leader PR was all that mattered. (Since they were not very interested in the subject, all forms of electoral reform were called 'PR' (proportional representation) by the Tories, even when, like AV, they are not proportional.)

If Cameron wanted more than a 'confidence and supply' agreement, he would have to move his party's position on PR. But far from rallying to the leadership's side, the first mutterings of disgruntlement were emanating from the party. Cameron set up an open door surgery, by phone and in person, for any unhappy Tory MP to express their views.

Even at the worst of times, talking to MPs would usually have perked Cameron up. But there was a deeper reason for his low mood – he thought he was being two-timed by Clegg. He had known in advance that the first meeting of his rivals would take place, but Clegg had not told him about the second round. This was the angriest Cameron ever got with Clegg during the five days. Osborne told him not to be silly – they would have done the same thing as Clegg, in his shoes.

The weekend was drawing to a close. In the morning the financial markets would reopen, the country would return to work, and people would expect some indication that, within a reasonable timeframe, a government might be constructed. Though narrow party advantage dominated the political calculations that were being made, with all three sides considering commitments against which they would be judged by the electorate for years ahead, the national interest was weighing heavily too. The troubles of the Eurozone made for an unsettling backdrop. Pressure was being exerted on countries like Spain and Portugal. France and Germany were having difficulty agreeing the best way to stabilise the currency. There was a risk that nervousness and uncertainty would hold. In such an environment, it was therefore plausible that if the City took a dim view of the progress of negotiations between the parties in Westminster, things might get very sticky, very quickly. Perhaps Osborne and O'Donnell's fears would be proved right.

Neither the Conservatives, Labour nor the Liberal Democrats would sacrifice their core interests in order to fulfil artificial deadlines or to please the markets. Nevertheless, time was moving on. They had had a decent crack at it – the Tories and Lib Dems through very public negotiations; Labour and the Lib Dems through meetings of the leaders, and those 'informal talks' behind the scenes. It could not go on for ever. As Sunday edged into Monday, the feeling was something had to give.

Paddy Ashdown thought it was time to force the pace. The former Liberal Democrat leader was at the forefront of efforts to make it work with Labour. Like many senior figures on both the Labour and Lib Dem sides, Ashdown has claimed subsequently that he always thought the odds were stacked against a deal. Whatever his doubts, that weekend he gave it one hell of a shot.

In the early hours of Monday, David Laws, who had succeeded Ashdown as MP for Yeovil, gave 'Paddy' one last chance to bring about the deal he'd relentlessly pursued when he was leader, the dream of a 'Progressive Century' dominated by Labour and Lib Dems working together. Naturally to make any progress on this, Ashdown would have to involve his sometime partner, the man who had jilted him back in 1997 thanks to the Labour landslide: Tony Blair.

Ashdown and a bunch of Lib Dems had enjoyed a 'jolly evening' first at the Prince of Wales pub in Kennington then at his nearby London home south of the river – dinner fuelled by 'several bottles of wine'. At around two o'clock in the morning, David Laws rang and gave Ashdown his version of how the latest Labour–Lib Dem talks had gone. The Labour team had been very bad tempered and insulting, the atmosphere had been awful. Laws also reported Clegg had 'a terrible meeting' with Gordon Brown in which the

Prime Minister had emphatically withdrawn his agreement to go before the recess or even at the party conference in September. This had been Clegg's interpretation of what the two leaders had agreed in the Foreign Office earlier on Sunday, that Brown would have space to 'go with dignity'. But now he was saying only that he would go 'sometime' – 'Sometime, Never' the old nursery rhyme rejoinder hung unspoken in the air.

Next Laws arrived in person at the Ashdown flat. It was time to play the last card. Ashdown called Blair's London home but, like many a late night carouser, he woke his wife. ' "Sorry to disturb you at this time of night" – she was very good about it actually. I said I really need to speak to Tony – "Oh he's in the Middle East."'

Cherie gave Ashdown Blair's number but said she would try to contact her husband first. 'Before I could finish the washing up', Ashdown's phone rang and it was Tony.

'I said I'm very sorry to disturb you, but this thing hangs in the balance. I'm not sure it'll work . . . And he said, "Yeah I'm not sure it'll work either . . ." And I said, "Well I'd like to see if we can give it a go", and he said "I agree."' In fact even on the phone, woken in the middle of the night 2,000 miles away in the Levant, Blair appears to have turned in one of those classic performances that had fobbed off Ashdown so many times before. Blair told Ashdown he didn't think the maths or the will were there for a Labour-led government but still promised, 'I'll see what I can do.' Not much it turned out. Rather more frankly he'd told Mandelson 'There'll be an outcry if we stay on . . . we'll be smashed [in a subsequent election].'

But it was enough for Paddy. Starting at about four in the morning, he called Andrew Adonis, Alastair Campbell and Peter Mandelson as well. In defiance of Labour's own party procedure, he was looking for Brown to step down as soon as possible and for 'the new potential leader to come out and say they are prepared to work for this [a Lib–Lab pact]'. Later in the day, he would make the same point to Gordon Brown himself on the phone. But by then events on the Labour side had moved on.

In a weekend of frantic, and tangled negotiations, this was the most notable and bravura example of scattergun diplomacy. There is a certain irony looking back on Ashdown's dusk to dawn barrage of Labour figures, since one of the main complaints raised by the Liberal Democrats about Labour when post-mortems have been conducted subsequently is that they could never really tell whose was the authentic voice of the party. Even within the Labour negotiating team, it has been suggested, the absence of Alistair Darling raised questions of legitimacy. While on the Conservative side the chain of command could not have been clearer, the Lib Dems wondered whether in the court of Gordon Brown, there was anyone in charge.

Paddy Ashdown is indignant at the suggestion that he himself was freelancing: 'I saw it as my role, and I told Nick this, as to try to give as much substance, or semblance of substance, to this pretty fragile proposition of a coalition with Labour. If we hadn't done that, we'd have had no bargaining power with the Tories. My job was to help sweat a better deal out of the Tories.' A cynic would say, heads I win, tails I preserve my reputation as a statesman. If bluff it was, it was a bluff Ashdown certainly took to extremes.

As the nation woke up, news was spreading of the extent of contacts between Clegg and Brown and their respective parties. The club of ex-Liberal Democrat leaders, none of whom was sympathetic to an agreement with the Conservatives, swung in behind Ashdown. David Steel (Lord or Sir, depending on which side of the Scottish border he's on) talked down the possible scope of any deal with Cameron, telling the *Today* programme that the Conservatives were only looking for a fixed-term deal of about a year's duration before another election (fixed terms were indeed a vital part of the negotiations, designed to ensure that each side got what it wanted before any pact broke down).

The City had returned to business without undue panic. Traders were reassured by the news that in the small hours of Monday, after ten hours of emergency negotiations, the European Union had approved a package to defend the common currency worth at least 750 billion euros. Although Britain was not a member of the Eurozone, Chancellor Alistair Darling confirmed that Britain's share would be some £8 billion – both the Conservative and Liberal Democrat spokesmen endorsed the deal. Markets from Asia westward rallied. There was space for more haggling at Westminster.

On his way to work, the current Lib Dem leader played for time and fobbed off the media with verbiage: 'All the political parties, all the political leaders are working flat out, round the clock, to try and act on the decision of the British people last Thursday . . . I hope people will equally understand that it would be better to get the decision right rather than rushing into something that won't stand the test of time.'

The big ticket diary event was the resumption of Lib Dem–Con talks at 10.30 a.m. at the Cabinet Office. On their way in, negotiators professed as usual to be 'optimistic'. However, with the issue of electoral reform continuing to bedevil progress towards a full coalition, the two sides confined their efforts to nailing down a full agreement, which would be struck on the basis of confidence and supply. Given the work they had already done, it did not take long. After no more than ninety minutes, the meeting broke up. Both sides returned to consult with their leaders and parties to determine whether the proposed deal was good enough. William Hague put on a brave face for the cameras.

The talks had 'made further progress', he told the waiting media, adding: 'The negotiating teams are working really well together.' A few moments later Danny Alexander agreed with this assessment that there had been 'good further progress and I am going to report to my colleagues.'

On the Conservative side, people were getting their hopes up that a limited deal might be ratified quickly. Among those with intimate knowledge of the negotiations, there was a widespread belief that the Lib Dems would not, at this late hour, walk away from involvement in government. Even without agreement on electoral reform, the common ground uncovered by the negotiating teams meant a minority Conservative administration could surely be made to work? Some in David Cameron's inner circle thought it was only a question of time, and getting the parliamentary parties' respective approvals.

But the Lib Dems were not going to give up their quest for involvement in a genuine coalition government without a fight. On the Labour side, one of the main obstacles to agreement was about to be removed. Peter Mandelson and Danny Alexander had arranged for a further meeting between their respective party leaders earlier that morning. Alexander was explicit: Brown's exit was item one on the agenda. Mandelson recorded that Ashdown backed up the message in a call complaining that Clegg found Brown 'lecturing, bullying, uncongenial'.

At last Brown put a firm date on his departure. A new Labour leader, he promised Nick Clegg, would be in place at Labour's annual party conference, which always takes place in the last week of September. In return, according to Mandelson, Clegg spelt out the options he would put before his parliamentary party. 1. Coalition with the Conservatives; 2. Confidence and Supply for a minority Conservative government; 3. Talks with Labour. Clegg described the two Tory options as 'sub-optimal' because he was not getting what he wanted on Europe and AV, Mandelson recalled. He said he would not recommend either, although the weaker 'supply' option remained on the table.

The mood in the Labour camp lifted. By half past eleven, Labour was teeing up its team for 'serious and formal' talks with the Lib Dems and Alastair Campbell was telling those around him that Gordon would go and a Lib–Lab deal would soon be in place.

There was a new sense of purpose in Downing Street. Brown called the Foreign Secretary David Miliband, the man most likely to win the leadership contest that would follow, and, somewhat disingenuously, agreed with him that it was time to start negotiating with the Liberal Democrats. Brown sat at the 'horseshoe', the open-plan desks he had set up as the government control centre in Number 12 Downing Street, working on his resignation statement for that afternoon. As he saw it he had delivered his own head as his side of the bargain: now it was up to Clegg to do his bit and deliver his party to Labour.

Clegg met with Liberal Democrat MPs just after 1.30 p.m. in the Grand Committee Room, a large Victorian extrusion jutting out into Parliament Square from Westminster's medieval great hall. Paddy Ashdown kept Alastair Campbell up to speed with what was happening by text messages. But the meeting did not go quite as Labour were hoping. The MPs were intrigued by the distance the Conservatives had moved towards them and wanted their team to go back and try for more. The veteran MP Malcolm Bruce summed it up graphically to his colleagues: 'We've had the heavy petting, now can we get full consummation?' Laws and co were instructed to go back to the Tories for 'clarification' on 'education funding, fairer taxes and voting reform'.

The fragile line to the Conservatives had not been severed. However a significant majority of the MPs present made it clear that they would prefer to get into bed with Labour if it could be made to work. Even those with reservations, including the four negotiators, embraced the logic of showing a willingness to cosy up to Labour in order to keep the Tories keen.

Gordon Brown and Nick Clegg spoke twice on the phone in the hour before Brown stepped out of Number 10 to make the new position clear. Mandelson recalled that Clegg told Brown his MPs were not interested in the 'watered down deal with the Tories', they wanted full coalition with Labour or the Conservatives. Ed Balls said the mood music coming from the Liberal Democrat leader was as encouraging as anything Labour had encountered over the past few days. 'I heard Nick Clegg say to Gordon on the phone that if the Liberal Democrats were to go into government with the Conservatives, his members would leave in droves because the Liberals were a progressive party, not a right of centre party and his people would want to be with the Labour Party.' Did Balls think it could work? 'When you hear him say that, you think maybe he's going to try.'

Nick Clegg also telephoned David Cameron. The call left the Conservative leader in the deepest depression his aides had witnessed throughout the election period. Clegg told him that the offer on electoral reform was not good enough for the Lib Dems, and that therefore he would open formal talks with Labour to try to establish a coalition. All the work that had been done on the Conservative side looked to have been for nothing. It was a bitter pill for him to swallow – 'And just when things were going so well' as he complained to Clegg.

At five minutes to five, media organisations were alerted that the Prime Minister was about to make a statement. Gordon Brown emerged from the door of Number 10 at five o'clock on the dot. For all that was going on between the three parties, the media had no real clue of where things stood. The journalists who were massed on the opposite side of Downing Street from the Prime Minister, the people watching live television pictures or listening on the radio – all were captivated. For all they knew, anything might happen.

It soon became plain that this was no mere holding statement from Gordon Brown. Things were moving. 'Mr Clegg has just informed me that while he intends to continue his dialogue that he has begun with the Conservatives, he now wishes also to take forward formal discussions with the Labour Party. I believe it is sensible and it's in the national interest to respond positively.'

Labour was back in the game. Brown explained that the Cabinet would meet that evening, and that the Cabinet Secretary was drawing up arrangements to facilitate talks between his party and the Lib Dems. Brown continued with words that he knew were music to the ears of many grassroots Lib Dems.

'There is . . . a progressive majority in Britain and I believe it could be in the interests of the whole country to form a progressive coalition government. In addition to the economic priorities, in my view only such a progressive government can meet the demand for political and electoral change which the British people made last Thursday.'

This was the forward-looking Gordon Brown, doing what he enjoyed best. Grasping events, shaping the future. The paradox was that he was also about to do what he had resisted stubbornly during each last-gasp, back-to-the-wall crisis after another . . . he was going to resign.

As he came to the crunch, there was magnanimity first: 'I have no desire to stay in my position longer than is needed to ensure the path to economic growth is assured and the process of political reform we have agreed moves forward quickly.' Then humility. 'The reason that we have a hung parliament is that no single party and no single leader was able to win the full support of the country. As leader of my party I must accept that that is a judgement on me. I therefore intend to ask the Labour Party to set in train the processes needed for its own leadership election. I would hope that it would be completed in time for the new leader to be in post by the time of the Labour Party conference. I will play no part in that contest, I will back no individual candidate.'

Brown's friends and aides were lined up in the front hall of Number 10 to applaud him when he stepped back through the door. They knew how tough this was for Gordon Brown. They also knew that for all his will to cling to office, this moment had been coming. For months Brown had been intermittently attracted to the idea of making a grand gesture; thoughts of quitting the stage had been a recurring theme of recent months. At one point before the election he had planned to tie his future to winning a referendum on AV: to sacrifice himself on the altar of electoral reform. But this, his friends would have it, was a still nobler cause. The 'ultimate sacrifice', as a Cabinet colleague described it, for the sake of the party, and perpetuating a Labour government.

As the applause subsided, Gordon Brown launched into an impromptu speech. Liberated, perhaps, by having finally set a date for his departure? Energised, certainly, by the immediate task he had set himself. 'This is not a valedictory speech,' he told his supporters. 'There is much more for us to achieve in the days ahead.' The thought must have occurred to at least one or two – does this man ever let up?

10

THE DEAL

'I'm afraid the meeting with Labour was terrible'

Imagine the disorientation Jim Knight must have felt as he walked up Downing Street to attend a meeting of Gordon Brown's Cabinet. In a gathering as surreal as it was unprecedented, Knight found himself the first person who was neither elected to the House of Commons nor appointed to the Lords to attend Cabinet. An hour before, the Prime Minister had announced his intention to step down. Four days previously, Knight himself had been turfed out of his constituency of Dorset South by more than 7,000 votes. In the intervening period, like most of his Cabinet colleagues, he had been nothing more than a bystander, transfixed as was the rest of the nation while Gordon Brown, Nick Clegg, David Cameron and their immediate coteries tried to sort out the fortunes of the nation amongst themselves.

If Knight and his Cabinet colleagues were cheesed off at being on the sidelines of such historic events, they kept it to themselves. Now that Gordon Brown had sidelined himself, the acting

Labour leader Harriet Harman endeavoured to set the emotional tenor of the meeting. She paid what colleagues described as a 'moving tribute', applauding the achievements of the outgoing leader and stuck to her pledge not to run for the top job (and thus hold on to her deputy leadership without a contest).

Brown and Harman's colleagues were nevertheless struck above all by the strangeness of being in the Cabinet Room at all having lost the election, and an awareness that it might not be destined to last was not far from many ministers' thoughts. There was a certain sense of being in the presence of the living dead, in political terms. Ed Balls recalls that, 'For most of us, the inclination was to believe that this was a prolonged ending of our period in government. But you couldn't one hundred per cent rule out the possibility that that might not turn out to be the case.' David Miliband describes the mood with characteristic understatement: 'There was a high degree of uncertainty. Gordon had made this big announcement. We'd lost the election but it wasn't totally certain we were out of government.'

Of course, the one man who believed utterly things could be made to work was Gordon Brown. 'Gordon himself believed that he was going to pull it off,' Balls insists. 'Gordon believed that he was persuading the cabinet that a coalition with the Liberal Democrats was the right answer.'

The statements the Prime Minister heard from ministers around the table could easily have confirmed him in his conviction that they were along for the ride. Harriet Harman told her colleagues, 'I cannot go back to my constituency and say that I let in the Tories.' Others spoke out in the same vein. Peter Hain pointed out that Labour and Liberal Democrats had worked together well in the Welsh government. Alan Johnson foresaw the 'fruition of the new politics'. Shaun Woodward argued that both the Nationalist and Unionist parties at Westminster would seal the deal because of their dislike of the Conservatives. John Denham, a key moral barometer in the Cabinet because he had once resigned from government over the Iraq War, said it was 'the right thing to do'. Culture Secretary Ben Bradshaw also joined the chorus.

Given what had happened shortly before, it might be said that the last Cabinet of the Gordon Brown era was surprisingly upbeat and united. With a leadership contest now beckoning (and reports already circulating that David Miliband would be first out of the traps to declare his candidacy), those around the table knew that if things could be made to work out with the Liberal Democrats, the prize would be not just the party's top job but the nation's top job as well. 'It wasn't a jolly occasion for the obvious reason that the Prime Minister had just announced he was standing down, and we'd lost the election,' David Miliband said afterwards, 'but there was in some people's eyes the tantalising sense that we just didn't know what the Liberal Democrats were up to.'

Depending on whose version you listen to, there was either uniform or near-uniform agreement that *finding out* 'what the Liberal Democrats were up to' was indeed the right course of action. Only Scottish Secretary Jim Murphy and Health Secretary Andy Burnham appear to have left other ministers with the impression they were seriously doubtful. Labour might well 'get killed in eighteen months' time' if the arrangement collapsed and a new election took place, Burnham said, as 'we would be seen to have lost the election' this time. His words almost precisely echoed what Tony Blair had been telling his friends. Ed Balls maintains that whatever discussion there might have been about the likelihood of the negotiations succeeding, no one dissented when it was proposed as the right course of action.

'I raised questions on two areas. I think one was about the maths,' David Miliband claimed. 'We only had about 315 or 316 seats at that time [Labour combined with Liberal Democrats] and there was real scepticism whether a coalition government could prosper in those circumstances, and, secondly, the fact that there was a legitimacy issue with second and third place parties coming into play.'

But in the end David Miliband went along with what he had been told by Brown, while hedging his position with 'ifs': 'My position was that we were absolutely right to open talks, because if Tory–Lib talks had failed, the country needs a government and we would be duty bound to form a government. So I don't think there was a division along "for and against" grounds – it was "What does it mean?" and "What are the chances of success?".'

Others couched their reservations with similar care. Even Jack 'You can never trust a Liberal' Straw went along with the negotiation. Alistair Darling, Sadiq Khan and Liam Byrne limited their comments to questions as to whether the numbers really stacked up for even a temporarily stable government. Ed Balls sums it up: 'The mood of the meeting was that this will be quite difficult, but we should try to do it.'

In any case, Ed Miliband (who was in principle in favour of a deal) felt that having just watched Gordon Brown step down from the position that meant everything to him, it would have been hard for anyone to voice profound doubts about whether he had done the right thing. 'Because Gordon had made this sacrifice, it would have been very difficult for anyone to come along and say, "Look, you've just made this sacrifice, but we think it's a waste of time and we're totally against a deal."' The more nuanced picture, which Brown did not fully appreciate, was that 'People thought it's a big ask, and it's not going to be easy,' according to Miliband.

This was not only the first meeting of the Cabinet since the election; it was the first formal meeting of any representative Labour body to discuss the unprecedented situation in which the party found itself. Gordon Brown's decision to step down had been made without any meaningful consultation with the party (partly owing to Brown's paranoia about information leaking out to the media).

The lack of grassroots involvement was becoming an embarrassment, and party chiefs knew it. On Monday afternoon it was announced that the NEC (Labour's National Executive Committee) had hurriedly scheduled a meeting for the next day. By the time Cabinet drew to a close, however, Harriet Harman, Leader of the House, Party Chair and now its Acting Leader, had still not yet made any announcement about bringing together the PLP (Parliamentary Labour Party, made up of Labour MPs and peers).

Even Ed Balls, not usually one to criticise his mentor, thought that Gordon Brown was missing a trick in failing to emulate the other parties. 'Gordon was making a big mistake at that time, which was that while the Labour party may not be the Liberal Democrats, where they had three- or four-hour meetings almost half-daily . . . But I think not to have had more broad-based consultations with the PLP on Monday . . . ? I think that made Tuesday more difficult.'

Jon Cruddas, the MP for Dagenham and influential intellectual beloved of the grassroots, agreed. His feeling was that freelancing by Number 10 made it much more difficult to keep the party together during this vital period than it was for their opponents.

The Conservatives and Liberal Democrats held meetings almost to excess. Cameron broke off from a Shadow Cabinet meeting to watch Brown's statement on television, before addressing a scheduled meeting of his MPs. Ashdown was able to take an advance copy of Brown's speech into a meeting of Lib Dem peers which coincided with it. Their Liberal lordships were said to be 'euphoric' at the news.

It was shortly after Gordon Brown had addressed the cameras in Downing Street that Alastair Campbell headed for the media village that had sprung up on Abingdon Green opposite the Houses of Parliament. He went knowing that this was a vital juncture in the news cycle with early evening news bulletins going out on all main channels, and yet the Cabinet was still tied up back in Number 10. Campbell was one of Gordon Brown's closest unelected aides, and perhaps Labour's most reputed expert on communications. At 5.39 p.m. he stepped in front of a Sky News camera to promulgate the Labour view as seen from Downing Street. Because this resulted in an on-air confrontation between Campbell and Adam Boulton, Adam Boulton takes up the next section in the first person.

When I started out in television, a news editor passed on a saying from his days as a tabloid reporter: 'Never sleep with or become the story'. Unfortunately while such advice undoubtedly protects star reporters like Simon Walters of the *Mail on Sunday* or Mazher Mahmood (aka the 'Fake Sheik') of the *News of the World*, it doesn't really work for television personalities such as me. We are part of our company's brand, we contribute to and defend its reputation and we are constantly in the unblinking gaze of the camera.

In the days after the election, we were on public view to an exceptional extent. For me, this was not just because of the Debates and the ten-hour-long election-night programme I had just presented, but because the political situation was fluid given the hung parliament, and people, even leading politicians, did not know what was going on. That is when rolling news, 24-hour news, comes into its own: a point not missed by the civil servants and other guardians of the constitution who had taken pains to ensure that we were well briefed in advance on the niceties of procedure should no party secure an outright majority.

At Sky News we were devoting all our resources, on-screen but far more off-screen, to finding out and reporting what was going on. Even during the weekday mid-afternoons, on Monday 10th and Tuesday 11th May 2010, we still had more than 750,000 people tuned in to the main channel in the UK, plus hundreds of thousands more following us abroad, online, via Twitter or our iPhone app.

During those fine May days those of us reporting from Westminster were also quite literally on view to passers-by. We and colleagues, including those from the BBC, CNN and ITN, were broadcasting in the open air from platforms purpose-built on Abingdon Green opposite the Palace of Westminster or from the pavement outside buildings in which key meetings were taking place. Political high days always attract demonstrators and cranks and they know where to come to try to get on camera. The Sky News platform was relatively low to the ground, positioned immediately next to the wide Millbank pavement. We attracted more than our fair share of attention, mainly because of BSkyB's links to Rupert Murdoch, that perennial soft target of the rabble-rouser. On the Saturday afternoon my colleague Kay Burley and I had nearly been forced off air, when the hard left faction of a voters' rights march surrounded our spot, blocked the view with their banners and tried to drown out our broadcast with electric bullhorns, shouting such witticisms as 'Sky News is Shit'. (Thus generating footage for rebroadcast on *Have I Got News for You*.)

A main reason why we set up camp opposite parliament at moments of high political volatility is that those involved in the drama know where to find the cameras. We don't exactly offer an open microphone, but the political players know that they stand a good chance of getting their opinions broadcast on several channels simply by turning up 'on the green'. Inevitably, the rolling news channels are always hungriest for the latest titbit from the latest interviewee.

Clever media managers have sometimes exploited this situation to get disproportionate coverage for their views. Most famously in 1995 when John Major resigned and put his continued prime ministership to a vote of Tory MPs, his supporters flooded the green with ministers declaring loudly what a fantastic result he had won, thus, by their own admission, converting a near-terminal close shave into a mandate that propped him up for another two years.

That Monday evening, I knew that we were near a climactic moment. I was conscious that live broadcasters had perhaps been guilty of a collective failure to challenge adequately what we were being told during similar circumstances in the past. I knew from the many contacts our team had exchanging information that there was deep unhappiness in many quarters of the Labour party – both with the outline deal with the Liberal Democrats that was becoming apparent and with the fact that it was being negotiated by a small clique of Brown advisors without any formal reference to Cabinet, party or MPs. Finally, at that hour I was no longer the channel's main presenter from Westminster. In the interests of variety Jeremy Thompson, the regular anchor of Live at Five, had taken over, relegating me to the role of reporter/commentator.

Suddenly Alastair Campbell strode onto the green – and no TV channel, alas, was going to turn down the opportunity of

Blair's former director of communications live. (Indeed, a few days later the BBC even had him on *Question Time* in preference to a member of the new coalition Cabinet.)

What followed was an on-air row between Campbell and me of which the best that can be said is that it added greatly to the gaiety of the nation. Many viewers have told me it was the highlight of their general election. A snowballing YouTube hit, it trended on Twitter that night, a new expression to me meaning it was one of the dominant topics of online chatter in the English-speaking world. But it was not one of my proudest moments as a broadcaster. I regret losing my temper, although I stand by the comments I made. It was a Harry Hill 'fight, fight' moment in which two unelected observers of the political scene squared up to each other – but there were no blows, or other physical contact between us – to the disappointment of many of those watching, as I subsequently found out.

Half past five that Monday evening was a great moment to hear from Campbell who had come straight from Number 10. An hour earlier Gordon Brown had made his dramatic and confusing statement proposing that he would form a new government with the Liberal Democrats before resigning in the autumn. The Cabinet was still meeting. There had been no authoritative statements from Labour over the weekend. Campbell had no official position in the current party team but Alastair was Alastair, famous for his intimate friendships at the top of New Labour.

My instinct was to leave the interview to Jeremy and I withdrew out of camera-shot to the edge of the scaffold platform. But just before going live Campbell challenged me to take part with words to the effect of 'Come on, let's have a dust-up.' Against my better judgement I agreed to move back into shot and join the discussion.

Jeremy Thompson: *I'm joined here in Westminster by Alastair Campbell. Good evening to you. A lot of people are trying to make head or tail of what the Prime Minister said. Your colleagues say it's a dignified and statesmanlike offering from him, those on the other side of the House saying that it's a blatant piece of party gamesmanship and has nothing to do with dignity.*

Alastair Campbell: *What it is I think, it brings sense to this very, very complicated and difficult situation, which the election result threw up. No party won, no party leader got a very clear mandate. The Tories got most seats, they got the biggest share of the vote and the options remain a minority Tory government, some sort of deal between the Tories and the Liberals and they can carry on their discussions with that. But what's happened today is that Nick Clegg has indicated to Gordon Brown that there may be sense in actually a discussion developing, there have obviously been sort of behind the scenes discussions going on, but a proper policy-based discussion developing between Labour and the Liberal Democrats to see whether the basis for a coalition government can be formed and I think actually a lot of people will feel that's not a bad . . . if that materialises it is not a bad outcome from this election. Let's just go back a bit where we were . . .*

Jeremy Thompson: *Do you think that's what the British people really voted for?*

Alastair Campbell: *Well I don't, what they certainly didn't, they certainly voted for change of some sort, no doubt about that . . . let me finish, they voted for change of some sort . . .*

Adam Boulton: *Oh I see, I thought you wanted to have a discussion.*

Alastair Campbell: *No, I wanted to answer Jeremy's question if I may.*

Adam Boulton: *Oh right.*

Alastair Campbell: *They wanted change of some sort, they did not go for David Cameron despite the utterly slavish media support that he got, despite all the money from Lord Ashcroft and his friends, despite the fact that we'd had the recession and so forth, they didn't really want Cameron. There's obviously been, Gordon accepts that there was also . . .*

Jeremy Thompson: *Well this was their least worst option. They certainly didn't give Gordon Brown a ringing endorsement did they?*

Alastair Campbell: *What Gordon said was no party leader and no party won the election.*

Adam Boulton: *Hang on . . . but let's be clear of the facts of the election. In the election we take three main parties . . .*

Alastair Campbell: *Yeh.*

Adam Boulton: *. . . there is one party that lost both in terms of share of the vote and seats – that is Labour. There is one party that is behind the Conservatives and on top of that we have now got a Prime Minister who wants to stay on for four months but is saying he is going to resign in four months' time. Now none of that, with all due respect to Alastair*

Campbell, can be seen as a vote of confidence by the voters in the Labour party.

Alastair Campbell: *But nobody is saying that it is, in fact that's the whole point . . .*

Adam Boulton: *But you're saying nobody won . . .*

Alastair Campbell: *Well they didn't.*

Adam Boulton: *What I'm saying is, if you look at the results there is a party which clearly lost in as much as it moved down . . .*

Alastair Campbell: *What you're therefore saying, but what you are saying though is that . . . look David Cameron didn't do that much better than some of his predecessors but I accept he got more seats and a bigger share of the vote but my point is . . .*

Adam Boulton: *A much bigger share of the vote.*

Alastair Campbell: *Right, OK but my point is that the situation constitutionally . . .*

Adam Boulton: *And the second point if I can just . . .*

Alastair Campbell: *Can I answer the first point?*

Adam Boulton: *The second point is if you put together the percentages of the vote or the parliamentary seats, a Lib–Lab combination doesn't do it.*

Alastair Campbell: *No, you'd then have to look at other parties . . .*

Adam Boulton: *It doesn't have a majority so you can't claim . . .*

Alastair Campbell: *But nor has a minority Tory government.*

Adam Boulton: *Yes, but a Lib–Lab, a Lib–Conservative coalition clearly has got a majority and a majority of seats.*

Alastair Campbell: *And that may happen, and that may happen, all that's happened today . . .*

Adam Boulton: *Well, why not do what Malcolm Wicks says and just go quietly, accept that you lost this election? Why not do what David Blunkett says and accept that you lost this election?*

Alastair Campbell: *No, because, well because I don't think that would be the right thing to do because I don't think that is the verdict that the public delivered.*

Adam Boulton: *What, the national interest is actually what you are seriously thinking about in this?*

Alastair Campbell: *Yes, it is actually, yes.*

Adam Boulton: *The nation needs four more months of Gordon Brown limping on until he retires?*

Alastair Campbell: *Well, Adam, I know that you've been spending the last few years saying Gordon Brown is dead meat and he should be going anyway . . .*

Adam Boulton: *I've not been saying that, OK show me where I said that once?*

Alastair Campbell: *Well you've pretty much, you pretty much have . . . Adam, I don't want to go and rewind . . .*

Adam Boulton: *But are you saying in the national interest what the nation needs is four more months of Gordon Brown and then resign having lost an election?*

Alastair Campbell: *I am saying, I am saying there are three options. One is a Tory minority . . . none of them are perfect, one is a Tory minority government. That would be perfectly legitimate, OK. It wouldn't be terribly stable, it might not last very long but it is legitimate. The second is a Lib–Tory deal either formal . . .*

Adam Boulton: *Which would be stable.*

Alastair Campbell: *. . . which could be stable but what's absolutely clear, Adam, you can't tell the Liberal Democrats to do things they don't want to do.*

Adam Boulton: *No, I'm not telling anybody to do anything.*

Alastair Campbell: *No, but you're sort of saying that it is an easy option for them and it's not and what's coming through loud and clear from a lot of the Liberal Democrats is that their activists and their supporters are saying, hold on a minute, we did not vote to get you to put David Cameron in power, we voted to stop that happening.*

Adam Boulton: *Well, did they vote to put, keep Gordon Brown in power?*

Alastair Campbell: *They voted, they voted . . .*

Adam Boulton: *Did they vote to keep Gordon Brown in power?*

Alastair Campbell: *No, they didn't and Gordon has accepted that today which is why . . .*

Adam Boulton: *No exactly, so on that basis you, he didn't win at all . . .*

Alastair Campbell: *Well what does he do, what does he do? He just sort of says here you go, David Cameron come on in, you didn't actually get the vote you should have done, you didn't get the majority you said you were going to do .*

Adam Boulton: *'You got a lot more votes and seats than me.'*

Alastair Campbell: *Yes I know. Adam, you're obviously upset that David Cameron's not Prime Minister.*

Adam Boulton: *I'm not upset.*

Alastair Campbell: *You are, you probably are.*

Adam Boulton: *No, no, no, don't keep casting aspersions on what I think . . .*

Alastair Campbell: *Adam, calm down.*

Adam Boulton: *I am commenting, don't keep saying what I think.*

Alastair Campbell: *This is live on television.*

Jeremy Thompson: *Alastair, Alastair . . .*

Alastair Campbell: *Dignity, dignity.*

Adam Boulton: *No, don't keep telling me what I think. This is what you do, you come on and you say no one won the election . . .*

Alastair Campbell: *No, I mean, Jeremy . . .*

Adam Boulton: *. . . no don't you talk to me, I'm fed up with you telling me what I think, I don't think that.*

Alastair Campbell: *I don't care what you think, I don't care what you're fed up with, you can think what you like. I can tell you my opinion . . .*

Adam Boulton: *Don't tell me what I think.*

Alastair Campbell: *I will tell you why I think you are reacting so badly.*

Jeremy Thompson: *Alastair, you're being, you're being very, you are being a bit provocative here and unnecessarily so.*

Alastair Campbell: *Well, sometimes politics is about passionate things.*

Jeremy Thompson: *I understand that.*

Alastair Campbell: *He is saying Gordon Brown is no longer legitimately in Downing Street . . . He is.*

Adam Boulton: *No, I'm saying Gordon Brown, I'm saying if you look at the performances in the elections, Labour did worse than the Conservatives, will you accept that?*

Alastair Campbell: *No. They got more seats, of course they did, the Tories got more seats . . .*

Adam Boulton: *So you do accept it?*

Alastair Campbell: *Yes. But equally Gordon Brown is constitutionally perfectly entitled to be Prime Minister and , , ,*

Jeremy Thompson: *Can we er, Alastair, just tell me how . . .*

Alastair Campbell: *Let me finish this point, Jeremy, let me finish this point. He has managed this situation I think perfectly properly. He has today announced he will not be the Prime Minister . . .*

Adam Boulton: *Well, can I ask you a simple question?*

Alastair Campbell: *Yes.*

Adam Boulton: *Why hasn't he had a Cabinet meeting before making this offer?*

Alastair Campbell: *He's about to have a Cabinet meeting now.*

Adam Boulton: *Yes, but he hasn't had it now, he has made the offer, what can the Cabinet do . . .*

Alastair Campbell: *He's spoken to his Cabinet, he's spoken . . .*

Adam Boulton: *. . . why haven't you had a meeting with the Parliamentary Labour Party like the Liberal Democrats and the Conservatives have had?*

Alastair Campbell: *He's having one tomorrow, he's having one tomorrow.*

Adam Boulton: *In other words it's you, you, you totally unelected have plotted this with . . .*

Jeremy Thompson: *Gentlemen, gentlemen.*

Alastair Campbell: *Me? What and you're elected are you . . . ?*

Adam Boulton: *Yes. You're up here speaking about him, no but . . .*

Alastair Campbell: *No but that's because the Ministers are going to a Cabinet meeting . . .*

Adam Boulton: *He's has got a parliamentary party. You're the one that cooked it up, you're the one that's cooked this up with Peter Mandelson.*

Alastair Campbell: *[laughing] Oh my God, unbelievable. Adam, calm down.*

Jeremy Thompson: *Gentlemen, gentlemen, let this debate carry on later. Let's just remind you what Gordon Brown said a few minutes ago that seems to have led to this latest debate, this is Gordon Brown's statement . . .*

Adam Boulton: *I actually care about this country.*

Alastair Campbell: *You think I don't care about it, you think I don't care about it?*

Adam Boulton: *I don't think the evidence is there.*

Alastair Campbell: *Well, OK, Adam, you're as pompous as it gets . . .* [unintelligible].

Jeremy Thompson: *This is Gordon Brown's statement* [cuts to footage of Gordon Brown].

Readers must draw their own conclusions about both of us. My view was that the tide finally going out on Campbell's influence-peddling exposed him for what he had always been. He had not expected to be challenged on his tendentious assertions but once he was, and was forced to concede their validity, he resorted to bullying, baiting, impugning his inconvenient challenger. It may possibly have worked for him during the Kelly Affair and the Iraq War, but it didn't, as history repeated itself as farce, with the attempted 'Coalition of the Losers'.

Although upset I was immediately heartened by the messages of support which pinged onto my BlackBerry from bosses at BSkyB – 'what he said was outrageous'. Experience told me to walk away and get on with the job of reporting the major political story. I decided not to blog, let alone Twitter, on the matter.

Regrettably, unjustifiable attacks on Sky News' political impartiality by some Labour figures had become commonplace since the *Sun* had taken its quite independent decision to switch its editorial allegiance from Labour to Cameron in September 2009. (As a matter of fact the *Sun* had informed Sky News of its change of line at exactly the same time as it told the BBC.)

Peter Mandelson had started the calumny. Prescott and Campbell had spread the attacks online. In an interview with the *New Statesman* during the campaign Ed Balls smeared 'Sky News and most of the newspapers are deeply partisan . . .', apparently backing off when challenged by me and others. All he was able to cite was a question, which I had asked of Mandelson, about cuts at an open news conference. So it was hardly a surprise when the Cabinet Minister Ben Bradshaw took up Campbell's tune later that evening on air and told me 'I know you feel very sore about this, Adam [the putative Lib–Lab pact].' By this stage I was quoting on the record views against the deal from across the Labour spectrum – from John Reid to Diane Abbott. Citing these figures, I impressed upon Bradshaw that 'this is nothing to do with my opinion'. He Twittered to his fifty-five 'followers' later 'What is wrong with him?'

The 'Boulton v Campbell' encounter quickly gathered a cult following. Every day since I have had strangers coming up to me to express their support. In Haymarket a bus driver jammed on the brakes to give me a double thumbs-up; I've had congratulations from policemen to Labour peers and Alastair Campbell has naturally claimed that he has made me famous. At the time, I declined to comment, except to the sketch writer Ann Treneman who I talked to outside the Conservative and Liberal Democrat coalition negotiations in Whitehall, as a passing crowd of demonstrators chanted my name. She reported in *The Times* that I regretted the incident. I repeated this view a few weeks later on BBC Radio 4's *Today* programme when I was invited on with John Sergeant on the somewhat unlikely pretext of discussing the thirtieth anniversary of the launch of CNN.

But even though Campbell instantly claimed to have won the encounter, and in spite of his insistence that he was interested in policies not personalities, he and his cronies set about trying to dominate the post-match analysis and to do me as much damage as they possibly could.

That night Campbell contacted the most senior people at Sky News who he could find in his BlackBerry to demand action against me. John Prescott, who seems never to have forgiven me or Sky for breaking the story that he had punched a member of the public, pointed his 22,000 Twitter followers in the fight direction: 'Inundated by people wanting link to report Adam Boulton,' he tweeted, 'happy to help', before giving the address of Ofcom.

Campbell also continued to try to settle scores on Twitter: 'When JP punched someone, pompous Boulton said he must go! Wonder if same rules for TV hacks losing it live. Thought the headbutt imminent . . . Really worried about Adam Boulton . . . Wonder if he might need some of my pills. Anji ought to come home from her foreign trip.' He variously referred to my 'on-air melt down', how I 'lost it live', and my 'live toys-out-of-the-pram tantrum'. He claimed that 'online there was a lot of comparisons between Sky and Fox News – not to Sky's reputational benefit I would say.' But Campbell couldn't quite work out who was threatening who during the publicity interviews for the latest volume of his diaries, telling the *Guardian*: 'There's one point where I start to move back a little bit. I was thinking "What do you do if someone headbutts you live on TV?"' but boasting at an awards ceremony according to *PR Week*: 'If

I hadn't thought about my mum watching at home, I'd have headbutted him.'

However along with the banter, Campbell made a more private and insidious attempt to throw his weight around and seemed to want to settle scores with me. The man who had impugned both my and the channel's professional integrity sent a letter by email that same week to John Ryley, the Head of Sky News, threatening to sue unless disciplinary action was taken against me. A copy of Campbell's email was supplied to me for my information. I reproduce quotations from it here without the permission of John Ryley or indeed Sky News. But I take this step in the firm belief that reading it reveals a lot about the man and his modus operandi.

Following the initial pleasantries, Campbell details that he has spoken that morning to lawyers:

> *Their advice is that I have every right to complain to Ofcom, and have set out the grounds on which such a complaint ought to be accepted. However, I see from the media that many others have done this already. So, other than giving publicity to an interview that needs no more, I see little point in doing this. Ofcom will doubtless look at it and make up their own minds.*

Campbell also states he had been advised that what I had said during the interview and afterwards was defamatory:

> *Lawyers draw attention in particular to his questioning of my motivations in seeking to discharge the duty I had been asked by the Prime Minister to fulfil, namely advising him in conjunction with the official government machine on how to navigate a complex constitutional position. Further, he questioned my integrity at various points including via allegations that Peter Mandelson and*

I were involved in an unconstitutional 'stitch up', that we were compulsive liars and that we were unpatriotic.

He claims that he has

been libelled and defamed many times, but in part because I believe in freedom of speech, and because I happen to think our libel laws are hopeless, I have rarely used them. Whenever I have, I have won.

I let most things go because there are more important things in life than wasting time on this kind of thing. Indeed, Boulton has defamed me in the past and, because the impact has been minimal, I have let it go. However, the attention given to this has been enormous, and worldwide. Yesterday as I went about my business, as many people raised this with me as raised the rather more important question about who our Prime Minister might be at the end of the day. It has been viewed by hundreds of thousands of people since the first broadcast, produced tens of thousands of comments online, and though the vast majority are in my favour, that does not negate the defamatory nature of what he said, and has been saying to others since. Even the Mail today, which libels me on close to a daily basis, seems to accept most professional journalists saw his outbursts as a disgraceful and unprofessional contribution to an important debate in which I was trying to engage in a responsible, restrained, if robust manner.

While Campbell writes that his lawyers are advising he consider whether to take legal action, he stresses that he would be

less minded to do so if Sky News were to take some steps, privately and publicly, to mark an acceptance that his behaviour was unacceptable and that I am owed an apology. For this not to happen would mean that Sky felt there was nothing wrong with his behaviour, when I know from senior executives at News that they think no such thing.

I think it is best at this stage if you, rather than I, make propos-
als as to what the private and public expression of this should be,
but be assured I am determined there should be such an expression
and I look forward to hearing from you.

Pestered by several more emails, 'Have you got anything for me?', Ryley eventually replied by letter that I had expressed regret about the incident and that that should be sufficient. Nothing further has been heard from Campbell.

Attempts by Campbell, Prescott and other interested online parties to involve Ofcom were no more successful. The regulator reported that it had 'received 1,116 complaints about this content, with complainants considering that Adam Boulton was biased towards the Conservative party and against the Labour party, and was confrontational, bullying and aggressive towards Alastair Campbell. Some complainants considered that it was inappropriate for a presenter to lose his temper on television.'

Ofcom's judgement pointed out that although the live programme went out after polling day the rules of 'due impartiality' still applied because 'the programme was dealing with arguments for and against Gordon Brown's attempt to form a coalition administration with the Liberal Democrats . . . discussions around the formation of the UK government was clearly a matter of major political controversy.'

However, it took the view that both sides had had the chance to air their opinions:

First, given that Alastair Campbell had effectively accused Sky News' Political Editor of wanting a Conservative Prime Minister, we consider that it was not unreasonable, and within the requirements of due impartiality, for Adam Boulton to defend his position. Adam Boulton did become visibly angry – but that does not, in itself, impact on the due impartiality of the content.

In terms of the issues under discussion on the programme, Alastair Campbell was able to argue that Gordon Brown was constitutionally able to remain as Prime Minister, in the particular circumstances of the post-election period following 7 May 2010, unless another leader was able to construct a coalition that would command a majority in the House of Commons. Within this context, Alastair Campbell was arguing that, although the Conservative party had won most votes and seats at the General Election, no party had won an overall majority. Therefore, Gordon Brown could legitimately, in his view, seek to form a coalition.

In contrast, Adam Boulton was able to press Alastair Campbell on whether, given that the Labour party had come second in terms of votes and seats at the General Election, it was appropriate for Gordon Brown to seek to form a coalition Government and remain in power, taking into account the Parliamentary arithmetic of the numbers of MPs of various parties that would be involved. We considered that it was legitimate for Adam Boulton to question a leading representative of the Labour party about whether it was appropriate for the Labour party to try to continue in Government in these circumstances. It was also legitimate for the programme to explore the stability of a potential Labour Government in coalition with a number of other political parties. Further, we considered that Alastair Campbell was able to effectively get his points across. While the conduct and manner of the discussion was certainly unusual, in terms of impartiality we consider that relevant views and issues were aired.

The regulator also considered whether the item had given 'offence' noting that some viewers had complained that the exchange was 'horrendous' and 'offensive'. But it ruled that:

> ... the discussion between Alastair Campbell and Adam Boulton may have proved surprising or even to be uncomfortable viewing to some, and we also accept that the exchanges were heated. However, given the nature of the programming (a live 24 hour news service), the important political issues that were being discussed and the overall context of the programme, we concluded that generally accepted standards were applied to this content. Two well-known personalities from the worlds of politics and journalism were taking part in a debate about a matter of topical and serious concern. We considered that although the tone and content of this exchange was unusual, it would not have been beyond the likely expectations of the audience for this channel. It should be noted that the discussion at no time resulted in any abusive language or gratuitous insults. Therefore to find that these heated exchanges could not be transmitted would be an unnecessary interference with the broadcaster's and the viewer's right of freedom of expression. We therefore considered there was no breach of Rules 2.1 and 2.3.

The Ofcom ruling was a great relief to me and effectively closed an incident which had always had its ludicrous side. I hope it has done no lasting damage to Sky News' reputation, hard-won over the last three decades. I have made mistakes during live broadcasts, and I admit them. What concerned me about this incident was that a political operative appeared perhaps by instinct to resort shamelessly to 'playing the man'.

As ever, family members can be relied upon to put things in their proper perspective. Over the summer Campbell and I ran into each other at parties given by mutual friends (some openly hoping our row would add a frisson to proceedings). Emotions were highest at a joint 60th and 21st birthday party for Blair's pollster Philip Gould and his daughter Grace. Campbell spoke movingly and at length about his friends and Philip's battle with cancer. He concluded with a jokey programme for the evening, to be rounded off with 'a naked mud wrestling match' between teams led by him and me. His only rule was that it should be 'a fight to the death'.

Grace Gould kept it shorter, advising the oldies present to 'grab a drink and, if you're lucky, a twenty year old!' Afterwards Campbell got his teenage daughter, also Grace, to confess to me that she was on my side 'because nobody has ever argued with Dad like that.' I replied that my wife, Anji, a former Downing Street colleague of his, 'backed Alastair'.

★ ★ ★

Time and again during the election campaign and the days since, David Cameron had shown his ability to adjust to unwelcome circumstances. Now he was going to have to do it again; to demonstrate once more the Cameron capacity to take a blow, pick himself up and move forward. David Cameron and the Conservative party had one last card to play. He determined to make his final offer.

It was what the Liberal Democrats had been waiting for. A vote in the House of Commons on an AV referendum, with the full backing of the Tories behind it. The Conservatives would not just put a vote on the referendum before parliament, as they had already suggested to the Lib Dems, but they would use the whip to support it. Since the Conservatives and Lib Dems would command a majority in the Commons, this pledge made it a certainty that a referendum would take place.

It was this proposal that Conservative MPs gathered to discuss at six o'clock – an hour after Gordon Brown had made his statement in Downing Street, and at the very same time the Cabinet was gathering. Not all senior party figures were delighted when they heard of this latest concession. Chris Grayling and Theresa May both expressed some concern. There was bound to be a degree of dissent from right-wing Tories, but the meeting of the parliamentary party was tightly managed and went better than many in Cameron's circle could have hoped.

The Conservative leader told his party that he needed to go further or the Lib Dems would walk away for good. He said he believed Labour had offered to legislate to introduce the alternative vote without first holding a referendum, and while the Conservatives could not match that they would have to offer a significant concession on electoral reform. Not promising to deliver AV like Labour, but promising to hold an early referendum on whether it should come in. Conservatives, including himself, he emphasised would be free to campaign for a 'No' vote in such a referendum against their putative coalition partners. Cameron was given the endorsement he needed. Journalists were told that the leader was cheered loudly when he explained that the AV compromise was necessary to win power. 'The sense of relief was palpable', one Tory strategist commented in the media. 'For a minute it looked like we were out of the game and there was panic at the top.'

When the meeting wrapped up after an hour, William Hague strode to the main pedestrian entrance to parliament, St Stephen's. He announced that the Conservatives 'will go the extra mile' on electoral reform and offer a referendum on switching to AV in return for a coalition government with the Liberal Democrats.

Questioned subsequently in the House of Commons, Nick Clegg denied that Labour had ever promised explicitly to deliver AV without consulting the people first. And no official Lib

Dem–Labour negotiations had yet taken place at the time that Cameron told his party such an offer had been made. This led to some suggestions that Cameron had lied to his own party to secure the concession he needed. Both Cameron and Osborne denied emphatically that their party had been misled. Osborne had heard from a number of sources, including the Lib Dems, that Labour were potentially offering such a concession. There was a widespread view at the top of the Tory tree that when it came to it, Gordon Brown would offer whatever it took. Even now, Cameron's closest colleagues maintain their belief that at the end, the Prime Minister 'just chucked everything onto the table' in his desperation to stay on.

The idea was explored at the instigation of the Lib Dems. On Saturday morning, a substantive conversation had taken place between Peter Mandelson and his old 'Britain in Europe' mucker Danny Alexander. During this, Alexander broached the idea of the Lib–Lab voting majority (if it could be called such a thing!) imposing the alternative vote without first holding a referendum. According to Mandelson, 'he said their worry was that a referendum would be lost because voters might see a Lib–Lab pact as a self-interested stitch-up on both sides, so it might be better to avoid such a test.' Alexander also pointed out to Mandelson, offering a precedent of sorts, that there was no commitment to a referendum on PR in his own party's manifesto; simply a commitment to deliver it.

On the Lib Dem side, it is argued that given a number of Lib Dem MPs raised the idea at their meeting on the Saturday, it was only proper that the leadership should test its viability with their negotiating partners. Fears that a 'coalition of the losers' would find it hard to sell anything to the British public (let alone a complex new system of voting) were at the heart of their attempt to ascertain whether a referendum could, in fact, be bypassed.

Peter Mandelson may have been willing tentatively to engage in the discussion, but looking back on the episode, some among his negotiating partners can barely hide their disdain. Ed Miliband maintains that a large part of one of the meetings with the Lib Dems was 'consumed by whether or not we could have AV without a referendum . . . or have it for by-elections. We didn't want it without a referendum but they said as a compromise, "Well, let's just have it for by-elections." We thought that was just for the birds, frankly.' (A senior Liberal Democrat describes that version of events as 'nonsense', insisting that AV was only a part of a wider discussion of electoral reform lasting a quarter of an hour.)

The constant media reports indicating that Labour was prepared to go the extra mile on AV contributed to Conservative unease. Sky News and the BBC both cited 'Labour sources' that AV without a referendum first was on the table, alongside records of conversations with other 'Labour sources' vowing not to support such a deal. It was, as the Tories would later say in their defence, 'in the mix'.

Whether or not Labour ever offered to legislate for AV without a referendum, as Cameron believed at the time and Clegg subsequently denied, there is no doubt at all that the Lib Dems tabled such a demand and that their hankering to change the voting system without necessarily asking the voters first provided a crucial counterpoint throughout the five days.

Mutterings within Labour ranks were not confined to the issue of AV. The consequence of Gordon Brown's failure to consult the parliamentary party was that individuals who felt shut out of the process began to make their dissatisfaction clear in public. That evening it was quickly apparent that large sections of the Labour party would not support a Lib-Lab coalition. Diane Abbott MP and John Reid said as much on air a few minutes after the Cabinet met. David Blunkett had already declared that his party had lost the election. Jon Cruddas let it be known that he and his supporters were unhappy about the likely ideological price a compromise with the Liberal Democrats might entail. Even mainstream party loyalists were protesting that they would never vote for 'PR'.

The noises off were a problem. Even the Labour negotiators knew it. One of the Labour team felt that 'People coming out and saying it was not going to work . . . spooked them [the Lib Dems] more than anything.' The problem was the Liberal Democrats viewed each MP voicing dissent as an MP lost to the coalition they were struggling to build with Labour. Soundings that were going on within the Labour party would only have enhanced their concern, had the Lib Dems known about them. When it had become clear that negotiations would start with Nick Clegg's party, Gordon Brown finally asked his aides to do an informal ring-round of parliamentarians to see where they stood. The results were not encouraging. Only about half were 'up for it'. Doubt, recalcitrance and suspicion were rife.

Most of this was not known to either the Labour or the Liberal Democrat negotiating teams when they met, just after 8 p.m. once again in Room 319 in Portcullis House.

This was a bad meeting. Labour, knowing the need to demonstrate a measure of goodwill, had come with what they viewed as 'goodies'. They agreed not to proceed with a third runway at Heathrow and made a further concession that, in their view, amounted to 'dumping' the controversial ID cards scheme. The Lib Dems were not impressed. The ID cards proposal, that they felt Labour was making a great song and dance about, was not what it was cracked up to be, in their view. According to a Lib Dem negotiator, Labour agreed not to proceed with ID cards for the length of a parliament, but insisted they needed to maintain the database on which the scheme was based. To the Lib Dems, this was a half-hearted postponement, no more.

The Labour side were unaware of the adverse impression they were giving. 'There's no doubt that on the Monday if there was any aggression or cold water being poured on the talks, it was from the Liberal Democrats,' Ed Balls complained.

Ed Miliband argued that the Lib Dems had had it too good with their Conservative interlocutors. 'The Tories were willing to throw anything out of the balloon in order to get this thing to happen. We were trying to engage in serious negotiations about things that would have credibility. We were probably more conscious of the need for credibility.' In sum, 'I just think that we weren't pushovers.'

The short-tempered Miliband and his Lib Dem opposite number on climate change squared up to each other on energy for a sticky moment: Chris Huhne said the aim should be for 40 per cent renewable energy not 15 per cent. Miliband stressed this figure was unachievable leading Huhne, it is recalled, to counter, 'Well you had a bad record in government and you can do it.'

The most damaging impression was coming from Balls, Miliband and Harman, according to David Laws. 'It was totally different to the Conservative discussions,' he asserts. 'The body language, and the sneering and so forth . . . There was much more of a sense of "We've been in the government, we've done all these things, we know all the answers . . ." and all these policy proposals you're making are ridiculous or undeliverable.'

Laws says the Labour negotiators tried to catch him out over the Lib Dems' central taxation proposal, raising the threshold of the basic rate to £10,000. 'There was an attempt to buy us off,' he says, 'by suggesting that the pensioner tax allowance could go up to £10,000. Since I pointed out that the pensioner tax allowance was already £9,600 . . . it was almost a trick since it was fairly worthless in terms of what it represented.'

Worst of all, things went backwards on the Lib Dems' top issue, electoral reform. The uniform Lib Dem view is that Ed Balls went out of his way to say that it would not be easy to guarantee Labour party support as many members were opposed to AV. Balls believed he was only being realistic: 'We said we will support an AV referendum and we will campaign for it. That is better for you than getting an AV referendum with the Conservative party which will campaign against you . . .' There appears to have been an attempt by Andrew Adonis to mediate by suggesting a referendum question on full PR, but by his own admission Balls crushed this, insisting, 'There will be no support within the PLP for going wider than AV within the referendum . . . even on the AV point, this is hard for us.'

The Lib Dems regarded Ed Balls's interventions as undermining the whole coalition endeavour. The numbers were critical. They argue that what the Schools Secretary did was to expose that the rock-solid support a Labour–Liberal Democrat coalition would require was simply not there. 'For Balls to be saying this could be very difficult for our people . . .' Danny Alexander explains, 'this was tantamount to saying there are parts of our party that will not allow this to pass. What Ed Balls did was to send a signal that a government that needed every single vote could not, in practice, rely on getting them.'

The Lib Dem team rapidly concluded that at least half the Labour side, and the dominant, elected side at that – Harman, Balls and Miliband – did not have their hearts set on reaching a deal. Adonis and Mandelson were in the end only glorified advisors. The talks broke up after a couple of hours, with the Lib Dems angry and disappointed. David Laws said, 'All four of us finished the meeting concluding that Labour were not adequately committed to making the thing work, and they were offering us considerably less in certain areas than the Conservatives were.'

Naturally that is not what they told the journalists waiting for arrivals in Westminster Hall outside the venue for the second meeting of the Liberal Democrat Parliamentary Party scheduled for late that evening. A Lib Dem source said the discussions had been 'constructive'. Ed Balls called them 'positive and constructive'.

'Terrible' was the word Nick Clegg used. 'I'm afraid the meeting with Labour was terrible,' he told his MPs after arriving just before 11 p.m. at their meeting to discuss the way forward. By now events were beginning to militate against a deal with Labour. The mood at the meeting hardened. Evidence of dissent in Labour ranks was mounting over any pact with the Lib Dems, and doubts about the mathematical viability of such a deal (never far from the surface) were becoming more pointed.

Given the intense and competitive courting they had been subject to, the Lib Dems' coquettish self-regard was more inflamed than usual, and the mood of the meeting changed as accounts spread of how their representatives had been treated. Senior figures in the party stood up and led the party in a new direction. Three of the most influential all came from constituencies they had personally won from the Conservatives in hard-fought battles: Norman Baker from Lewes; Don Foster from Bath; and Vince Cable from Twickenham. Now they all spoke in favour of a deal with the Tories. Vince Cable was both uncharacteristically vehement and characteristically understated. 'I hate the Tories. I have spent my whole life fighting them. But I think we could be quite influential if we go with the Tories.' Cable's intervention seemed to be decisive, since it was generally known that he had spent the past four days talking to Brown and trying to stitch up a deal with Labour.

All the same, Nick Clegg told the negotiators to hold one further session with Labour the next day. The Lib Dem parliamentary meeting broke up after two hours at a quarter to one in the morning with an official statement that said: 'current negotiations need to be concluded rapidly to provide stable government that lasts.'

The Lib Dem team were far from enthusiastic about the task that the party leader had set them for the coming morning. They were, in David Laws's words, 'fed up'. He confesses they thought it was a waste of time. Clegg gave his men a pep talk. 'You are going to have to go back in and find out whether they feel better about this tomorrow and are willing to be more serious,' he told them, 'because we need to test their true intentions and make sure you've understood them correctly. We've got to show that we've seriously tested all the options.' Grudgingly, they agreed.

Back home, and knowing nothing of the state of the talks with Labour, David Cameron was resigning himself to the worst. He consoled himself with the knowledge that he had done the right thing, but had no great expectation it would do the job. Labour, he thought, would give the Liberal Democrats what they wanted, and a Lib–Lab pact would emerge. Before leaving work, to staff who had been preparing to move out of the opposition offices, he had given weary instructions: 'Put the pictures back on the wall.' At dinner, he told his wife Samantha that he expected to be leader of the opposition for a few years more – 'I hope you don't mind.'

It was the lowest point for the Conservatives but there were some compensations. As William Hague remembered, 'That was the only night we had a good night's sleep because . . . well there's nothing more we can do now, we'll just see how the Liberals react to the various offers, and we all went home to our wives and had a good sleep. But while we were asleep it all turned in our favour . . .'

Britain woke up to a changed mood. A Lib–Con coalition seemed to be possible again. A second Lib–Lab pact no longer looked like a certainty – even if there were some still fighting fiercely for it. Paddy Ashdown gave an interview to the *Today* programme, which was tetchy even by his standards. He insisted that: 'A minority Lib–Lab coalition, I think, can provide stability because, although there is a technical majority against it, I can see no political circumstances in which that can be assembled.' Even though only 52 per cent of the electorate would have voted for either party in the government, he was persuaded by that narrow majority of the popular vote: 'I call that legitimacy.' Ashdown closed by saying that he knew what his advice to his party would be at the decisive meeting but refused to say what it was, even after it was pointed out to him gently that he had dedicated his political life to a progressive alliance with Labour.

Cameron and Clegg managed to preserve their dignity. After the meeting of his MPs the night before, the Lib Dem leader now had a clear idea of where things were headed. And David Cameron was starting to receive intelligence – positive intelligence. That morning, Danny Alexander told his opposite number, William Hague, that the meeting with Labour had been very difficult, and in stark contrast to the Lib–Con talks. Alexander informed Hague he felt now as though they were only going through the motions with Labour, but that they needed to give it a final try; at least so that the Liberal Democrat grassroots had a clear picture of the governing party's offer, approach and unity. It was music to Conservative ears.

A breezy David Cameron left his West London home at 8.45 a.m. declaring he had made a 'very full, very open, very reasonable offer' and that it was now decision time for the Liberal Democrats.

Half an hour later, outside his home in Putney, Nick Clegg still tried not to be drawn between the two other parties, confirming only that negotiations to decide Britain's future were at a 'critical and final phase' and that he was 'as impatient as anyone else' to resolve the political impasse and hoped to make an announcement 'as quickly as we possibly can'.

What would indeed turn out to be the final session of official Lib–Lab talks began at 10 a.m. in what by now must have become the very familiar, though dispiriting environs of Room 319. Mandelson picked up on 'a new mood of prickliness, even truculence, from the Liberal Democrats'. He 'inconspicuously texted' Danny Alexander, who was sitting in the room across the table from him, 'If this goes on we'll get nowhere.' But what really broke the back of the meeting was the opening announcement from Alexander, the Lib Dems' team leader, that the Lib Dems had unilaterally cancelled a mooted meeting between Alistair Darling and Vince Cable. Labour had long regarded Cable as their inside man, but it now appeared that he had been turned. 'I knew then and there,' Lord Adonis said later, 'that the Lib Dems were not serious about a deal with us.' Another member of the Labour team commented, 'The fact that Vince was not at the talks was in itself very telling, but the fact that he was stopped from seeing Alistair made it clear: they had already decided to go with the Tories.'

Shortly after noon Gordon Brown left Downing Street for a quick meeting with Clegg in parliament, but twenty minutes later the formal talks between their parties broke down terminally. Labour initially stated there had been 'good discussions' but the Lib Dems complained of 'bad body language and bad attitudes' from the Labour team. According to Andrew Adonis, the claims that increasingly gained currency among Lib Dems, that the numbers had never been there for a Labour deal in the first place, were mere 'alibis'.

Apart from the serially inconclusive and seemingly uncomprehending Clegg–Brown talks, there was now no way forward together for Labour and the Liberal Democrats. From lunchtime onward straws thickened in the wind that a deal would be done. Andy Burnham became the first Cabinet minister to state on the record that Labour should not attempt a coalition with the Lib Dems because his party 'didn't win' the election. Ed Balls's claims that things were going positively were slapped down by Diana Johnson, one of his own junior ministers; the 'numbers don't stack up' she asserted. Even the Lib Dem MP Evan Harris, who had just lost his seat in Oxford to the Conservatives after a vicious campaign, asserted that the Tories were willing to offer much more than Labour.

But still there was no official word. After an hour of face-to-face talks, Cameron and Clegg instructed their teams to revive the coalition agreement that they had set aside because of the earlier stalemate over AV, and ready it for publication. Official negotiations between the two sides resumed at the Cabinet Office at 2 p.m. A restless David Cameron, prowling the corridors and tearooms of the Palace of Westminster, was cornered by reporters around lunchtime. 'I'm in the dark, like all of you,' he protested.

Like an angel of political death, Christopher Geidt, the Queen's Private Secretary, appeared in the Cabinet Office that day. Geidt had the responsibility of arranging the audiences with the monarch that would seal any transfer of power. According to Mandelson, Geidt must have gone down the connecting corridors to Number 10 that afternoon, where he delicately discussed with Brown 'how developments might unfold'.

Between 4 and 5 p.m., not all the activity was centred around parliament and Whitehall. Amid the hubbub and speculation,

David Cameron checked in with party workers at Millbank HQ, and did his best to reassure them things would work out. The Lib Dems announced they were convening a joint meeting of their parliamentary party and the Federal Executive for that evening. A photographer captured Clegg carrying a piece of paper listing Tory 'red lines', but which also seemed to say that the Lib Dems would have a minister 'in each department'.

By 5 p.m. television teams had relocated around the corner from outside the Cabinet Office to outside Number 10, in anticipation of developments there. The street was brightly lit because the broadcasters had been allowed to keep the special structures erected for election night – but there were also strict orders to dismantle them from midnight that day. As Adam Boulton walked up the street the assembled journalists, photographers and technicians broke out in applause and cheers following his encounter the previous night with Alastair Campbell. Meanwhile, Vince Cable told Sky News viewers that a deal was 'very close to being done'.

But the real drama, by now, was taking place inside Number 10. Gordon Brown had returned from his lunchtime meeting with Nick Clegg knowing there was little room for optimism. Further calls he made to Paddy Ashdown and Cable confirmed the Prime Minister in his belief the game was up. He began to make the final preparations to leave, unwilling to be left dangling on a string by the Lib Dems as they tried to exert the last concessions from David Cameron's party.

By three o'clock, flights were booked to return Gordon Brown, his wife and children to Scotland that night; and shortly after four, he told his staff it was all over. Harriet Harman, as expected, would take on the job of interim Labour leader. The remaining hours were spent saying goodbyes, thanking the staff, writing a letter to the incoming Prime Minister David Cameron and (of course) making and taking more telephone calls. As Peter Mandelson returned to Downing Street at around 6 p.m. from a scheduled meeting of the Privy Council at Buckingham Palace, he found Gordon Brown in his office with the whole team grouped around him. A comforting call from Tony Blair had been put through.

Nick Clegg had telephoned around fifteen minutes before Mandelson's arrival. The Lib Dem leader was insistent Gordon Brown should not resign straightaway, but should allow the negotiations to play out to the end. He requested a further hour. Gordon Brown took the opportunity to call in a barber. As Brown's hair was being cut in preparation for his final Downing Street performance, the weight and tension of the past few days lifted, and he began sharing jokes with colleagues about the experiences they had enjoyed over the past few years.

Clegg rang again not long before seven. The exchanges between the two men had become increasingly acrid. At one point Brown warned Clegg that the 'progressive realignment Tony and Paddy had so wanted would be lost for a generation at least'. But Clegg represented a new Liberal Democrat party – he was interested in his own future and not their past. He retorted, 'rather brutally' in Mandelson's view, 'the reality is that your party is knackered after thirteen years in power.'

In extremis, in the final moments of his premiership, Gordon Brown, a politician who had always found it so hard to take decisions and so easy to vacillate, obfuscate, evade and prevaricate, had managed to tap into inner reserves of courage to bring an end to his life's desire, his period in power. Just after seven, Clegg was still wittering away on the phone asking for a few more minutes, perhaps out of politeness and embarrassment at the crisis his party's decisions had precipitated. The Prime Minister cut him short: 'Nick, Nick, Nick, Nick . . . I know the country's mood. They will not tolerate me waiting another night. You are a good man and you have to make a decision. I have made mine. It is final. I am going to the Palace. Goodbye.'

First Brown had to face the cameras for his resignation speech. At 7.10 p.m. a podium was placed in the street. A round of cheers were heard through the door and then the staff started to line up on the pavement outside Number 10.

There are moments when you see a man you know well afresh; as though for the first time. Here was such a moment. At 7.19 p.m., when Gordon Brown walked composedly to the lectern in Downing Street, his wife Sarah at his side, it was as though years of comment and caricature at Brown's expense, barbs and acid contempt were put aside, and in return the bluster and arrogance, the glowers and stony obduracy – the walls that this proud but uneasy Labour Prime Minister had built around himself – fell away.

The words were formal enough. They were the words that David Cameron had dreamed of hearing.

'I have informed the Queen's private secretary that it is my intention to tender my resignation to the Queen. In the event that the Queen accepts, I shall advise her to invite the leader of the opposition to form a government.'

Still, the name 'David Cameron' could not quite make it across Gordon Brown's lips. Nevertheless, Brown's sentiment was generously expressed.

'I wish the next Prime Minister well as he makes the important choices for the future.

'Only those that have held the office of Prime Minister can understand the full weight of its responsibilities and its great capacity for good. I have been privileged to learn much about the very best in human nature and a fair amount too about its frailties, including my own. Above all, it was a privilege to serve.'

Gordon Brown in Number 10 had always been, in some respects, a square peg in a round hole, and he knew it. 'I loved the job not for its prestige, its titles and its ceremony – which I do not love at all. No, I loved the job for its potential to make this country I love fairer, more tolerant, more green, more demo-cratic, more prosperous and more just – truly a greater Britain.'

Of all that was flung at Gordon Brown, if there was one thing that had got under Brown's skin in the previous months, it was the suggestion that he did not care about the sacrifices of Britain's armed forces. This, at the last, was something he determined to remedy. It was the final time that, as Prime Minister, Gordon Brown would allow a hint of the sense of grievance and injustice that always bubbled angrily within him, to rise to the surface.

'And let me add one thing also,' he insisted. 'I will always admire the courage I have seen in our armed forces. And now that the political season is over, let me stress that having shaken their hands and looked into their eyes, our troops represent all that is best in our country and I will never forget all those who have died in honour and whose families today live in grief.'

There were thanks for colleagues, ministers and Labour MPs, but above all this was a moment for the Brown family, not just Gordon and Sarah, but their sons John and Fraser, who through their parents' choice had been obscured from public view up until now.

'As I leave the second most important job I could ever hold, I cherish even more the first – as a husband and father,' Gordon Brown concluded. 'Thank you and goodbye.'

Gordon and Sarah Brown turned to the door, inside which his young boys were waiting. The children had wanted to share a moment in Downing Street with their father. For most of the watching nation, this was the first time they had ever seen John and Fraser, and the picture was as touching as it was unexpected. With their mother and father looking on proudly, the pair posed for the cameras, smiling, bright-eyed, smart in long trousers, checked shirts and blazers.

As they walked hand in hand down the street to where a government Daimler awaited, it might have occurred to an onlooker that alongside the political drama of the past five days, a minor family drama had played out too. The mother, who, even on Friday morning, had begun packing in expectation that things would most likely not work out . . . who told friends in Downing Street on Sunday that 'Either Gordon is going to be happy, or we are all going to be happy and get our lives back' . . . the father who, the night before, had taken time to put his two boys to bed, and warned them that the next day, they would be leaving, and they would not be coming back.

This was a side of Gordon Brown he never permitted the world to see. How perverse, in a senior politician, to refuse to show one's best, most human side! Yet how expressive of Brown's unique (mostly unfathomable), but undeniable sense of principle.

As Gordon Brown's car passed through the gates of Downing Street, and on to Whitehall, the journalists lined up on the other side of the road looked at one another. What next? It was pretty clear that DC had to turn up sometime, but nobody was quite sure where the Prime Minister-in-waiting had got to.

In fact, David Cameron had been caught on the hop as much as anyone else by the rapid turn of events. With the Tory and Liberal Democrat negotiating teams still meeting, the expectation was that Gordon Brown would hang on until a deal was signed and ratified. His irritation at feeling used by Nick Clegg to try to lever a better deal out of the Tories, coupled with a conviction that leaving Downing Street after nightfall would be demeaning, made that impossible.

As speculation mounted that events were coming to a head in the late afternoon, Cameron and his entourage wondered whether the endgame might really be upon them? 'I phoned Samantha,' explained Cameron, 'and said, "What are you doing?" "Feeding the children." I said, "You'd better get your frock on, this might happen tonight."'

As the Camerons readied themselves to see the Queen and make their long-awaited entrance into Downing Street, the Conservative leader's advisors hotfooted it from his parliamentary office, across Whitehall and into the Cabinet Office. There was some concern when chief of staff Ed Llewellyn was mislaid en route, but once the new Prime Minister's team entered the very same building where the coalition talks were still taking place, they were greeted by civil servants holding brand new Downing Street passes. There was some unfounded anxiety that the Labour team might have left some stragglers, but once they had recovered their bearings, the second 'Cameron family' were taken through the corridors from the Cabinet Office to Downing Street. After the proper interval had been observed, and 'events' began to occur, they stationed themselves in the street – in front of the door of Number 11 and therefore out of the main camera shot – and waited.

Entirely unnoticed amid the momentous events in Downing Street and at the Palace, the Lib–Con talks broke up for the last time at 7.35 p.m. – a final meeting of some five and a half hours. The negotiators would have been well aware they were no longer the only show, and a competing attraction round the corner was now rather more of a draw. Nevertheless, professional to the end, William Hague kept his cards close to his chest. The meeting had been 'very positive' and he had 'some recommendations' to take back to Cameron. Danny Alexander observed that there had been a 'good atmosphere' around the table. No one seriously doubted that a deal had been done.

All eyes were on the Palace. Journalists could not believe that there still had been no announcement about audiences with the Queen. Neither party had been willing to confirm that formal agreement had been reached between the Conservatives and the Liberal Democrats. Yet just after 8 p.m., television helicopters identified the silver Jaguar bearing David Cameron gliding towards the palace, its shark-like motion broken only by encounters with a learner driver and a motorcycle courier.

The live cameras in the inner courtyard of Buckingham Palace were still warm from Gordon Brown's coming and going and the careful viewer might have noticed a change of style. While Brown had been alone except for his officials, entering the building swiftly, Cameron tried to hop round his Jag to open the door for Samantha before a flunkey got there. He introduced his pregnant wife to the waiting Lady Susan Hussey, 'woman of the bedchamber', and then followed them up the stairs to the audience room.

On being asked by Her Majesty to form a government, Cameron agreed but said he didn't know what sort of government it would be yet, minority or coalition.

Waiting back in Downing Street was the world's media and the Cameron faithful; inside the front door was ranged an expectant fleet of civil servants. Looking up between the tall buildings of Numbers 10 and 11 on one side of the street and the Foreign and Commonwealth Office on the other, the narrow strip of sky was matted with dark, black clouds. A piercing, late evening glow of sunlight persisted, adding drama to events that hardly needed nature's help. It was the sort of light that precedes a storm, or might be left when one has passed.

After the high emotion of Gordon Brown's departure, David Cameron could scarcely hope to compete. The decision had in any case been taken to ensure the choreography of his arrival was spare and undemonstrative. The children stayed at home. There were no flag-waving crowds lining the street as in 1997. As David Cameron spoke, his wife Samantha stood modestly a few paces from his side. A vague hubbub could be heard from Whitehall a hundred yards away – a mixture of anti-war demonstrators and the Tory faithful bellowing.

The most unexpected touch in David Cameron's speech was its opening. Just occasionally, a British political leader can pretty much say what they like without fear of internal party reproach. Cameron took his opportunity to praise, in words that he would have weighed carefully, the legacy of New Labour.

'Her Majesty the Queen has asked me to form a new government and I have accepted. Before I talk about that new government, let me say something about the one that has just passed. Compared with a decade ago, this country is more open at home and more compassionate abroad and that is something we should all be grateful for and on behalf of the whole country I'd like to pay tribute to the outgoing Prime Minister for his long record of dedicated public service.'

With the agreement that Cameron knew had been reached between the Liberal Democrat and Conservative negotiators still to be ratified, Cameron could only refer to his 'aim' to form a coalition. He nevertheless asserted that he and Nick Clegg were both committed 'to put aside party differences and work hard for the common good and for the national interest. I believe that is the best way to get the strong, decisive government that we need today.'

There was little that was unfamiliar to those who had listened to David Cameron over recent months; little that reached beyond the normal campaign rhetoric. As ever, he was poised and fluent. And Cameron would have known that with that famous front door behind him, the night drawing in and the camera lights brightening, words that might have sounded prosaic in some other setting would take on a greater lustre.

'I want to help try and build a more responsible society here in Britain. One where we don't just ask what are my entitlements, but what are my responsibilities. One where we don't ask what am I just owed, but more what can I give. And a guide for that society – that those that can should, and those who can't we will always help.

'I want to make sure that my government always looks after the elderly, the frail, the poorest in our country. We must take everyone through with us on some of the difficult decisions we have ahead.

'Above all it will be a government that is built on some clear values. Values of freedom, values of fairness, and values of responsibility.'

David and Samantha Cameron posed affectionately on the doorstep of Number 10 before going inside to their new life. It would take some getting used to. Neither husband nor wife slept in Downing Street that night, and it would be several weeks before Samantha moved with the children into 'the flat above the shop'.

The immediate task was to secure the coalition agreement. Both Cameron and Clegg still faced party meetings that evening. The Tories were now back in government and the party's 'secret weapon of loyalty' was likely to kick in, even though, or even precisely because, it had been sorely tested in the years since the fall of Thatcher. Conservative party democracy was in any case comparatively rudimentary and tribal and no single parliamentary meeting could derail a coalition deal.

The Liberal Democrats were quite another matter. Clegg's meeting started first, around 9.30 p.m., preceded by equivocal comments from party grandees. Simon Hughes hailed 'a surprising coming together', but ever-Eeyorish Vince Cable insisted 'nothing has been formally agreed'. The most influential participants who were also potential troublemakers were the ex-leaders, David Steel, Paddy Ashdown, Charles Kennedy and Ming Campbell. It was difficult not to detect the whiff of sour grapes mixed in with their undoubted left-of-centrism.

Ashdown intervened emotionally early on: 'I can't do this. I'm off to my garden and my grandchildren.' But then he got his hands on the document outlining the agreements reached which was beginning to circulate. He changed his mind and stood up to speak again: 'Look I came into this room prepared to say I don't like this. I don't like it because I've fought the Tories all my life. I don't like it because it's the abandonment of the strategy of equidistance. I don't like it because I've spent thirty years getting Labour out of the West Country and now they'll get a chance to get back. I don't like it because we're being used by Mr Cameron to reform his Tory party and I can't think why that's our role. He obviously wants to be Disraeli, but who's going to be Gladstone?

'But now I've seen this agreement I have to tell you very bluntly my reaction. It's amazing. Fuck it! How can I stay out of this fight? If you are going to fight on this, and I grant you this will be a fight, you'll have to count me alongside you. You know I can't resist a fight especially in the company of my friends.'

Ashdown's 'fuck it position' prevailed. A share of real national power for the first time in their lives was too much for the professional politicians to resist. The Lib Dems endorsed the agreement 'unanimously', although Ming Campbell and Kennedy let it be known that they were still unconvinced, with the Scottish parliamentary election due in 2011.

Nick Clegg, who had been named as Deputy Prime Minister even before the Lib Dem meeting had wrapped up, made a brief speech to the cameras shortly after midnight. He hoped his party's coalition with Conservatives would mark the creation of a 'new kind of government' in Britain. He also paid tribute to Gordon Brown. Asked by reporters for his reaction to the coalition deal Lord Ashdown rose to the challenge in one word: 'Hooray!' he said simply.

Late that evening inside Number 10 Downing Street, David Cameron sat in his private office with newly appointed Foreign Secretary William Hague and the Chancellor of the Exchequer George Osborne. The three men were joined by the close civil service staff Cameron had met just hours ago, but would come soon to rely upon. They sat around chatting and eating pizza. What an evening!

Following his arrival in Number 10, Cameron had within minutes been whisked off for briefings by his new Foreign Policy Advisor Tom Fletcher ahead of a conversation with the US President. Having received the congratulations of Barack Obama, next on the line were Angela Merkel, the German Chancellor, and the Canadian Prime Minister Stephen Harper. President Sarkozy of France would have to wait – he had retired for the night by the time the call was attempted.

The international pleasantries over, Cameron and his wife returned to the Palace of Westminster. First they went to the Norman Shaw offices that would soon be occupied by Harriet Harman, the incoming leader of the opposition. Tory staffers who had spent most of the evening celebrating in the Red Lion Pub on Whitehall cheered the new Prime Minister to the rafters. There was a similar reaction from Conservative MPs gathered in the Grand Committee Room when Cameron made his entrance. Shouting, banging of desks; general euphoria. The Tories were back!

In a quieter moment, David Cameron sat down to read the letter Gordon Brown had left him. Truly, the ink was barely dry: Brown had taken the time to write amid all the chaos and comings and goings at five o'clock that very afternoon. The letter, in the famous Brown scrawl, was generous and heartfelt. David Cameron, he said, should know that the civil service staff he was inheriting were an exceptional group of people. And, from one Prime Minister to another, Gordon Brown told Cameron that this would be the most privileged role either of them would ever experience.

PART III

COALITION

11

INTO GOVERNMENT

'Did you really say that?'

It was third time lucky for David Cameron. Nick Clegg had twice before rebuffed his outstretched hand of friendship. After Clegg's leadership election victory in late 2007 Sam and Dave thought it would be nice to have Nick and Miriam around for dinner, but the Cleggs turned down the invitation. By the conference season of 2009, the defeat of Labour seemed certain but an outright Conservative majority was not guaranteed. Dave tried an approach in the workplace and went public with a suggestion to Nick that their two parties should cooperate shaping 'progressive' policies – 'There's barely a cigarette paper between us' – only to meet the fisheye once again.

But now here was Clegg standing and smiling next to Cameron as his Deputy Prime Minister.

The two men's joint news conference in the Downing Street garden was one of those events that just worked. The dramatic conclusion to the five days of bargaining was only a short night's sleep behind them. The sun shone. It was the 12th of May when most tended English gardens are near their best.

British weather means that prime ministers don't often hold public events in their large garden, which stretches behind Numbers 10, 11 and 12 Downing Street, behind walls on two sides abutting Horse Guards Parade. In June 1995 John Major temporarily resigned there, and two years later the Blairs hosted Bill and Hillary Clinton, in what they inaccurately renamed 'the rose garden' (not that there are very many more actual rose bushes in its White House namesake). The double act of 2010 was at least as memorable as either of these.

Both men strolled together down the steps from the patio, beloved of Tony Blair, to identical lecterns, Clegg to Cameron's right. Conscious that this occasion was being broadcast live around the world, they were careful to keep chatting animatedly to each other and to ensure that neither fall even a step behind the other. It was a sketch and headline writer's dream – 'A Special Relationship', 'The Happy Couple at No 10', 'HisTORY Boys . . . but how long will the love-in last?' Here were very similar fortysomething young men. Both white, English, fit-looking products of public schools, Oxbridge and special advisordom. They were dressed in similar dark-blue suits and white shirts. You could tell the difference by heights (six foot one-plus Clegg edges over Cameron who doesn't quite hit six foot) and by their plain ties: Clegg prudently stuck to his party's golden colours (even though they don't suit him); Cameron went for purple, accidentally striking off the slightly purplish hue of Clegg's suit.

But neither man would have wasted much time thinking of such sartorial details. Cameron got quickly to the point, claiming their government would mark an 'historic and seismic shift' in British politics in 'a direction of hope and unity, conviction and common purpose.' He said they had considered a minority Conservative government but dismissed it as 'uninspiring'. Instead theirs would be 'an administration united behind three key principles – freedom, fairness and responsibility . . . united behind one key purpose and that is to give our country the strong and stable and determined leadership that we need for the long term.'

Clegg admitted that both sides were taking 'big risks' – but he too stressed the national interest rather than the party political: 'It's a new kind of government, a radical reforming government where it needs to be and a source of reassurance and stability at a time of great uncertainty in our country too.'

A list of the new government's top appointments, including five Liberal Democrat Cabinet ministers, was released to coincide with the joint news conference, as was a document headed 'Conservative Liberal Democrat coalition negotiations – Agreements reached 11 May 2010'. This ran to eleven numbered sections: deficit reduction; spending review – NHS, schools and a fairer society; tax measures; banking reform; immigration; political reform; pensions and welfare; education; relations with the EU; civil liberties; and the environment. This document mostly followed the concessions and red lines hammered out at the Cabinet Office talks. There was more detail on political reform than before, designed to give something to all interested parties.

The mob waving torches and pitchforks over expenses were given the right to vote out their MP on a 10 per cent turnout in a local petition. For the Liberal Democrats, the government pledged to hold a referendum on AV, and to implement it if there was a 'yes' vote. For the Conservatives there were 'fewer and more equal sized constituencies'. The Tories were firmly convinced that redrawing boundaries in this way would redress the imbalance in the electoral system whereby it takes more votes nationally to elect a Conservative than a Labour MP. Senior Tories even claimed Cameron would have had an outright majority in a fair voting system. Most experts disputed both the analysis and the dividends that the Tories would get from new boundaries. (2010 was already a much 'fairer election' in this respect than 2005. Dividing total votes cast for each party by the number of MPs gained, in 2010 it took 34,989 votes to elect a Conservative, and 33,350 to elect a Labour MP. In 2005 the disparity was much larger, 26,896 for a Labour MP, 44,531 for the Conservatives. Things actually got worse for the Lib Dems, their votes/MP ratio rising from 96,487 to 119,788!)

Most intriguingly the reform section of the document revealed how the two parties planned to keep the show on the road. Fixed-term parliaments of an ambitious five years' duration rather than four, as had been widely expected, reinforced by legislative handcuffs designed to prevent either side forcing an early election by collapsing the government. The coalition government was subsequently forced to abandon its over-engineered proposal for a super majority of at least 55 per cent of MPs required for a dissolution of parliament but only in a way that will make it even harder by adopting Labour's two thirds majority as specified for the Scottish parliament.

Questioned on this, Nick Clegg produced the best soundbite of the morning (he and Cameron are both too fluent for odd phrases to simply slip out). 'We will succeed through our success,' he argued tautologously. In other words, he accepted that it was likely his party would take a hit for joining the Conservatives, but that it could redeem itself over time through a sustained and substantial record of achievement in government – five years at least by this reckoning.

As often on such occasions, Channel Five News' political editor, Andy Bell, came up with the best question. Remarkably

Bell had found something interesting in the orotund book of pensées *Cameron on Cameron*, which the young leader had vouch-safed to the editor of GQ, Dylan Jones. (By being mostly boring, Cameron did rather better than Clegg, whose GQ interview with Piers Morgan resulted in his notorious claim of 'no more than thirty lovers'.)

Bell reminded the Prime Minister that when asked for his favourite political joke he'd replied: 'Nick Clegg'. Clegg acted surprised, 'Did you really say that?' 'Yes, I'm afraid I did.' 'I'm off, I'm off,' Clegg said and feigned walking away. 'Come back!' Cameron shouted, going on to predict with confidence, 'We're all going to have things thrown back at us. We're looking at the bigger picture . . . and if it means swallowing some humble pie, and if it means eating some of your words, I cannot think of a more excellent diet.'

The comedy double-act summed up the first joint appearance of Prime Minister and his Deputy in a way that both wanted: edgy but relaxed, light but serious-minded, forward-looking but aware of the past, above all united and purposeful. There was a remarkable rapport, especially considering that Clegg had spent more time talking to Brown over the previous few days than he had to Cameron.

But in fact this was not quite rapport at first sight. A year before, in spite of Clegg's calculated reluctance to be caught in Cameron's potentially suffocating embrace, the seed of the two opposition leaders' regard for each other had been sown. They had been forced together with Gordon Brown to try to deal with the non-partisan political crisis that engulfed all MPs – the revelations about MPs' expenses, chiefly in the *Daily Telegraph*.

Both Cameron and Clegg spotted the fundamental repu-tational danger to parliament more quickly than Brown, who in its early stages had encouraged the Speaker to deal with the matter as quietly as possible. The two younger men had immediately refunded their own purported 'overpayments' for expenses claimed on such items as gardening or cleaning, and left their parties' MPs little alternative but to follow their example. To the dismay of many of those closest to him, Gordon Brown was paralysed by rage when it was suggested that his cleaning expenses, shared with his brother, had been too great. It was one of those occasions when he really did kick a waste-paper bin across the floor and shout at his wife. More significantly, he lost crucial days worrying about the stain on his own integrity, so allowing his political rivals to take the lead on dealing with the matter.

In an attempt at recapturing the initiative, Brown invited Cameron and Clegg to meet with him in the imposing Prime Minister's Room in the House of Commons. But the day before they were to have their supposed discussion, he announced his own plan in a widely derided video on YouTube. Instead of expenses, Brown wanted MPs to be paid a per diem allowance for each day they attended parliament. This had the merit of following a system (since changed) for covering the costs of (unpaid) members of the House of Lords. But it was an obvious non-starter for the Commons – 'Being paid twice for just turning up to do the job,' as one of the opposition leaders put it.

When the three men sat down together, Brown 'just banged on' about his idea. Clegg and Cameron raised possible problems and came up with alternative suggestions but they felt that they were just being brushed aside. Brown insisted that he 'needed' their support, and repeated his arguments. Like two head prefects in the study of an eccentric master, the question was one of how matters could be brought to a close. Clegg was more annoyed and less resigned than Cameron, who was impressed by how robust and determined the Liberal Democrat had been. This turned to admiration as Clegg rose to his feet and declared, 'There's obviously no point in going on with this meeting' – his time would be better spent reading a bedtime story to his kids back at home. The two men, in shared anger and exasperation, left the Prime Minister's room together, Cameron musing that there was more to Clegg than he might have thought.

Cameron and Clegg were born within three months of each other on 9 October 1966 and 7 January 1967. Both came from wealthy backgrounds. Cameron's father was a successful stockbroker, while Nicholas Clegg CBE was chairman of United Trust Bank. Regardless of future prospects, by the time they came into government both men were millionaires in terms of personal assets.

Both Clegg and Cameron pronounced 'properly' as 'propply' and 'create' as 'crate'. Both were educated entirely at private school – 'prep' school until thirteen, and then 'public school' until eighteen, Eton for Cameron, Westminster for Clegg. Both went to 'Oxbridge', Brasenose Oxford for Cameron, Robinson Cambridge for Clegg. Given the small percentage of children who do either – yet alone pass through both educational stages – it was worth noting that neither the Prime Minister nor his Deputy was an exception in a government in which both private education and Oxbridge were disproportionately represented. A majority, sixteen members, of the Cabinet went to private school, a similar number to either Oxford or Cambridge.

Plus ça change. David Cameron was the first Old Etonian Prime Minister since Sir Alec Douglas Home in 1963. Nick Clegg the first Old Westminster in government since, well, Ruth Kelly. And he arrived in power with two other senior ministers from the old school, Dominic Grieve and Chris Huhne, so equalling the score with the Old Etonian cohort of Cameron, Oliver Letwin and Sir George Young (aka 'the bicycling baronet').

The two public schools the two men attended are those that historically have had the closest ties to Britain's political power structure, taking first and third place in terms of number of old boys who became Prime Minister. Eton is bigger, older and less academically competitive – it can lay claim to some nineteen British Prime Ministers compared to six from Westminster.

For Cameron, Eton and politics were both family traditions. On his mother's side a Mount family forebear had lost his seat thanks to the Corn Laws (Cameron still has the poster which did for his ancestor, 'the most effective campaign I've ever seen', which lists item by item the price rises necessitated by Mr Mount's votes at Westminster). Another cousin, Old Etonian and Oxford graduate, Ferdinand Mount, was head of Mrs Thatcher's policy unit.

It was a well-trodden path. When one of Cameron's Brasenose College contemporaries was asked what Cameron did at Oxford, he replied, 'hang out with the other Etonians.'

What all this boiled down to was that both men came from an elite background which accustomed them to mixing with powerful people – either as parents of school mates or visitors invited to speak to the students. The cloistered surroundings of the Palace of Westminster would be familiar to both men. The cloisters and yards of Westminster Abbey and School are just over the road!

Their background and upbringing had a lot in common but the world chose to see them differently. Cameron's name was hardly ever mentioned without the words 'toff' or 'Etonian' attached. But Clegg largely avoided aspersions of privilege and elitism.

In the labyrinth of the British class system the explanation was simple. Cameron was 'posh', upper class, different from everyone else; Clegg was merely upper-middle class, at one edge of what most people considered themselves to be and thus unexceptionable. The difference between the two is itself embodied in the two very expensive public schools they attended.

But this is 'the narcissism of small differences' again. The big difference between the two men was that media comment often defined Cameron by his background but Clegg escaped this fate – even though he was perhaps the more elitist and aloof figure. By the standards of modern celebrity, Clegg had the flashier school friends including media stars such as Louis Theroux and Helena Bonham Carter. Cameron relied on Sam to supply the boho glitz such as her Bristol art school acquaintance with the graffiti artist Banksy. Compared with Clegg's exotic Russian, Dutch and Spanish relatives, Cameron was a shire Tory brought up away from the bright lights of London. Cameron was gregarious, ready to strike up friendships across party lines, but Clegg had few friends in the Westminster parliament, sticking instead to the more cosmopolitan circle built up at school, Cambridge and, above all, his time as a Eurocrat in Brussels.

Even so, the two men had much more in common than separating them – except of course party politics. Perhaps that explained why Cameron and Clegg and many of their ministers from both parties settled down to work together so harmoniously. The civil service may have faced massive cuts, but the Cabinet Secretary, Sir Gus O'Donnell, was pleasantly impressed: 'The new government has set out a clear agenda in its programme for government and has moved quickly on to its key priorities such as cutting the deficit and reform of areas such as schools and the health service.' The Cabinet Secretary also professed to being 'impressed by the way in which ministers from the two coalition parties have worked together productively and have sat in some very serious and substantial discussion of issues in the Cabinet and Cabinet Committees.'

The view from the bridge was pretty balmy as well, at least according to one senior Conservative Cabinet Minister, a month or so into government: 'If you came down from Mars and looked in the window and listened to us, you'd be quite hard put to work out who's in which party.' The 'Lib Dem in every department' rule amongst ministers extended to their advisors. The two parties had been coordinating their messages to the public ever since the uninformative utterings from Danny Alexander and William Hague during the Cabinet Office talks (the negotiations with Labour were characterised by a lack of coordination even within the same party). Now the Lib Dem Jonny Oates was official deputy to Andy Coulson, heading up the communications team. And Polly Mackenzie, Clegg's ideological sounding board, actually shared an office with Steve Hilton (now on the government payroll and so being paid only £10,000 per year more than her £80,000, a jolt down from his reported previous party-funded salary of £270,000) to form the hub of the policy unit.

But there were grumbles from both sides in the engine room.

The inescapable truth was that Cameron was almost certainly the only politician who got exactly what he wanted out of the 2010 election – becoming Prime Minister with a comfortable parliamentary majority behind him. Even Clegg still stated that he wanted to be Prime Minister. None of the other Conservatives really wanted to share power. And many Lib Dems still would have preferred entering into a partnership with Labour.

The political contortions needed to make the coalition work were, at least in the early stages, more a source of amusement within the administration than a serious inconvenience. On the Conservative side, it was noted that David Cameron would bend over backwards to accommodate the Lib Dems in areas where he determined that to do otherwise might endanger the long-term survival of the government. Even in Conservative strategy meetings, Cameron would volunteer to 'help' the Lib Dems, though this bias was balanced, perhaps deliberately, by an increasing reliance on those with the sharpest political elbows in the Tory team. For example Steve Hilton, whose ideas might have been described as the most coalition-friendly in the close Cameron circle, saw somewhat less of the Prime Minister in the early months of the administration than before; whereas George Osborne's influence grew even stronger. (The Chancellor confounded those who had predicted he would buckle under the initial pressure of office.) There was enough space within the Downing Street operation for the two sides to let off steam from time to time – hence Andy Coulson's description of a parliamentary week that took in the publication of AV legislation and the establishment of an inquiry into alleged collusion with torture by British intelligence agents as 'a festival of Libdemmery'.

But at the head of a government after thirteen years of Labour, Conservative gripes were hardly a major concern for Cameron, even though he found that managing his own party was taking up far more time than he had bargained for. This was likely to be a recurring problem both for the new Prime Minister and his Deputy who share a healthy attitude to the correct work–life balance. Both have wives who are successful career women in their own right, and both expect to spend time with their young families. To many Conservatives, the purpose of their party continued to be to exercise power. As Cameron carried on trimming to appease Lib Dem sentiment, even one of his critics, Tim Montgomerie of the volunteer ConservativeHome website, could comment with equanimity, 'the trajectory of the coalition is clear; it is heading leftwards or it is heading for breakdown.'

Most of the initial discomfort lay with the Lib Dems. Having lain in the bed they had made, some, including the strategist Lord Rennard, seemed to feel that David Cameron was having more fun. 'It's very, very clear that Cameron's driving motivation is to complete the detoxification of the Conservative brand, which when you look at the election result he clearly failed to do in opposition,' he protested. Perforce in his role as Lib Dem chief executive, Chris Rennard became an expert on coalitions and he knew what his party had to avoid: 'There's always the danger in coalitions that you get the blame for everything and the credit for nothing as the junior partner.'

Complementing Cameron's rhetorical argument, Clegg habitually fell back on his duty to the national interest, insisting he was serving his party's core beliefs if not quite everything which it had recently put into small print. 'I am a Liberal politician to my fingertips . . . and I think there is something morally wrong with sitting on our hands and risking a double-dip recession,' he argued a few weeks into office.

Clegg knew better than anyone that his decision to go into office had 'caused both surprise and with it some offence'. He was also aware that he had made enemies in each party, 'both on the left and right who are united in thinking this should not have happened.' But his conclusion balanced the pragmatic with the idealistic. On the one hand 'the truth is this: there was no other responsible way to play the hand dealt to the British people at the election. The parliamentary arithmetic made a Lib–Lab coalition unworkable, and it would have been regarded as illegitimate by the British people.' But on the other, there was great work which needed to be done: 'Equally, a minority administration would have been too fragile to tackle the political and economic challenges ahead.'

These points, and more, were hammered home by both leaders in the Downing Street garden. It was their moment, and if they had to share it with each other, they were going to make sure it was going to work.

Making the event seem more like a marriage service than ever, flunkeys held back the congregation of correspondents as the partners made their ceremonial exit from the garden back into Number 10. Since those gathered together that sunny day had no affiliations to either side, perhaps even more witnesses in the crowd than usual wondered just how long it was going to last.

MANAGING CAMERON by Joey Jones

The occasion David Cameron lost his rag with me sticks in my head. It was the first time I had met the Conservative leader, and a minor meltdown was not what I had expected. In the run-up to local elections in May 2006, Cameron was campaigning in Newcastle, a visit designed to show his determination that even Labour strongholds should not be 'no-go areas' for the Tories. I was sent to cover him for a day or so on the stump. As I was not a political journalist at that point (more a general reporter), Cameron did not know me, nor I him.

The piece was entirely uneventful and good-natured until we sat down to talk at the end. As is ever the way, the party leader had run short on time, and Gabby Bertin told me the fifteen minutes I had been allotted for a formal sit-down interview had become five. Maybe seven or eight, at a squeeze. With no time to waste, after a couple of general questions about his hopes for the forthcoming poll, I decided to hammer away on a single issue – his relationship with the Conservative party. The day before, as we were filming on a train from Waterloo to Kingston-upon-Thames, Cameron had told me how he 'woke up every morning thinking how can I change the Conservative Party . . . ?' I put it to him that the whole thing was a bit of an obsession, and an obsession furthermore that some party loyalists (who quite liked the old-style Tory party) would not appreciate. Cameron stonewalled vaguely, so I tried again and then again. Following my third variant on a theme, he began to respond, then broke off abruptly in mid-flow and looked up at his press secretary. 'What am I doing here? Why are you asking all these questions?' Realising the camera was rolling, and he probably looked a bit of a prima donna, Cameron gathered himself and continued, but when the interview closed asked me, 'You won't be using that bit in the middle, will you?' Not getting the answer he was after, he stormed off, leaving Bertin to try to clear up the mess behind him. (The Tory leader's displeasure took a while to fade. The next time we met for a short recorded interview on a subject I forget, he insisted sternly 'No tricks this time, right?' before we got underway.)

The whole thing was a storm in a teacup, and worth mention-ing now mainly because it illustrates how far David Cameron has come since. Getting under the skin of Prime Minister Cameron is formidably difficult. There is more focus, more discipline and with the government machine now on tap, complete command of pretty much whatever subject area you might choose to address.

To my mind it was telling that Cameron's anger was prompted by my questioning the necessity of the reforms that he was imposing on the party. That issue never did go away. David Cameron's lack of patience with those who, in his view, did not 'get it' sparked trouble even in the immediate aftermath of the formation of a government. Then, Cameron's desire to insti-tute new rules for the Tories' backbench talking shop, the 1922 Committee, prompted a revolt. Cameron may have had a bee in his bonnet about ministers being excluded from the work-ings of the committee (Parliamentary Labour Party meetings had no such restrictions, he would point out), but his attempt to force change looked high-handed; and then, when he was beaten back, it looked high-handed and weak. Cameron came to accept that the business of running a coalition would involve a far more assiduous courting of his party than he had expected. In the wake of the 1922 fiasco, senior MPs had dinner with the PM; and every Conservative member received an invitation to Downing Street at one time or another.

Thinking back to 2006, it is notable that accompanying David Cameron were the same Gabby Bertin and Liz Sugg who came later to join him in Downing Street. Some of his closest team were very young (at the time, both these two were under thirty) and without a great deal of experience. In allowing such individuals to grow, and ultimately to flourish, Cameron showed considerable loyalty. The reward for him was a close team at all times fiercely protective of their man, but also with a sixth sense for danger – knowing the warning signs that Cameron might be struggling or (just as bad!) that he might be showing too much confidence, with the risk of overreaching himself.

Along with loyalty, perhaps the best managerial quality David Cameron possesses is his willingness to step back and let others do the work when it suits. Downing Street staff were astonished to find the new Prime Minister, mid-morning just a couple of days after taking office, with his feet up reading the paper, and no apparent desire to be seen in public doing anything. 'Today is George's day,' he explained airily. It would never have happened under Gordon.

In general, senior civil servants have been gratified to find Cameron eager to involve them. Even the cosy morning meeting at which George Osborne is the only Cabinet attendee features three civil servants – Permanent Secretary Sir Jeremy Heywood, Principal Private Secretary James Bowler and Foreign Policy Advisor Tom Fletcher. All three worked under Gordon

Brown and have helped smooth the path to a very different style of administration.

Back in the autumn of 2009, journalists from the *Daily Telegraph* sat down to dinner with the leader of the opposition, David Cameron. It was the sort of occasion that tends to happen once a year or so with major news organisations; a formality really – a friendly chat to make sure things are on an even keel . . . an opportunity to raise issues of concern on both sides.

During the meal there was general discussion of the scale of the economic challenge that would confront an incoming administration. Cameron was in no doubt that dealing with the deficit would be an enormously difficult task. Given how hard it was going to be, asked Will Lewis, the then editor, 'Why do you want to be Prime Minister?' Cameron shot back: 'Because I think I'd be good at it.'

The story was later heard by Gordon Brown's team (Peter Mandelson referred to it around the time of the publication of his memoirs). In Labour circles, it tended to be recounted with mock horror – 'Has this man no soul?'; 'Could he be any more shallow?'

With hindsight, another explanation occurs. David Cameron is a less complicated character than those who peopled the New Labour psychodramas. Profiles of the Conservative leader that try to probe beneath the surface – to unearth the 'real' David Cameron – are missing the point. Yes, he can get angry, as I witnessed, though an equable calm is most characteristic now. He can make mistakes, as the 1922 Committee know, but endeavours to learn from them. There is no tortured soul; no writhing snakepit of motivations . . . With David Cameron what you see is pretty much what you get. And one man's shallowness or superficiality is another man's straightforwardness.

'I think I'd be good at it.' Maybe, but with all administrations the honeymoon only lasts so long. Remember, Cameron and his operatives remain reasonably untested – their worst crisis was way back in 2007 when Gordon Brown threatened a snap election. 'I think I'd be good at it'? It's a thought. And if he's right of course, who will seriously complain?

12

PRIME MINISTER HOME AND AWAY

'You're a crazy guy!'

David Cameron was as well travelled as most Englishmen in his class – part of gap year spent in Hong Kong, good works in Africa, lots of holidays in the sun around the globe, even the United States as a small boy, when a classmate, a young Getty, took his prep school mates over on Concorde for a luxury tour.

Yet Britain's new Prime Minister had never displayed much interest in foreign affairs for their own sake. His expensive education left him with no particular grasp of a modern European language. And his two main mentors in the Conservative party, Norman Lamont and Michael Howard, came very much from the eurosceptic, almost Little Englander, wing of the party. Their pragmatic, mildly suspicious and opportunistic view of the world was probably where his outlook coincided most precisely with the man he chose as his Foreign Secretary, William Hague, a former leader of the Tory party, memorably described as 'an intellectual with sardonic humour and advanced baldness' by the Belgian newspaper *Le Soir*.

On the few occasions that 'abroad' came up during Cameron's election campaign, he pledged to cut the number of immigrants coming *in* from there, and expressed sympathy for the soldiers sent *out* there by Labour to fight in Iraq and Afghanistan.

Yet the rest of the world forces itself immediately to the attention of a new national leader. Within the first hundred days of his premiership, Cameron had completed a carefully choreographed sequence of visits overseas. Brussels and Canada for regularly timetabled leaders' summits of the EU and G8; courtesy calls to the closest European neighbours who matter, Sarkozy of France and Merkel of Germany; Afghanistan, to deliver tonic to the troops and the Karzai government; a 'special relationship tour to Washington and New York'; visits of choice to two newly identified strategic partners, Turkey and Israel; a quick you-matter-too dash to Silvio Berlusconi in Rome.

Many British Prime Ministers have trodden these pathways to visit their opposite numbers before, so inevitably there was a ritualistic quality to much of this political tourism, made more stark by the palpable excitement of many of the Prime Minister's personal staff for whom it was all an exciting first – and yes, the real West Wing really does look like it does in the TV series.

So far so obvious, but was there a Cameron doctrine discernible along with the predictable itinerary? It was left to William Hague to lay out the new government's foreign policy philosophy in a well-advertised speech: no nation owed Britain a place in the world. It would have to be earned and the priority must be to increase trade. This unsentimental and utilitarian approach was reinforced by the Prime Minister himself at a conference for all ambassadors, who were recalled to the Foreign Office on economy-class return tickets.

Of itself there was very little surprising in this 'new' foreign policy; in fact there was a certain element of reinventing the wheel about it. For at least the past four decades, improving business links has been at the core of British diplomacy. And although the Cameron camp made much of his mission to India, accompanied by a planeload of British business, sporting and cultural leaders, there was a certain element of déjà vu about the trip. Cameron was by no means the first British Prime Minister to lead such a trade mission – both his immediate predecessors Blair and Brown had also done so for example, with the twin Asian tigers, India and China, as the target.

But after perestroika and glasnost, Reagan and Gorbachev, the fall of the Berlin Wall, Croatia, Bosnia, Kosovo, Kuwait, Iraq, and Afghanistan – the point about the new doctrine was that it didn't dwell on any of the above. Where the Blair and Brown governments had talked about a morally driven foreign policy with an ethical dimension, and the Thatcher and Major governments had reluctantly shouldered the global policing burdens of the rich west, Hague and Cameron were now talking about earning a crust. David Miliband, Labour's last Foreign Secretary and, he hoped, next leader, picked up on the change, writing in an op-ed that 'the real worry is that Mr Cameron has a shrivelled notion of Britain's role in the world.'

Shrivelled or not, the new policy demanded a big change of approach, on Britain's bloodiest remaining entanglement: Afghanistan.

When travelling abroad, foreign leaders, having left their regular pulpits at home, become more dependent than usual on the media who are along for the ride to carry their message home. On most trips, the British Prime Minister often does a number of interviews with his accompanying TV network reporters – an arrangement which can make it worth the journey for both sides. Given the cost-cutting and improvisation which typifies most British prime ministerial trips, interviewer and Prime Minister have often found themselves crammed together in a nondescript hotel room or office, with furniture piled in a corner and only a purloined flag, plant or lamp for set dressing.

Cameron's team would have none of this – they demanded a spectacular backdrop for their man. Thus the Indian news network ND24 built an entire studio set in a hotel suite, complete with a model Palace of Westminster. ABC News interviewed Cameron on the balcony of Washington DC's splendid Newseum, while Sky caught him over a rooftop overlooking the US Capitol – 'Oh yes we went right in there [on the prep school tour]!'

The G8's country retreat in Canada had only nature's majesty on offer. Cameron stood with his back to a balcony, facing his TV interviewers with the endless forests and lakes of Ontario stretching behind him. That morning he had quenched his lifelong passion for taking a dip, or 'wild swimming' as it is now known, by plunging into the lake nearest to his country club accommodation. A feat which emphasised his youthfulness compared to most of the other summiteers and which earned him the accolade 'You're a crazy guy!' from President Obama, who had arrived fashionably late, having that morning overseen the passage of the financial reform bill before flying north to Canada.

Interviews have to fit round the timetables of both the broadcasters back home and the schedule of the visit itself. In order to make the early evening British TV news bulletins, Cameron was speaking a few minutes before the G8 sessions began. This meant that there was no particular agenda pressing for discussion. But Afghanistan was bound to come up, especially in a host country whose Conservative Prime Minister, Stephen Harper, had just called time on his troops' decade-long commitment to the mission. So Adam Boulton of Sky News asked a 'fishing question' but one with a discernible worm on the end of the hook: 'Will the [British] troops be home before the next election?' Cameron was happy to take the bait: 'Well, I want that to happen, but make no mistake about it, we cannot be there for another five years, having been there effectively for nine years already.'

Cameron had been definitive and he had gone beyond the agreed line to take. Both his governmental spokesman, Steve Field, and his political fixer Andy Coulson immediately claimed that Cameron had said pretty much the same thing during the election campaign. The difference of course was that he was a new Prime Minister now, and one who wanted to set a fixed five-year term on the duration of the parliament. Cameron's words were not a problem hours later when he had a meeting with Obama. The American President had already committed to a similarly political timetable with plans to draw down US troop levels from summer 2011, just as the 2012 White House campaign would begin.

A few days later, the Prime Minister visited Afghanistan itself for the first time in his new role. Even in opposition, Cameron had tried to put a new complexion on such visits – placing the lives of the ordinary troops (rather than the commanders) at the centre – all designed to get out the message: 'This is not my war but I'll do my best to clean up the mess.'

Cameron had had a dry run for this visit at the end of 2009 as leader of the opposition. This trip now as Prime Minister would be very different to those of Blair and Brown on tour in Iraq and Afghanistan. Unlike Blair's fly in, fly out style, he spent the night on the ground at the British base and even tried his hand at some barrack room games. The morning saw him heading for a jog with some soldiers before sharing a hearty full English breakfast back in the troops' mess. He also made a point of coming into contact on camera with ordinary Afghan civilians. Unlike Blair and Brown, he suffered no awkward wardrobe malfunctions and avoided unfortunate juxtapositions with body armour and weaponry. Leaning heavily on his fellow Old Etonian Johnnie Boden's mail order catalogues, 'Cameron Casual' was already a well-established style – black or dark blue shirts and trousers or shorts.

And unlike any other Prime Minister since John Major, he had no trouble getting on the same wavelength as the serving men and women. There were no toe-curling moments such as when Gordon Brown boasted of a 44p increase in their daily allowance, or ended his address to people standing in 40-degree heat in full body armour: 'So enjoy your summer!' Instead, speaking in shirt-sleeves, Cameron told his audience to cheers, 'I couldn't do your job,' and doubled the operational allowance to around £5,280 per six-month tour of duty. He promised to restore the 'military covenant' to make the British people once again 'revere' their armed forces: 'You do so much for us. We're going to properly look after you. We're going to rewrite that covenant.' Although Cameron is no football fan, he avoided sounding patronising as Brown and Blair always did in similar circumstances. When the subject of the imminent World Cup was raised he deftly produced and read out a message of support for the troops from the England manager Fabio Capello.

This Afghan visit was about looking after the troops, not winning the war, or even supporting the Karzai government. Instead, Cameron's tone was about endurance: 'This is not a war of choice, it is a war of necessity. This is not a war of occupation, it is a war of obligation.' The gritty tone was further enhanced by the cancellation of a planned visit to a forward post in Helmand because of a feared assassination plot. Shortly after Cameron's trip it was confirmed that 30,000 troops under American command would soon take over three quarters of Helmand, all of which Britain had attempted to control with only around 10,000 troops.

Such dexterous public presentation replicated in his trips around the world earned widespread accolades. The *New York Times* had welcomed Prime Minister Cameron before his first visit with an editorial paean, 'likeable, quick on his feet, informal, self-assured, his easy charm a vivid contrast to the tortured, self-lacerating intensity of former Prime Minister Gordon Brown.' But Cameron's relaxed self-confidence led some critics to find him callow and careless as he began to develop a distinctive new style in foreign capitals.

For whatever reason, whether through accident, design, or inexperience on the part of Barack Obama, Gordon Brown's final visit to the White House as Prime Minister was a public relations failure, and widely judged in the British media to have been a snub by the newly installed President. Brown was the first leader outside of North America to see Obama in the Oval Office, and the words spoken were warm enough but his treatment seemed peremptory. Obama did not find time for a proper news conference, and Brown's agonisingly well-chosen present of an appropriate historical relic was reciprocated with a pile of 'Region 1' DVDs, unplayable in Europe. The Cameron team worked for weeks not to repeat such mistakes. This time both the precise timing of the exchange and the nature of gifts was carefully negotiated. The presents were both cheap and intimate enough to stand a chance of actually being used by the recipients: pairs of Sloane Ranger-brand Hunter wellies in bright pink and purple for the Obama girls; perfumed candles from the exclusive Mayfair store Miller Harris for Michelle; a baby blanket for the expectant, and absent, Samantha; a DC United football shirt for Elwen Cameron, four; a White House charm necklace for Nancy, six; and an exchange of modern art between the two sets of parents.

David Cameron was given the full treatment in Washington – Oval Office talks, a tour of the private quarters, lunch with Obama and a proper East Wing news conference (if just two questions from each country's press pack can be considered proper). Naturally reserved, Obama tried to force the charm, yet again rehearsing the beer bet they'd exchanged after the England and United States 1–1 draw in South Africa (Goose Island 312 from Chicago from the President, Hobgoblin from Wychwood Breweries in Oxfordshire from the Prime Minister). His words gushed on 'excellent talks . . . truly special relationship . . . I appreciate David's steady leadership and his pragmatic approach.' Cameron was equally cloying with 'Barack', failing to quite get the tone right as he crashed into an anecdote about the relative tidiness of their children's bedrooms. For Obama, the mood was warm; American officials reported that the President enjoyed Cameron's company. With a fair electoral wind the pair are likely to partner each other for some years to come. But, there was no evident personal 'special relationship'. They remained firmly apart in their respective national safety zones on cuts versus spending stimulus and on the issues raised by the reporters' questions: US Senate demands for a public inquiry into BP; the release from a Scottish jail of the convicted Lockerbie bomber Abdelbaset Ali Mohmed Al Megrahi; and the proposed extradition from Britain to the United States of the mentally disturbed Internet hacker Gary McKinnon.

Obama and Cameron had yet to work on a pressing issue in the way that can forge close working relationships, as had happened with previous Presidents and Prime Ministers. Neither was committed emotionally to the wars their predecessors had begun in the Middle East. Speaking in his favourite 'direct' mode, Cameron would not claim a special affinity with Obama. Such bonds cannot be sweated, so it seemed gratuitous that Cameron deliberately used his visit to recast Britain's relationship with America in a way that flattered his hosts and, perhaps, belittled his own country.

In an op-ed piece for the *Wall Street Journal*, Cameron complained about those who 'over-analyse' the US–UK special relationship and went on to offer his sympathies for this annoyance to his hosts: 'I know how annoying this is for Americans and it certainly frustrates me. I am hard-headed and realistic about US–UK relations. I understand that we are the junior partner – just as we were in the 1940s, and, indeed, in the 1980s.'

Nobody could deny that the United States is a richer, more populous and more powerful nation than Britain – but his language was original. Was 'junior', with its dictionary associations of 'subordinate' and 'less experienced' really the right word? Cameron was picked up on it by the ABC's Diane Sawyer in his major, if rather slangy, US TV interview of the trip. He defended himself: 'I'm a realist right. I mean, I think you shouldn't try to pretend you're something you are not.' But Downing Street had to issue an apology to British veterans after the Prime Minister told Sky News 'we were the junior partner in 1940 when we were fighting the Nazis' – a serious historical error since 1940 was in fact the year when Britain stood alone as Winston Churchill tried to persuade President Roosevelt to bring his country into the war.

As Cameron left the United States, the question remained why he had made such an odd comment? What purpose did it serve? The Americans had not been looking for it and seemed rather to look the other way once it was made. It didn't seem likely to enhance Britain's trade links with the United States. Back home in Britain, if anything, concern was that a previous Prime Minister, Tony Blair, had been too subservient to the American presidents of his time, George W. Bush and Bill Clinton.

With or without such a statement, American politicians from across the spectrum continued to assume that Britain was a highly reliable ally if one of limited capacity. But by challenging the convention of 'not talking down your own country when abroad', Cameron did not seem to have helped his cause. If anything, the public avowal of weakness encouraged the senators, led by the populist Democrat from New York Charles Schumer, to increase the shrillness of their demands over BP. Cameron gave them the concession of a meeting with him, although British ministers and ex-ministers later refused to attend American hearings.

On the right, Republicans were bemused, not least because so many of them revere twentieth-century history. They applauded him on cutting the deficit at Obama's expense, and in spite of the profligate federal spending under the last Republican President. But elsewhere 'the junior partner' comments chimed loudly with the growing realisation that in both policy and outlook Britain's new right-of-centre government mapped closely with the Obama administration's outlook. Cameron and Hague are neither ideologues nor neo-Conservatives. In such circles their half-muzzled Defence Secretary Liam Fox was likely to continue to be the most welcome British guest.

The best explanation of Cameron's use of the word 'junior' in the first place and, of his refusal to withdraw or even qualify it, was psychological. As a product of a privileged background, Cameron was used to being belaboured by such adjectives as bumptious, overconfident, even arrogant. He became proficient at countering such charges with considerate good manners and conscious displays of humility. In the United States he appears to have conflated personal presentation with the national stance. This trait would develop further on his swing eastward to Turkey and India.

David Cameron was not grand. He set about the trappings of office with an axe. British parsimony had always prevented the Prime Minister from having his own 'Air Force One' like other comparable foreign leaders. So on most trips outside of the EU, it was customary for the British government to charter a plane from British Airways or Virgin – Prime Minister's party at the front, lesser officials in the middle and travelling journalists stringing out to the back. But on becoming Prime Minister, Cameron imposed austerity on both the nation and his own budget. A review determined that the taxpayer was subsidising official charters to an unacceptable degree and Cameron suspended them except in exceptional circumstances. Thus on his trip to the United States by scheduled airline, accompanying journalists joked about him making spoons with his chief of staff, Ed Llewellyn, as they lay side by side on flatbeds.

For India, a Jumbo jet was chartered from British Airways. The justification was that this was a business mission. To the usual planeload of officials, staff and media, a party of more than sixty was added, made up of corporate CEOs, cultural leaders such as the Director of the British Museum, Olympic ambassadors including Sir Steve Redgrave, Dame Kelly Holmes, and Lord Sebastian Coe. These guests were scattered about the aircraft in different classes reflecting the attitudes of their different organisations. But Cameron did not pass up the chance to make a gesture. He left first class to the plutocrats, some of his senior staff and a few print journalists on upgrades, basing himself in business class in the upstairs cabin.

Not that the cheese-paring always benefited the Exchequer – the business mission flew directly from London to Turkey, where it picked up Cameron, and then on to India. To get to Ankara for their Turkish meetings over the previous twenty-four hours, Cameron and William Hague had each taken separate, chartered executive jets.

The Indian visit was of course not the innovative new departure which the Cameron camp presented it as being, given the similar trips made by Blair, Brown and Cameron himself, as leader of the opposition. Doors may have been opened, and ties forged more strongly but, by Number 10's own admission, it did not mark the signing of a profusion of new deals. (At a rather anaemic ceremony in the presence of both ministerial teams, culture ministers exchanged a pact on swapping museum exhibits and an existing BAE contract to supply trainer aircraft was accelerated.) But it was by far the largest such mission ever undertaken by a British Prime Minister, and by a fresh Prime Minister with charisma still to burn at that. It was also a mission that had been planned meticulously by the Business Department's UK Trade and Investment arm in particular. (This was actually Cameron's third trip to India. The first was a romantic 'fantastic beach holiday' in Kerala. His second, as leader of the opposition in 2006, held less happy memories after a minibus carrying Cameron's entourage ran over and seriously injured an elderly woman. Cameron later visited her in hospital.)

Here again though Bangalore and New Delhi witnessed unexpected, and not-obviously productive, bursts of candour from David Cameron. He chose the 'campus' of the high-tech company Infosys for his major speech in India. It was an appropriate venue for the Prime Minister's comments on trade and India's future but the surrounding audience of young IT boffins looked a little incongruous as he moved on to international affairs. Cameron now broke another diplomatic taboo as he spoke out on Indian soil against India's bitter rival Pakistan. 'We cannot tolerate in any sense the idea that this country is allowed to look both ways and is able, in any way, to promote the export of terror, whether to India, whether to Afghanistan or anywhere else in the world', he extemporised, going beyond his prepared text.

In a pattern familiar from the United States visit, Cameron also tried to ingratiate himself with his hosts by writing an article for a prominent local newspaper (probably a good idea since the visit to India seemed to attract less attention in the local media than his visit to America). Once again the Prime Minister's choice of words was highly personal and quite possibly a little clumsy. 'I have come to your country in a spirit of humility,' he wrote in the *Hindu* newspaper. 'I know that Britain cannot rely on sentiment and shared history for a place in India's future. Your country has the whole world beating a path to its door.'

Both comments – about Pakistan and humility – delighted the Indian audience. Indians remained notoriously susceptible to flattery and super-sensitive to British attitudes because of the legacy of Empire. Conversely, and not surprisingly, the remarks went down badly in Pakistan. A visit to Britain by Pakistani security officials was cancelled and Pakistan's High Commissioner in London dismissed Cameron as 'inexperienced'. Despite the furore and even though his country was experiencing severe floods, the Pakistani President went ahead with a scheduled visit to Chequers the next week, during which David Cameron accorded a rather warmer welcome than he might otherwise have planned. President Asif Ali Zardari gave several interviews in the British media pointing out that he needed no lectures on fighting terrorism; terrorists had murdered his wife, Benazir Bhutto.

And again, was 'humility' really the right word? For sure India had enjoyed impressive rates of economic growth in recent decades but it still contained hundreds of millions of the world's poorest people. It was only on this visit that Cameron confirmed that Britain wanted to cut its foreign aid donations to India. Even on the most optimistic projections, it will be several decades before India will overtake Britain in the GDP tables, and many, many decades after that before it could surpass Britain on a per capita basis. For many western visitors the most humbling experience is watching Indians trying to overcome the limitations of abysmal infrastructure both conventional and high tech. Cameron's 'spirit' seemed a bit premature.

As in the United States, it was difficult to trace any practical positive changes in Anglo-Indian relations stemming from the visit. Indians still complained about restrictions on immigration and student numbers to Britain. The British businessmen on Cameron's plane had received expressions of positive intent on the lifting of bureaucratic restrictions that prevent them from expanding their business in India. But given the slow pace at which the cogs of bureaucracy were likely to turn, any really significant benefits from Cameron's visit would most likely materialise only after he had left office.

The stopover on the way to India allowed David Cameron to make his first official trip to Turkey. The decision to visit this country, and to try to elevate relations with it, was the most discretionary choice Cameron and Hague have yet made, although, here again, they were following down a track already beaten by predecessors including Thatcher, Major and Blair. Hague signalled the upgrade by hosting the Turkish Foreign Minister as his first major guest in London, but he was simply reinvigorating an established dynamic in British foreign policy. Most of Britain's closest European neighbours had long wanted to 'deepen' the EU into an 'ever closer Union' of member states – the Euro currency was perhaps the most vivid example of this approach. Britain always opposed 'deepening', countering it with proposals to 'widen' the Union to new members instead. This strategy witnessed the successful expansion of the European community, to include Britain and Scandinavia as well as many former members of the Soviet bloc and Cyprus. Given the wide disparities in economy, democracy and the rule of law, the 'wider Europe' also helped to keep it shallower as a trading union rather than a political one. It also made it much closer to a civilian version of the NATO military alliance – both Britain's preferences in any case.

Cameron took up these traditional British themes in his speech to Turkey's equivalent of the Chamber of Commerce, championing the country's bogged down application to join the European Union. He made an emotive case, and claimed that Turkey's opponents were either 'protectionists' (who feared Turkey's growing economic strength), 'the polarised' (who believed in the clash between Western and Eastern civilisations), or 'the prejudiced' (who wilfully misunderstood Islam, and believed that a moderate Islamic nation such as Turkey had no place in 'Europe'). In a direct challenge to some of Europe's most powerful leaders, Cameron declared, 'it makes me angry that your progress towards EU membership can be frustrated in the way it has been.'

Cameron's strong rhetorical position was a direct challenge to the European Union's most powerful Conservative leaders – Angela Merkel of Germany and Nicolas Sarkozy of France, both of whom had recently entertained the new Prime Minister and met him on several other occasions, though with much less fanfare than on his visits further abroad. Turkey remained an applicant country to join the European Union, and had fought successfully to maintain its formal status at one of Gordon Brown's EU summits. But both the German Chancellor and the French President had given strong indications that they opposed Turkish membership ever coming about in practice – for both of them it would almost certainly have been electoral suicide to do otherwise.

Even though many economists would argue that a large, young Turkish influx is just what sclerotic Western Europe needs, fear of mass immigration is what motivates Merkel and Sarkozy. France is already struggling to assimilate the comparatively large percentage of Muslims in its population, mainly from former North African colonies. Germany fears a return, with full rights this time, of the Gastarbeiter (guest workers) population it successfully exploited to fuel its Wirtschaftswunder (economic miracle).

There were cultural considerations as well. During the painful process to reform the EU Treaty, most European countries had resisted an attempt, inspired by the Vatican, to define Europe as an essentially 'Christian' entity. Most pointed out that their societies were now diverse and multi-ethnic. But do Europe's boundaries really extend to borders with Iraq, Iran, Syria and Armenia, as they would if Turkey were to become a member state?

These were very real concerns for any politician, and ones shared by Cameron in the context of other arguments. He had championed Turkey's cause but had he made it any more likely that Turkey would ever join the EU? Would his support lead to any discernible increase in Britain's trade with Turkey?

The diplomatic, or undiplomatic, initiatives of Cameron's early months in power were dismissible as muscle-flexing, shadow-boxing or simply being of no great impact or significance. Once his government was in the grip of real and powerful events they could be forgotten quickly. It was not surprising that a new Tory Prime Minister should present himself to the world as pragmatic, self-deprecating, friendly, and pro-American; the last Tory Prime Minister, John Major, had started out in pretty much the same way.

But there was a big difference between John Major and David Cameron, which showed what had happened to their party in the years in between the two Prime Ministers. Unlike Major, who began with hopes of rebuilding Britain's place in the European Union, Cameron and Hague could barely bring themselves even to mention it as an entity. Their preferred formulation was to refer to the EU as a grouping of nations, with each of which Britain enjoyed strong bilateral relations. Yet for Turkey, or India, or even the United States, Britain's membership of the world's largest integrated trading and political bloc was the greatest single reason for wanting closer relations with the UK as a nation – and it marked the truly decisive break with history and tradition which Cameron said he wanted.

During their period in government, Cameron and his ministers would unavoidably spend more time dealing directly, on an equal basis, with their European counterparts than with representatives from any other part of the world. Yet this was a fact which Cameron appeared unwilling to talk about, yet alone exploit, because of the deep wounds left by the matricide of Margaret Thatcher on all in his party, including himself.

Cameron had few friends in Europe. During his inaugural visit to Paris, Sarkozy was impressed by his charisma and boldness but that was hardly bankable. Merkel is visibly impatient with him – she has not forgiven his refusal of her request not to withdraw the Conservatives from the European People's Party grouping. During the G8 summit Merkel tried to chum up by watching the West Germany–England World Cup game with him, but the atmosphere turned frosty when the TV coverage cut away to two England fans in the crowd, unfortunately decked out in Battle of Britain costume of flying helmets and handlebar moustaches. Cameron's best friend in Europe is a relatively marginal player, the Prime Minister of Sweden Fredrik Reinfeldt. When Cameron was leader of the opposition, Reinfeldt did him the favour of devising a way to exclude any chance of Blair becoming Council President. (The two jobs on offer were divided between the two main political blocks – ironically from which

Cameron was withdrawing his party – President for the right, High Representative for the Socialists, et voilà, Blair was suddenly out of the running.)

Privately, Cameron used the coalition to warm his government's stance towards the EU. With the exception of Hague, strongly eurosceptic Tories were moved out of the engine room. European spokesman Mark Francois became a whip instead and the impeccably moderate David Lidington went into the Foreign Office alongside the Liberal Democrat Jeremy Browne. And the Brussels veteran Nick Clegg was licensed to lead a permanent European charm offensive, even speaking to many of them, fluently, in their own languages. (To be fair there were far more linguists in the new government than its predecessor which seemed to boast only Blair's French and the polyglot verbal diarrhoea of Denis MacShane.)

The Cameron government started to build up one other strategic alliance to stand it in good stead in the difficult years ahead: the civil service liked it. These were early days but good manners certainly helped. As one senior civil servant confided: 'As you know we public servants are all a bit lefty, but we're getting on famously. This lot actually ask us to do things, not just barking orders, and thank us for work done.'

The Conservatives and Liberal Democrats seemed less suspicious of civil servants than Labour and more prepared to rely on their offices. The coalition agreements lay at the core of its policy-making and permanent secretaries were allowed to set up a network in parallel to coordinate all government activity with these principles. The civil service version of this mechanism met regularly, all the way to the top, at least once a week. A political trouble-shooting committee structure of ministers was also established. But it only met at Cameron's level a couple of times before the summer recess.

Britain's foreign policy apparatus was restructured, placing a career diplomat at its head with the appointment of Sir Peter Ricketts as the first National Security Advisor, at the head of a new National Security Council (although Ricketts soon announced that he would be in the role only for a 'limited period'). From the first meeting Cameron styled himself as chairman of the board, making sure everyone worked through the agenda and frequently dismissing items with the words, 'That's not a matter for the Prime Minister and this committee, take it up with the Departmental Minister.' In the view of a veteran civil servant present: 'Gordon never would have said that. Tony might have but he would have immediately checked out the minister to make sure he saw things his way.'

Cameron encouraged civil servants and diplomats to play a direct part in policy-making and diplomacy – as he made clear at two government summits – one for diplomats, the other for home civil servants. When travelling abroad he reverted to Thatcher and Major's practice of staying at the residence of the British Ambassador. Blair in particular avoided the diplomatic cocktail party circuit and would normally set up his foreign HQ in the most luxurious hotel he could find. Much to his satisfaction, Cameron saved the taxpayer hundreds of thousands of pounds in this way in his first months in power.

Cameron's commitment to foreign visits meant that he missed the two final Prime Minister's Questions sessions before the summer recess. Nick Clegg had a torrid time standing in on the first Wednesday, so the Commons conveniently wrapped up its affairs in haste, obviating the need for a second Clegg–Jack Straw bout. And having clocked up the air miles as parsimoniously as possible, it was no surprise that the Cameron family opted to holiday at home, returning to the beaches of Cornwall which had provided such excellent photo opportunities both on previous holidays and during the election campaign. It was a gift to newspapers weathering the story drought of the silly season. 'Is Cornwall the New Tuscany?' the headline writers panted. Well no, but it was likely to see much more of the Camerons in future, not least because of the surprise early arrival of their second daughter, Florence, who was given the middle name Endellion to reflect her birthplace. The 'staycation' was a fitting destination. David Cameron's foreign policy had not really yet left these shores.

13

HANGING TOGETHER?

'The whole thing now will turn on three ninety-minute sessions in front of the cameras five years from today'

On the Sunday before George Osborne's 'Emergency Budget' was delivered, and the Sunday before that, Osborne and David Cameron, Danny Alexander and Nick Clegg met and discussed the speech in detail. Meeting in Cameron's flat upstairs in Downing Street in mid-June, a little over a month after having taken office, they pored over 'The Scorecard', an A3 sheet with all the proposed Budget measures annotated on it, weighing up what worked and what did not; what must stay, and what could safely be changed or dispensed with.

David Cameron likes to describe it as 'the most collaborative Budget in thirty years', and there was evident pride on the part of the four men involved not just in what they produced, but in the way it was done: a process that was courteous, calm and with a recognition of the need for give and take on both sides. (On Budget day itself, when the Chancellor announced an increase in the threshold of the basic rate of tax, a key Liberal Democrat policy, Nick Clegg turned to David Cameron, his neighbour on the front bench, and said: 'Thank you.')

So far, so good. The Budget was a crucial milestone for the coalition, binding the Conservatives and the Liberal Democrats together for a period of profound reductions in departmental spending, job losses in the public sector and associated industries, tax increases (2.5p in the pound on VAT), and, in short, a lot of angst all round. The Budget measures passed through the House of Commons with only a mild whimper of dissent from Lib Dem MPs. Two, Mike Hancock and Bob Russell, voted against the rise in VAT (the pair show every sign of becoming known as the Liberal Democrat 'Usual Suspects'); and Simon Hughes, the Deputy Leader of the party, briefly toyed with the idea that there might be amendments to parts of the Budget that were inimical to the Lib Dems, before jumping back on-message.

It is not as though the coalition had it all its own way in the early weeks. Some in the government had not prepared for the increased scrutiny that would come with office. The Chief Secretary to the Treasury, David Laws, might have been drunk on rave reviews of his first days in the job, but he was brought back to earth with a bump. As it had for Clegg at the height of Cleggmania, the *Daily Telegraph* went back over its files and turned up a corker. There had long been speculation that Laws was 'in the closet'; now the paper had evidence that he had claimed expenses to pay another man as his landlord. Once it was established that the two were in a relationship, something Laws seems to have had difficulty admitting even to himself, the new Chief Secretary appeared to be in clear violation of guidelines prohibiting payments to partners. Laws was contacted by the paper early on the Friday of the Whitsun bank holiday. He decided immediately that he would step down, the news however was kept secret, even from most members of the Cabinet, until an announcement shortly before the Sunday papers went to press.

In general, it is expected that things will get harder rather than easier for the Lib Dem–Con alliance in the future. A large part of the reason controversial legislation passed smoothly in the early weeks is simply because the Labour party was distracted by a drawn-out leadership election. With a leader in place, the government will have to assume the need to prepare themselves for tougher scrutiny, and a more focused political attack.

Michael Gove, the Education Secretary, got a taste of what 'real' opposition will feel like from Ed Balls who, owing to his personal candidacy for the leadership, was one of the few Labour spokesmen who had not adopted a position of semi-retirement. Gove made serious errors in his presentation of the case for scaling back Labour's flagship school-building programme, the 'Building Schools for the Future' scheme. (Not least, his department furnished him with a list of the establishments that would be affected that was so riddled with errors it had to be corrected a further four times.)

Nevertheless, as Michael Gove found himself increasingly bogged down in trying to explain and justify the cuts process, he enjoyed widespread sympathy on the part of coalition colleagues. They recognised Gove's discomfort was in large part the result of trying to fend off a fired-up Ed Balls, a man needing no additional motivation to harry, hassle and make a giant nuisance of himself. The word in government approaching the summer recess was that they should view this episode as a cautionary tale. Not only would it be necessary to check, check and check again when future announcements on cuts were promulgated, but they should assume that once the Labour party got its act together, there would be no more easy rides.

Pinpointing the sources of pressure on the coalition in the months and years ahead is the easy bit. Judging how the two parties may respond is a much harder business. All the inhabitants of the Westminster Village – politicians, civil servants and journalists – are feeling their way. Political journalists whose core business has tended to be identifying splits at the top are adjusting slowly to an environment in which a split is the dominant feature of government, yet not necessarily a negative one. Civil servants are torn between relishing an environment in which their political masters are primarily focused on the basic tasks of bedding in and making things work, and dreading the Whitehall cutbacks in which they will be embroiled. Politicians are acclimatising to government, easier said than done particularly for the Lib Dems, who have grown used to their status as perpetual outsiders.

As if the red boxes and decision-making were not enough, this bunch of governmental virgins (Ken Clarke and the like excepted) are confronted with the most intimidating task of cost-cutting to face any administration in generations. Little wonder, perhaps, that there has not been much occasion for party squabbling.

In time, thoughts will turn to ballot boxes, and ensuring their own parties prosper. The 5th of May 2011 will be a key date, with local elections in England as well as elections to the Scottish Parliament and the Welsh Assembly. As if that were not enough, the Liberal Democrats will be gearing up for their big day: a referendum on the alternative vote electoral system – only the partial realisation of a dream for them (PR is the ultimate goal), but not to be sniffed at.

Like many things to do with the coalition dynamic that were forecast to be troublesome – the Budget, for example – it may be that the situation of coalition partners campaigning against one another will be less traumatic than widely anticipated. Senior

Labour figures are not expecting the coalition to implode. They are looking to the long haul.

Nevertheless, if there is one thing that will breed unease, whether on the Conservative or the Liberal Democrat side, it is electoral failure. In the weeks after coming into government the Lib Dems saw their poll rating slide, whereas many expected a bounce owing to their (and their leader's) increased prominence. The Conservatives have far more reason to be sanguine, but both sides know the coalition must be made to work not just for Britain, but for them.

There is an argument widely disseminated within the Labour party that the Lib Dems have signed their own political death warrant by entering into a Tory-led government. In the words of one of the Labour negotiators. 'The truth is that all parties are coalitions of one set of people who are right-wing on economics, and one set who are left-wing on economics. That's OK when you're in opposition because you can pretend to one set of people you're right wing and another set you're left wing, then run away before they can properly test you out. The problem now is that they've jumped one way.'

Conventionally, political commentators and pollsters tend to look at the numbers and project them downwards, extrapolating the impact of a national swing constituency by constituency. Politicians preparing for an election are more minded to look from the ground up. It was this approach that made David Cameron, George Osborne and their colleagues so wary of anticipating overall victory in the run-up to the 2010 poll. Looking constituency by constituency was a salutary process, making them realise, as their key strategists describe it, that they had to win everywhere . . . demolish Labour in the South, do well in Wales, well against the Lib Dems in the West Country and West London and pick up some seats in Scotland.

Assuming the Lib Dems adopt the same approach, it may give them nightmares. In Labour/Lib Dem marginals, the opposition believes, David Cameron's partners are riding for a fall. Remember, Ed Miliband says, 'They have spent their time in Labour urban seats saying don't listen to these Labour people – we're the party of fairness, social justice, public spending and public services. They have forfeited any credibility they had for any of this for seats around the cabinet table.'

David Miliband shares his brother's view that if the Lib Dems continue to pursue seats with the tactics they employed in the past, they will struggle. 'Look at someone like Norman Baker,' Miliband warns (re the Lewes MP), 'with a majority of 5,000. There are at least 5,000 people in his constituency who wouldn't have voted for him if they'd known he was going to end up as a transport minister in a Tory government.'

In the end, whether it be 2011, 2015 or whenever, the coalition marquee, so elaborately constructed, will be taken down. Two parties will need to disentangle themselves from one another. Assuming both the Lib Dems and the Conservatives stay intact (defections from the right-wing of the Lib Dems may be an occupational hazard in the run-up to a general election), it seems on the face of it that the Tories have far less explaining to do. They will not have to justify their very involvement in a coalition as the Lib Dems will – what else could David Cameron's party have done? They made the best of a messy business. The key preoccupation for the Conservatives is more straightforward on the face of it, though perhaps equally problematic in practice: simply to keep the show on the road. The task against which the Tories will be judged is ensuring that cutting back the public sector does not cripple the economy, that growth is maintained and by the end of the parliament that the country is coming out of the woods. No mean feat in itself. Not surprisingly, the distant prospect of fighting alone, and on their record as a party, has barely come to occupy the minds of even some of David Cameron's most senior Cabinet lieutenants.

The one thing that will be done seriously and without unnecessary hullabaloo is to look at why the 2010 campaign failed. The Conservatives refuse to consider the campaign a failure, and object strongly when it is described as such. They have been spared a good deal of soul-searching because neither Labour nor the Liberal Democrats managed to scrape the dozen or so seats (maybe even a half-dozen?) that would have made a Lib–Lab coalition not just viable, but likely. The fact that David Cameron made it into Number 10 made all the difference. Now the Tories can look back and congratulate themselves on the organisational triumphs of again and again readapting to the unexpected . . . They can revel in the audacity and foresightedness of their leader, now Prime Minister. The bald fact is the Tories aimed to win, and fell short. Is Ed Balls really so wrong when he concludes, 'The reality is he [David Cameron] didn't establish a connection with the electorate, but he got bailed out after the election by Nick Clegg'?

Next time round, the Conservatives will fight on their record. If they can hold her steady, keep the economy moving forward over a parliament, demonstrate their competence in office, it will feel so very different to 2010. Above all, they will be led by Prime Minister David Cameron. If ever you doubt the advantage that holding the highest office of state confers on a political leader and his party, ask Cameron. He will tell of his, and his advisors', overwhelming sense of frustration and impotence as they watched Gordon Brown win applause and acclaim for doing the basics – managing the response to natural disasters, praising the troops, haranguing the banks – and thereby leaving the opposition (who would have done the same or better, they say), in his wake, adrift. At times, David Cameron used to fight by hook or by crook to break into the news cycle. Was it really necessary for him to comment on Jonathan Ross leaving an unpleasant message once on someone's answerphone? It was if you were leader of the opposition and wanted to be seen to exist.

All that is behind Cameron now. An opposition leader's polish will become a Prime Minister's aura. The trappings, and also the fearful responsibility of power. That brilliant black door, the fancy notepaper; the constant demands on your time, 'Prime Minister . . . ?'; the bonhomie and pitfalls that attend your contacts with world leaders; cameras following your every arrival and departure. Never again, the St Stephen's Club in St James's.

One day, it may be that David Cameron will make another speech so accomplished, so resolute and unanswerable in its comprehension of an event that, though nearly forty years past, seeps uneasily still into the present; so fluent and compassionate as that statement he made in the House of Commons on the publication of the Saville Report into what happened on Bloody Sunday. When he does, there will be an opposition leader sitting on the other side of the chamber who will be torn. On the one hand, a grudging admiration for the Prime Minister's ability to articulate the best of what could be clawed from an ugly business. On the other, saying to himself, 'I wish I could have been standing there. I'd have made an even better fist of it.'

Being Prime Minister may be a burden, but it is also the most terrific platform, and one David Cameron and the Conservatives will exploit to the full. Some within the Labour party fear that in their indignation at the Liberal Democrats' 'treachery', and their expectation that the third party will have a heavy price to pay, their own party may forget who they are really fighting. The next election will not be won for Labour by exploiting divisions within the Lib Dems. As Ed Balls puts it: 'If you make your sole focus, "Are the Liberal Democrats falling apart?" you completely let the Tories off the hook.'

David Miliband, too, cautions Labour against expecting an easy ride next time around. The portents, he recalls, are not good, warning: 'History suggests that Labour, when it loses office, loses it for a long time. 1931 out of power for fourteen years . . . 1951 for thirteen years. 1979 out of power eighteen years . . . We've got to buck the historical trend.'

The party that will continue to agonise over its fate for the length of the parliament is the Liberal Democrats. In part, it is in their nature. Beyond that, the decision to work in coalition with the Conservatives was, whichever way you look at it, a defining moment for the Lib Dems, and one whose consequences can be evaluated only once the British people have passed judgement at the ballot box.

Looking back at the five days during which the coalition negotiations played out, Nick Clegg feels there is nothing to regret. The Liberal Democrats went into the discussions with two objectives – to ensure their core policies were enacted, and to construct a stable government. (If they tied themselves to an administration which collapsed within months, not only would their best ideas be cast to the four winds, they would most likely be punished at the next election.) Both were accomplished.

Many Lib Dems will continue to feel with their hearts that this was a Faustian pact. Using their heads, they explain that to understand a Liberal Democrat, you must understand that they see themselves as having embarked upon a long and tortuous journey towards proportional representation. As Paddy Ashdown always said when he was leader, the story goes, the country will not accept PR until it has seen how a coalition government can work.

According to Chris Rennard, the trick for the Lib Dems at the next election will be to demonstrate that their involvement in the government was to the good, indeed that the Lib Dems were the best bit of the coalition cocktail. 'The challenge for the Lib Dems is to have a list that is sufficiently strong come the election – things we will say are there because the Lib Dems are there.' That list, it is argued, can be made up of positive changes that the Liberal Democrats have fought for (raising the threshold for basic rate taxpayers); or policies the Conservatives would have forced on the nation had they not been stymied by the heroic Clegg and Co (favouring the rich on Inheritance Tax).

It will be tough, but even those who struggled most with the prospect of alliance with the Conservatives say there was no real choice. Paddy Ashdown admits, 'If we manage this badly, we'll be terribly damaged in a year, two years, three years,' but the alternatives were worse. 'If we had gone in with Labour, we'd have been shot the day after . . . If we had let the Tories govern on a minority basis they'd have had another election in September; they'd have got a majority and we'd have been fucked. So there were three choices – we could either be shot on the morrow, shot in September or you could be shot in two or three years' time if you do things badly and don't make a success of it.'

When they themselves reflect and draw conclusions from their campaign of 2010, the Lib Dems will look with particular anxiety at the final week in which they were pitilessly squeezed by Labour and the Conservatives alike. How to avoid that next time around? The 'last week strategy' so harshly criticised by Paddy Ashdown and Simon Hughes was in essence to maintain a concentration on key policies, and not to be drawn into talking about a hung parliament. Even had it worked, it is hard to see how the second part of that equation will be effective at the next election, after however many years (one must presume years!) in coalition.

The Liberal Democrats have tended to aim high even at the risk of being ridiculed – insisting they be judged on their own terms, indignantly maintaining their right to dream, as Nick Clegg did during his final party conference speech before the election, of claiming the highest office; to dream of overturning the accepted hierarchy of Westminster parties, and becoming the second most powerful force in the House of Commons. As to the latter objective, David Miliband says the 2010 election was a painful corrective. 'If the Lib Dems think we should watch out, and they're serious about replacing us as the progressive force in politics, I think that argument is quite hard to sustain now,' he maintains. 'I think they underestimated what it would take to replace Labour, because they don't have the social roots across the country.'

The long game for the Liberal Democrats is one that most of them dare not even think about, let alone discuss. Just as the twentieth century witnessed the strange death of the Liberal party, with Labour displacing it as one of the two dominant groupings in British politics, might not that process be reversed in the twenty-first century?

The alternative vote system may fall well short of true proportional representation, but if it is endorsed by the electorate, all experts agree that the likelihood is a sharp increase in the number of Liberal Democrat MPs. This in turn would heighten the chances of further hung parliaments in future in which the Lib Dems would again play a central role, further cementing their standing in the national consciousness.

David Miliband may not be alone in arguing that Labour is too entrenched as a nominally 'socialist' party ever to be overtaken by the Liberal Democrats, but stranger things have happened. The United States have grown accustomed to party politics without a true 'left-wing party' at all – the Democrats staking out the centre, while leaving the Republicans to the right. And remember, until the mid-1980s Scotland was a relative powerbase for none other than the Conservatives.

Labour's class base has been steadily eroding along with organised labour and the trade union movement. In 2010, both Labour and the Lib Dems polled between 20 and 30 per cent of the popular vote. It would seem that like Eurosocialism before it, New Labour ultimately failed to recast itself as a party for all. Gordon Brown's successor will inherit a party financially just as reliant on trade union money as in the pre-Blair era.

Suppose the Cameron/Clegg government could be all of caring, creative and competent? Suppose the Liberal Democrats could walk away from the whole thing standing tall? That is the objective, after all. And then maybe, just maybe the cracks might start to show in the mould of twentieth-century politics.

If that is the ultimate dream, the next step on the road may, paradoxically, be to show a willingness to limit the party's immediate ambitions. First, following the election of 2010, the Liberal Democrats need to demonstrate that they are able to manage a hung parliament. Next time, as political allegiances become increasingly fragmented, might they not welcome one?

That would mean a willingness on the part of the Lib Dems to moderate their headiest aspirations – 'I want to be Prime Minister' and suchlike – and talk openly about their appetite for working with other parties even before polling day. If the Liberal Democrats were to brand themselves 'The Hung Parliament Party' explicitly in future, it would change the whole dynamic of British election campaigns for ever.

But for the moment, that idea is a step too far for Paddy Ashdown. 'The whole thing now will turn on three ninety-minute sessions in front of the cameras five years from today,' he maintains, 'at which time Nick Clegg has to be able to present himself credibly as an alternative Prime Minister. I think he can do that.'

When those television debates happen, the dynamic will have been completely changed because of the events of 2010. The viewers will be watching the three potential candidates for the highest office not just as rivals, models for running the country that should be seen as mutually exclusive. Instead they will weigh up how each man might function with the other as partners in government, should the electoral arithmetic once again leave them hung together.

POSTSCRIPT

A lot of water has flowed under the bridge since *Hung Together* was signed off. Europe was plunged into financial crisis; the Arab Spring transformed the foreign policy landscape; most of the government's legislative programme was passed, though not without some bruising lessons along the way; Ed Miliband secured the Labour leadership and has started to bed in at the head of the opposition.

In the round it is no surprise that David Cameron and Nick Clegg have told us they look back on their first period of government with satisfaction. They have made coalition government work through a combination of good sense, compromise and determination; and the general expectation is that the bargain will hold for the full term up to 2015.

One judgment we made at the time of publication that has proven right is that splits in the coalition would not be a major issue. A number of factors have reinforced the sense that trying to elicit fractures in the government is a sterile and frequently misguided endeavour – the very solid relationships and constant communication at the top of the administration lock the whole thing together; the unassailed supremacy of David Cameron and Nick Clegg within their own parties means that they are largely able to dictate terms to cabinet and parliamentary colleagues; the deepening of the economic crisis means that a general election has little appeal for either governing party in the short term; and in any case the collapse in the Liberal Democrat vote means that Nick Clegg's occasionally recalcitrant troops have nowhere else to go. A degree of tension is viewed on both sides as positive, and even necessary to keep their respective constituencies happy. Nothing pleases Liberal Democrat strategists more than Tory backbench MPs like Nadine Dorries or Peter Bone piping up to complain about the Lib Dem tail wagging the dog. Many of the 'rows' that are played out in public are sanctioned and stage-managed from the summit. One occasion when things got really strained – in the days after David Cameron walked out of the December 2011 EU Summit – can be put down as a rare example of the perils of misunderstanding and communications failure. Nick Clegg told colleagues he had explicitly been promised that Cameron would call him before opting for isolation (splendid or otherwise); Cameron meanwhile was equally convinced that in final discussions involving Clegg and his team, he had been given authority to act as he deemed best. The other moment when tensions boiled over – the AV referendum – had been identified from the start as unavoidably tricky. In the event, Liberal Democrats nursed grievances over the targeting of Nick Clegg in the No campaign literature; but the crushing nature of their defeat means that the only thing that would be gained from perpetuating the row would be a reputation as sore losers.

Writing in 2010 we allowed ourselves to speculate on whether the coalition might mark the beginnings of a recasting of the British party political mould, with the Liberal Democrats as the big winners. Looking at the polls two years later, such musings probably seem far-fetched even to the most ardent Lib Dem! Defeat over AV has set back the cause of electoral reform for the foreseeable future, and the process of boundary review has exacerbated the siege mentality among Liberal Democrat MPs, with many fearful of extinction at the ballot box even if they manage to cling onto a seat to fight in 2015.

Nick Clegg's own position in terms of popular esteem is parlous. Seasoned observers within government suggest that he himself must know that his personal ratings are irrecoverable. Having an unpopular chief is not quite such a problem for the Lib Dems as it would be for Labour or the Tories; in the case of the major parties, the electorate weighs the leader as a potential Prime Minister – rightly an unforgiving yardstick. Still, it cannot be easy for Liberal Democrats to have to accept that they may go into the general election with a leader who is not merely a passenger, but a positive drag on their electoral fortunes.

The Conservative leadership has shown considerable sensitivity to the Liberal Democrat predicament, and has gone the extra mile to try to shore up Clegg and his troops. Not only do the Tories give the Lib Dems space to claim maximum credit for popular policies like uprating the income tax threshold, they allow their coalition partners to knock chunks out of them when things go wrong as with Andrew Lansley's Health Bill.

Such manoeuvres provoke a good deal of squealing on the Conservative backbenches, and clearly irritate the hell out of the Tory grassroots. But the high command is playing a long game, a game in which Nick Clegg's survival at the head of a viable Liberal Democrat Party is a key component. In Downing Street there is undisguised satisfaction that Chris Huhne's implosion as a cabinet player confirms Clegg's unrivalled authority within the parliamentary party, (and personality politics play a role too – not too many Tories mourn the chippy former Energy and Climate

Change Secretary). But regarding the Deputy Prime Minister, concern lingers among intimates of the Prime Minister: will Liberal Democrat activists be prepared to hold the coalition line in the teeth of repeated pummellings in local elections where they have enjoyed such success in the past, they wonder? There is an arcane rule in the Lib Dem constitution (where else!) which states that if seventy-five constituency parties write to the party president requesting a leadership contest, he is duty bound to grant it. It is not likely to happen, but nor can a grassroots revolt be ruled out with the popular president himself, Tim Farron, the most plausible beneficiary.

What should one make of the fact that such a scenario provokes shudders of horror in Number Ten? Losing Clegg 'would be a disaster', one key advisor confides; and yet many if not most Conservative MPs would recoil, appalled (if not surprised), at the insufferable indulgence of such a view. In part, this shows that the coalition has resulted in splits – not between the parties but within them, with a pragmatic leadership faction on both sides wedded to the idea of sticking it out right through the five years on one side, and on the other a fractious and resentful parliamentary crew impatient of the whole project and itching to get back to what they view as a normal state of affairs.

Such tension is exacerbated by the nagging suspicion that there is just a chance that (perish the thought!) 'normal' politics might be slower to resume than the traditionalists hope. David Cameron tells us he is dead set on trying to win an overall majority, and must be taken at his word. But should he fail or win only a small majority, he could be forced straight back into the arms of Clegg and Co. It is a simple calculation. Much as the Lib Dems may drive the Prime Minister and his colleagues to distraction from time to time, at least they can be reasoned with. The same (in the opinion of the Tory hierarchy, including the Whip's office), cannot be said of some of David Cameron's Eurosceptic colleagues. If it comes to the crunch, it is easier for this Prime Minister to humour Simon Hughes than Bill Cash. So could it all happen again? Of course. It will come down to mathematics, pure and simple.

In the meantime, negotiating a complex love affair with his own party will become a full-time preoccupation for David Cameron. The new Conservative intake of MPs are an interesting bunch. As a body they are young, talented, ambitious, headstrong, unbeholden, impatient (extremely so), comparatively baggage-free, fizzing with ideas and they are bored. Bored by the demands of the party machine, bored by the drudgery of casework and the load of management. Bored by the lack of government business – the Lords have been much more in the thick of the action overall. And that boredom will only grow – already some fear the government's reforming zeal is calcifying, and it is a fact of life that towards the end of the parliament the whole legislative programme will grind to a halt.

The new intake constitutes half of the parliamentary party. They are a force to be reckoned with. David Cameron is torn: plainly attracted to the idea of revitalising his ministerial ranks with new blood, he nevertheless needs to show to the rest of his parliamentary colleagues who have waited longer, brooded, resented Liberal Democrat advancements, that they are not unloved, that they can be the future too. The Prime Minister cannot please everyone. The fallout from the one big reshuffle of this parliament could be momentous. Egos will be bruised, grudges stoked. The objective is to ensure the number of Tories who feel themselves to be 'outside the tent' is reduced ideally, or at least not significantly swollen.

In 2010 we remarked upon David Cameron's calm, level-headed approach to the job. If anything, since then the Prime

Minister's equable temperament (one close colleague claims never to have seen him seriously lose his cool in Downing Street) has been still more resilient, and pretty remarkable in the circumstances. One thing that does get under Cameron's skin though is when colleagues or commentators suggest his unruffled exterior is a manifestation of a man lacking in drive and application – an article by the *Telegraph*'s Ben Brogan, which said the Prime Minister spent too much time watching boxed sets with his wife and too little with the ministerial red boxes, particularly irked him.

David Cameron's riposte to this critique would be stronger were not carelessness an occasional and bedevilling trait of his administration. Blame can be shared around liberally for the legislative calamity of the first parliamentary term, the Health and Social Care Bill, but the Prime Minister knows he should not have allowed the situation to get out of control. An ability to delegate and grant autonomy to colleagues in this case blew up in his face. Not only did David Cameron inadequately supervise the progress of Andrew Lansley at the start, when trouble arose and the party looked to him for a lead, the Prime Minister again and again failed to articulate the case for reform powerfully, leaving the whole government on the back foot.

The policy challenges that confronted the government in 2010 – education and health reform, an overhaul of the welfare system, above all revitalising the economy – have all been taken forward with varying degrees of success and will continue to be the government's bread and butter through to 2015. In the second half of the parliament constitutional issues will also come to the fore. Nick Clegg has the Prime Minister's support in pressing ahead with reform of the House of Lords, and the government is now fully engaged in trying to thwart Alex Salmond's desire for an independent Scotland. David Cameron fears that if he mislays Scotland during his period in office, he may be remembered for little else. The Tories' unpopularity north of the border means the Prime Minister will need to operate largely behind the scenes, but he has left colleagues in no doubt as to his determination to maintain the Union, and the full muscle of government will be drawn to the cause.

At the time of writing *Hung Together*, the Labour leadership contest had yet to be decided. We considered that the distraction of so protracted a contest risked handing the government a head start, a judgment that has only been reinforced by the passage of time – on a raft of fronts Labour under Ed Miliband is struggling to make up ground that was lost in 2010.

On education, once over his initial hiccoughs, Michael Gove streaked away with a ready-made package of reform. Once in situ, the Shadow Education Secretary Andy Burnham tried to oppose Gove even though his opposite number was already out of sight (and despite the fact that the changes were in any case rooted in Labour's own academies programme). On health, Labour was almost entirely absent, though gratifyingly the government gifted them a mess of their own making. On welfare reform, Labour is in a muddle. The heart says oppose, the head says support – the rather forlorn best hope is that Iain Duncan Smith makes a mess of his monster shakeup. Most importantly, on the economy, the argument that the government was 'cleaning up Labour's mess' gained such currency that it became nigh on impossible to counter. Ed Miliband's initial choice of Shadow Chancellor, Alan Johnson, might have worked but did not; it was spring 2012 before Ed Balls started getting into gear and by then the damage was done.

Lagging in the polls on the key terrain of economic competence, Labour also struggles with dire approval ratings for its leader. Ed Miliband has negotiated a stormy initial period at the helm of the opposition, and there are precious few signs to encourage the Miliband team as they survey the months ahead. Supporters insist that after a dreadful result in 2010, it was always bound to be a hard road back for Labour, and one should not expect the public suddenly to rally to a party they comprehensively rejected. Still it is clear that Labour is in a period of painful readjustment: grumpy about being in opposition and fearful of prolonged irrelevance.

On the positive side, Ed Miliband knows there is virtually no chance of a leadership challenge before the general election. He also has the advantage of a parliamentary party that (like the Tories) has been significantly revitalised by a large intake of new MPs. The one thing that stops Labour old hands in parliament from wallowing in gloom is the enthusiasm and fervour of their young, bright-eyed colleagues. Miliband has tried to harness some of that excitement by drafting some of the most talented straight into the shadow cabinet and other shadow ministerial roles. Such changes may help to persuade voters that Labour is undertaking a period of renewal, but there is a long way yet to go.

Reading again what Ed Miliband told us in 2010, it is striking how hostile towards the Liberal Democrats the soon-to-be Labour leader felt. Since claiming the top job there have been no serious signs of a rapprochement between the two parties. Miliband and Nick Clegg could not bring themselves to campaign together for AV, and the mood music during key parliamentary occasions is ugly, with Labour MPs expressing noisy, undisguised contempt for the Liberal Democrats. The inevitable consequence is that Lib Dem MPs circle the wagons and bind in still closer to the coalition project.

As 2015 approaches, not only will the Conservatives and Liberal Democrats have to find ways of unravelling the coalition without dismantling a working government, there will also have to be bridges built between Labour and the Lib Dems in case of a future hung parliament with a different balance of power. Neither process looks easy from this distance; both will be fascinating to observe.

AN INTERVIEW WITH DAVID CAMERON AND NICK CLEGG

This interview was completed towards the end of February 2012. Questions were submitted by email separately to the Prime Minister and Deputy Prime Minister – it was left to them how much they conferred, although the final text was collated in Number 10.

Our original request had been for a joint face-to-face interview with the two leaders. This was made in the autumn of 2011, for our publication date corresponding with the second anniversary of the formation of the coalition.

The idea was taken up enthusiastically by Craig Oliver, director of communications at Number 10 and by Olly Grender, who has been seconded to assist Clegg. When asked about the interview directly, Nick Clegg seemed less keen. He questioned whether it was 'too early' to talk about the coalition 'at mid-term'. In this fixed five-year parliament, mid-term itself is not actually due until November 2012.

The hope shared by the authors and the politicians was that some time could be found for a meeting during the quiet period around the turn of the year. But the coalition side were in the end unable to schedule one. This is certainly an indication of the obvious and heavy time pressures on senior members of the government. But it is also perhaps an indication of how little of the government's business is conducted in tandem by the two men alone. As Cameron's comments indicate, he doesn't even like looking at his role in that way.

So in the New Year we pursued the idea of doing the interview in writing. The interview for Hung Together *with the then cabinet secretary Gus O'Donnell had been done this way. The justly celebrated* Paris Review: Writers at Work *series provided another inspiration as did the more prosaic celebrity questionnaires now included in many magazines. Maybe it was our background in television news which led us to think that an interview should be a personal encounter as well.*

Even completing the interview in writing took much toing and froing – again indicating the sensitivity of Cameron/Clegg channels – and we are grateful for the help provided especially by Olly and Julian Glover, David Cameron's recently appointed speech writer.

As the reader can see, the Deputy Prime Minister proves generally more expansive than the Prime Minister. But even guarded answers can be revealing . . .

In your mid-term year how well do you think the coalition is doing?

DC: These are challenging times but I believe the government is taking the right steps and, as a coalition, it has been able to work through difficult decisions.

NC: Coalition government is working out to be strong government. Think back to before the election: headlines screamed that a hung parliament would be the end of the world. Then, once the coalition formed, the pessimists predicted that the government would either collapse soon or be condemned to perpetual deadlock. Nearly two years in and those fears have been confounded. Yes, the coalition is evolving, but it works and it will see things through.

Can you tell us about the practical ways in which you make the coalition work? What are the means by which the Conservative and Liberal Democrats in the government consult across party lines?

NC: The key thing is that coalition government has to be much more open and deliberative, otherwise the whole thing would grind to a halt. The rejuvenation of cabinet committees is a good illustration of a much more collective approach. I chair the Home Affairs Committee, which covers most domestic policy, so immigration, social care, policing, education and so on. The bulk of the cabinet actually sit in it, but we have much more time to debate the detail. That can lead to lively, sometimes fierce, debates. But it's much more rigorous than having a few people sat on a sofa cooking up all the big plans.

I also meet with my ministers and parliamentary party every week, to make sure my side of the equation is involved and on board. And David Cameron and I have regular meetings, along with phone calls and email exchanges. Issues usually come to us when others can't agree or when we ourselves don't. Resolution can take a while sometimes, but we just stick at it until we get somewhere.

DC: Look, anyone who knows the government would agree we're working through the proper systems – not sofa government but cabinet government, committee government, ministers working together. So I think we've found ways of making coalition government work effectively.

I have regular meetings with Nick Clegg and the two parties also work through what we call 'The Quad'. That consists of me, George Osborne, Nick Clegg and Danny Alexander – with other ministers coming in as appropriate – and it's the process that has worked well to deal with fundamental things such as the budget or welfare reform. At the start we set up a formal coalition committee, but because of 'The Quad' and bilaterals it hasn't met as often as we'd expected, though it does on occasions.

Do you feel that government works better because of the formal strictures of a coalition, and agreements to refer to, or does that just mean creative policy making is more circumscribed?

DC: We've agreed the priorities, we're meeting them and I think we're doing that in interesting and creative ways. I challenge anyone to say that ministers feel held back from bold policy making.

NC: It's impossible for any government to take all its decisions on day one. Situations change; policies evolve as they develop; events surprise you. So the Coalition Agreement is our blueprint, but no one ever expected it to contain all the answers. Clearly, decisions are sometimes stalled by individuals and departments digging their heels in, like in all governments. But, on the whole, there's an energetic and creative dynamic. You have two parties forced, constantly, to justify their preferences and assumptions to one and other. That encourages people to be innovative and resourceful and can lead to quite radical outcomes. And, on a whole range of areas – bold budgets, public service reform, welfare, social mobility – you're more likely to hear our critics accuse us of doing too much, rather than too little.

Would the coalition have been formed or held together without the shared challenge of deficit reduction?

DC: Well, the challenging nature of the times helped create the coalition, as it was obvious that the country needed a strong and stable government. And I think that judgement's been proven right by events.

NC: Two things brought this government together. First, no one won the last election and a Lib Dem–Conservative coalition was the only option the parliamentary arithmetic would allow. But, yes, second, our economy was on very thin ice and politicians had to work together to avoid further instability. The need to tackle the deficit remains a strong glue between the two parties.

Has either of you ever threatened to end the coalition? What have been its most difficult moments? Tuition fees? The EU veto?

NC: No, neither of us has threatened to end the coalition. It's no secret that there have been some strained moments. But this coalition will live or die on its ability to navigate those moments calmly and we simply have to stay focused on the job of governing.

DC: There's been no threat to end it, but of course there have been difficult moments. It's a deal for this parliament, and we're making it work.

You have both stated that you are not 'friends'. How would you describe your personal relationship now? How has it evolved? Are your wives friends?

NC: We don't socialise, it's not that kind of arrangement. Neither of us came into government to find new friends. But you do have to understand each other and particularly each other's political constraints. More broadly, I actually think working with people you know you disagree with simplifies things. Your starting point is that you differ but you have to find a way through.

That's healthier than, say, what happened with Blair and Brown's government. Everyone assumed they would – or at least should – share enough ground to make it work. But they didn't and the result was a government destabilised by profound differences of opinion at the top.

DC: We get on well; it's a practical, businesslike relationship.

How worried are you that those in government are losing touch with the party political feelings of backbenchers, activists, and supporters?

DC: In any government it can be a problem. Ministers can get so busy they start to forget about keeping in touch with MPs. That's why I try to spend a lot of my time talking to MPs from all parts of my party, meeting activists, getting out there and hearing their views.

NC: The twin challenge for any government is keeping your party and supporters content with the direction of travel while also dealing with circumstances that are often beyond your control. I suppose the added complexity for coalition is a greater perception, on both sides, of parties having to do things they otherwise wouldn't for the sake of compromise. You have to work hard to contain that perception. The Liberal Democrats punch well above our weight – there's more of our manifesto in the Coalition Agreement, for instance. But I still invest a lot of time in explaining decisions to my party.

Conventional wisdom is that Conservatives are doing well out of the coalition because they get to govern with a generally secure majority while Liberal Democrats are on a hiding to nothing for propping up an antipathetic right-wing government – do you agree?

NC: There are two polar opposite narratives here. If you read the right-wing media and listen to some Conservative backbenchers you'll hear that David Cameron is a puppet on a string and that string is being pulled by Liberal Democrats. If you read the papers on the left and listen to some members of the Labour Party, you'll hear that this is a Conservative government in all but name and we are being pulled along haplessly. Clearly, neither is true.

DC: Both parties sometimes have to accept they can't get everything all their own way. It's a partnership government. There are things Conservatives might like but can't have and of course that's true for the Liberal Democrats, too. My view is that if we make a success of the difficult decisions we've taken both parties will be able to explain what they've done at the next election.

Given psephological realities will the Conservatives ever again form a majority government?

DC: That's up to the people of Britain, of course, but I hope the answer is yes and it is what I will be fighting for at the next election.

NC: It's not for me to comment on the Conservative Party's electoral prospects. But in terms of majority governments in general, I do believe the days of the pendulum swinging from red to blue and back again are increasingly behind us. The two-party system suited a Britain divided along rigid class lines, at a time when the ideological conflicts of the Cold War dominated politics much more heavily. Britain doesn't look like that any more. Over the last few decades we have been inching towards a much more diverse, more plural political era. I think one day historians and political scientists will look back on this coalition as part of that bigger shift.

Do the Lib Dems face wipeout at the next election?

NC: No, certainly not.

DC: I think people will respect them for the strong and bold role they have played in government.

Whatever happens next, does five years of good, competent government make it worth it for you both?

DC: Look, the whole point of politics is public service in the national interest and that's what government enables you to do. Clearly these are very challenging times and that makes the importance of acting in the national interest all the more compelling.

NC: Will I be proud if, after five years, we can say we put the economy on an even keel? We began the long task of rebalancing our economy away from its overreliance on financial services and the South East? We made headway on key liberal priorities: social mobility; political reform; improving the life chances of disadvantaged children? Absolutely. Who wouldn't be proud of that?

Has the presence of prominent Scottish Lib Dems in the coalition significantly strengthened your chances of seeing off the SNP independence challenge?

NC: I'm sure that having two Scottish, Liberal Democrat cabinet ministers, along with figures like Charles Kennedy and Menzies

Campbell in our senior ranks has contributed to the measured and intelligent tone the coalition has taken on the referendum challenge. My party believes the future of Scotland is best served by more devolution rather than either the status quo or yanking Scotland out of the Union. That view seems to be winning out.

DC: Clearly having more voices in and from Scotland helps the government engage in this issue. But the future of the United Kingdom isn't a party issue: I want people of all parties – and none – who support the Union to get involved.

You have both expressed some sympathy for Ed Miliband. Do you expect that he will be the Labour leader at the third podium in the 2015 General Election debates?

NC: I suspect he will be. The Labour Party faces some very big challenges, not least because they continue to hanker for a politics of plenty that isn't going to materialise any time soon. For the moment, at least, I don't see any rivals on the opposition's front bench offering any answers to that dilemma.

DC: It's hard enough running your own party without trying to work out who should run the other ones too.

In 1997 and 2001 the British electorate showed it can deliver mirror image election results – if things came out effectively the same again in 2015 would you seek to continue the coalition? Would your respective parties let you?

NC: I'll start from the same position then as I did in 2010. Coalitions aren't deals between individual party leaders. They're a response to whatever instructions voters give politicians at the ballot box. They'll give us our orders and I'll always seek to follow them.

DC: As I've said already, I am fighting for a Conservative majority at the next election.

What advice would you give to any future politicians trying to form a coalition?

DC: The public are the boss, you have to deliver good government whatever the outcome of the election and be bold about getting the really big things right.

NC: Be utterly candid about the nature of compromise and know what your priorities are. My party's four priorities were printed clearly on the front of our manifesto. That clarity helps guide you, even in the very difficult times.

COALITION GOVERNMENT TIMELINE

2010

May

11   The Liberal Democrats and Conservatives form the first coalition government since the Second World War

13   The first cabinet meeting of the new government agrees a 5% pay cut for all ministers

15   Ed Miliband announces he will stand against his brother David for the Labour leadership

16   Incorporating voices from the left, it is announced that Labour MP Frank Field is to advise the government on poverty and columnist Will Hutton is to conduct a review of public sector pay

17   Chancellor George Osborne claims that the new Office of Budget Responsibility (OBR) will make it impossible to 'fiddle the figures' in future

19   Deputy Prime Minister Nick Clegg promises to 'tear through the statute book' in the 'biggest shake up of our democracy' since the Great Reform Act of 1832

20 The coalition's full programme for government under the framing principles of 'freedom, fairness and responsibility' is published

24 Financial markets are soothed as £6.2 billion of spending cuts are outlined for 2010/11

25 The Queen's Speech, earlier leaked to Sunday newspapers, heralds reforms to parliament, a referendum on electoral reform and the repeal of authoritarian legislation

29 Lib Dem Treasury Minister David Laws resigns from the cabinet and is replaced by Danny Alexander, Clegg's former chief of staff

30 Lib Dem Energy Secretary Chris Huhne warns of risks to coalition cohesion after reports that Osborne is considering concessions on capital gains tax

June

3   The range of 'special' responsibilities being transferred to Clegg are announced, including the alternative vote (AV) referendum, introduction of fixed-term parliaments and Lords reform

6   Labour MP Frank Field agrees to lead an independent review into poverty and life chances for the coalition government

7   Cameron uses a speech to mark his first month in power to warn that the economic problems facing the country are 'even worse than we thought'

8   Former Prime Minister Baroness Thatcher visits Downing Street for tea

13 A poll claims Lib Dem support has slipped below 20% for the first time since the first leaders' debate, although 40% of voters declare satisfaction with the coalition versus 23% who are dissatisfied

14 Britain's growth forecast for 2011 is downgraded in the first independent figures released by the OBR

16   Osborne announces the restoration of the Bank of England's macroprudential powers ahead of his first Mansion House speech

22   The emergency budget sees an increase in the rate of VAT and reduction in welfare payments

      Clegg faces the Commons for the first time in the new forum of Deputy Prime Minister's Questions

28   Home Secretary Theresa May announces a cap on the number of non-EU immigrants

29   Two Lib Dem MPs become the first to vote against the coalition government over the plans to raise VAT

      A poll reveals a third of those who voted Lib Dem at the election would not do so again now

30   Justice Secretary Ken Clarke prompts right wing ire by calling for a 'radical' change to prison policy

July

1   Foreign Secretary William Hague sets out a new vision prioritising Britain's engagement with Europe and emerging powers rather than the United States

5   Clegg announces the date of the AV referendum as 5 May 2011

7   Education Secretary Michael Gove apologises for misleading the Commons after claiming building projects were underway at schools where they had in fact been cancelled

12   Cameron and Clegg restate the case for the coalition in a joint newspaper article, while acknowledging 'the differences that exist between us and our parties'

14   The number of long-term unemployed reaches the highest figure since May 1997

21   Clegg's first appearance in Cameron's stead at PMQs proves controversial for his description of the 'illegal' invasion of Iraq in 2003

22   Support for the Lib Dems hits its lowest level since Clegg
      became party leader
25   Cable concedes that working with the Conservatives in
      government is 'difficult'
30   The Work and Pensions Secretary Iain Duncan Smith
      unveils plans for a 'radical' shake-up of the welfare system

August

3   Cameron and Clegg write a joint letter to cabinet members
      calling on them to not lose sight of the need to cut public
      spending
15   Clegg assures party members and voters 'We will govern for
      the long term and we'll stick to our plan'
16   Clegg clarifies his role while Cameron is away on holiday as
      'holding the fort' but not serving as acting prime minister
          Deputy Lib Dem leader Simon Hughes rules out a coali-
      tion pact at local elections and the next general election
      stressing 'We will fight the next election in every seat'
          Labour former minister Alan Milburn is branded a 'collab-
      orator' on agreeing to become the coalition government's
      social mobility tsar
18   As the coalition government marks its first 100 days in
      power, Cameron tells the *Sun* of his determination to make
      'difficult decisions' early on, having learnt the lessons of
      both Thatcher's and Blair's first terms in office
          The TUC takes a different view, publishing its list of
      '100 cuts in 100 days'
          A survey finds 43% of voters view the new government's
      performance as better than the last, while 26% regard it as
      worse
22   Following sustained rumours, former Lib Dem leader
      Charles Kennedy confirms he is not defecting to Labour

23 Labour leadership candidate Ed Miliband exploits the sense of instability to urge Lib Dem MPs and voters to switch their allegiance

24 Health Secretary Andrew Lansley's proposals for reform are branded 'the most fundamental changes to the way the NHS operates since it was created' by Unison as it launches legal action aimed at derailing them

31 A survey of Lib Dem party members reveals that 84% would reject any further electoral arrangement with the Conservatives at the next election, although the same percentage support the current coalition

September

2 Cameron backs Hague following the resignation of his special advisor and faces further pressure as a report claims his own communications head Andy Coulson was aware of the practice of 'phone hacking' while editor of the *News of the World*

6 Theresa May states that the government will not be taking action over phone hacking, instead leaving the matter in police hands

9 A Commons debate on the phone hacking row prompts the setting up of an inquiry by a committee of senior MPs

13 The head of the TUC tells its annual conference that the preoccupation with spending cuts has resulted in a 'demolition' rather than coalition government

Conservative MP Nick Boles suggests the coalition should be put on a permanent footing, with just one candidate chosen to stand in each constituency

14 A poll indicates growing unease at the pace and depth of spending cuts with three quarters of respondents believing they are happening too quickly

16 Support for Labour draws level with the Conservatives for the first time since 2008

17 Cable attacks the coalition's immigration cap policy prompting speculation he may resign

20 In his speech to party conference, Clegg calls for Lib Dems to 'hold our nerve'

25 Ed Miliband wins the Labour leadership contest and asserts 'a new generation has taken control of Labour'

28 Defence Secretary Liam Fox's letter to the Prime Minister claiming 'draconian' reductions in military funding could have 'grave consequences' for the government is leaked

October

1 An opinion poll places Labour ahead of the Conservatives for the first time since 2007

5 Duncan Smith tells the Conservative conference that his universal credit reform will restore 'fairness and simplicity' to the welfare system

6 Osborne's plans to withdraw child benefit entitlement from higher earning parents prompts a party backlash, while Cameron ends conference telling Conservatives to work together as 'Your country needs you'

12 Cable comes under pressure for endorsing 'the main thrust' of the Browne report on university funding, contradicting the Lib Dem manifesto promise not to raise tuition fees

14 The so-called 'Bonfire of the Quangos' begins as the future of 900 public bodies is revealed

15 The terms of the Strategic Defence and Security Review (SDSR) are revealed with 17,000 military personnel and 25,000 civilian staff set to lose their jobs

20 Osborne presents the Comprehensive Spending Review (CSR) to parliament, confirming that the average budget

cuts across government departments will be 19% and that nearly half a million public sector workers are likely to lose their jobs as a result

21   The Archbishop of York decries the CSR as 'the swinging axe that follows the cuddly blanket and soothing words of "The Big Society"'

22   Opinion polls indicate the Lib Dems are taking the brunt of the blame for the cuts as their support plummets to 10%, while the Conservatives maintain a 41% to 40% lead over Labour

24   Clegg reveals his struggles of conscience over the cuts to Radio 4's *Desert Island Discs*, saying he has found the CSR process 'morally difficult'

25   Simon Hughes states that the Lib Dems will vote against the reforms to housing benefit unless there are major changes

November

4   Cable refers the planned takeover of BSkyB by News Corp to Ofcom

10   While Cameron calls for greater political freedom in a speech delivered to students in Beijing, back in Westminster a march by thousands of protestors against the increase in tuition fees turns violent as splinter groups occupy Conservative HQ and cause extensive damage

12   The Metropolitan police hand a file to the Crown Prosecution Service raising the prospect of prosecutions over *News of the World* phone hacking

December

6   Dissension within the party over tuition fees is laid bare as two Lib Dem ministers reveal they are considering resigning over the issue

9   Violence erupts throughout central London as student protestors attack government buildings. The vote to increase tuition fees three-fold is passed, although the coalition government majority is slashed from 84 to only 24 as 21 Lib Dem and six Conservative MPs rebel

13   Communities and Local Government Secretary Eric Pickles unveils the Decentralisation and Localism Bill while calling for councils to do 'more for less'

17   Facing plummeting personal ratings, Clegg launches an attack on the banking sector and bonus culture in an attempt to re-establish his political credibility

21   Cable is stripped of his media sector brief after telling undercover reporters from the *Telegraph* that he had 'declared war' on Rupert Murdoch

        Attempting to present a united front, the Prime Minister and Deputy Prime Minister hold a joint press conference, Cameron insisting the coalition is 'a very good fusion of Conservative and Liberal Democrat policy' which 'makes it incredibly powerful', while Clegg dismisses questions over its stability: 'Shock horror – two parties have different ideas'

        The Office for National Statistics (ONS) reveals public sector net borrowing broke all previous figures in November, rising to £23.3 billion

23   Further revelations from the *Telegraph*'s undercover sting operation give a candid insight into how Lib Dem ministers view their Conservative colleagues

2011

January

5   A 'poll of polls' finds the Lib Dems at their lowest level of support since the party's formation

7   Clegg heralds a new age of civil liberties in his attempt to convince Lib Dem voters of the achievements secured within the coalition

13   Following talks with his French counterpart, Cameron declares Britain is 'neither joining the euro, nor are we going to be drawn into fresh and new mechanisms within the euro'

14   Labour wins the Oldham East and Saddleworth by-election as the Conservative vote is more than halved

18   The day after Cameron declares he is not to be 'held back' in his public services reform, a Conservative MP, who is also a doctor, describes the proposed changes to Primary Care Trusts as feeling like 'someone had tossed a grenade' in

19   Andy Coulson resigns from his position as Downing Street's director of communications

20   Shadow Chancellor Alan Johnson resigns and is replaced by Ed Balls

24   The outgoing head of the CBI attacks the coalition's lack of strategy for economic growth claiming 'It's not enough just to slam on the spending brakes'

25   Fears of a double-dip recession are sparked as the ONS reports that the economy contracted by 0.5% in the final quarter of 2010

26   Theresa May reveals plans to review counter-terror laws following months of negotiations with the Lib Dem leader – Labour brand the move a 'political fudge'

      The Metropolitan police reopen their investigation into phone hacking at the *News of the World* after 'significant new information' emerges

February

1   Bowing to pressure, William Hague provides a charter flight from Cairo to evacuate British citizens during the political unrest in Egypt

3   Clegg reacts with anger following revelations of a child's detention at an immigration removal centre over Christmas which undermines his pledge to end the practice

5   Cameron remains 'absolutely unapologetic' despite accusations of stoking extremism by delivering a keynote speech on the failures of multiculturalism at the same time as a march by the English Defence League

8   Nine Lib Dem MPs call on the coalition to 'reconsider' its plans to privatise the Forestry Commission

9   The deal dubbed 'Project Merlin' struck between the coalition government and banks is unveiled. It promises to curb bonuses and increase lending to small- and medium-sized enterprises by 15% during the year but the Lib Dem Treasury spokesman in the Lords resigns, branding the terms 'pitiful'

14   Cameron defends his 'Big Society' agenda against criticism that it is a cover for cuts

17   The government backs down on both its woodland sell-off and plans to cut housing benefit

24   Polling shows support for the 'yes' campaign in the AV debate leading by 42% to 35%

March

2   The chairman of the Police Federation predicts 'morale meltdown' if the coalition persists with its plans to cut police pay and funding

4   While Wales votes to give more lawmaking powers to its Assembly, the Barnsley by-election result sees the Lib Dems crash from second to sixth place

7   Hague is criticised for authorising a 'bungled' SAS mission to rebel-held eastern Libya

8   Clegg and Energy Secretary Chris Huhne launch the coalition's new carbon plan and green apprenticeships scheme

10 Lord Hutton publishes his report on public sector pay which recommends the scrapping of final salary pensions

11 As police and barriers ring the venue, Clegg tells his party's spring conference, 'Difficult choices, especially at these difficult times, provoke controversy and sometimes protest. And it is not easy for us as a party to be the focus of those protests'

14 Following a party grassroots rebellion, Clegg holds talks with Cameron on changes to the proposed NHS reforms

18 Cameron announces RAF jets will help enforce a UN no fly zone over Libya as rebels continue their attempts to oust Muammar Gaddafi

23 Delivering the terms of the Budget, Osborne declares that while last year's 'was about rescuing the nation's finances, and paying for the mistakes of the past', this year's 'is about reforming the nation's economy, so that we have enduring growth and jobs in the future'

26 As a quarter of a million join the TUC's 'March for the Alternative' against spending cuts, small breakaway groups attack banks and luxury stores. Addressing the rally in Hyde Park, Ed Miliband declares that the marchers represent 'the mainstream majority'

28 The AV referendum proves polarising as Huhne accuses the Conservative-led 'No' campaign of stooping to 'the politics of the gutter'

April

4   In a humiliating statement to the Commons, Andrew Lansley acknowledges the 'genuine concerns' regarding

NHS reforms and announces that time will now be taken to 'pause, listen and engage'

5   Clegg insists that the coalition is likely to make 'substantial' changes to the NHS reform Bill

6   Shadow Chancellor Ed Balls declares the start of the new tax year 'Black Wednesday' for families affected by tax credit and child benefit changes

14   At its local election campaign launch, the Lib Dem deputy leader Simon Hughes describes the coalition as 'a practical business arrangement' rather than a 'love affair'

18   Vince Cable denies rumours of impending resignation having described the Prime Minister in previous days as 'very unwise' and accusing him of 'inflaming extremism'

27   Figures show the economy returning to growth in the first quarter of the year but not reaching official expectations

28   Scottish Lib Dem leader Tavish Scott states the party is stopping the Conservatives from 'doing their worst'

29   Politics pauses for the day as Cameron, Clegg and Miliband attend the wedding of Prince William and Catherine Middleton

May

3   Facing likely defeat for his 'yes' to AV campaign, Clegg sees a silver lining in how the referendum has 'amplified the fact this coalition government is composed of different parties' and that 'the Liberal Democrats are the progressive party in this arrangement'

5   Following a higher than expected turnout of 41% for the AV referendum, the 'No' vote triumphs by 67.9% to 32.1%. The Lib Dems also take a beating in the local election results as Labour make significant gains, while the Conservative vote holds more strongly than expected

The SNP secures a majority in the Scottish Parliament for the first time since devolution, paving the way for a referendum on full independence

7   In the aftermath of the AV referendum, Cable brands his coalition partners 'ruthless, calculating and thoroughly tribal'

8   As Ed Miliband calls on Lib Dem ministers to quit the coalition, Clegg promises the party will have a more assertive voice in government

18   Breaking ranks with Cameron, Clegg rejects the key NHS reform of a regulator to promote competition

June

1   A senior Conservative aide to the Health Secretary reportedly loses her job after criticising Clegg

5   A group of economists demand Osborne formulate a 'Plan B' for the economy arguing that the 'breakneck deficit-reduction plan is self-defeating even on its own terms'

6   Vince Cable is heckled at the GMB union's conference when he warns against co-ordinated strike action

7   Cameron bows to Lib Dem pressure, though angers his own backbenchers, as he makes a series of major concessions on NHS reform

9   The Archbishop of Canterbury questions the democratic mandate of the coalition asserting that 'With remarkable speed, we are being committed to radical, long-term policies for which no one voted'

13   Clegg assures his MPs that all concessions demanded on NHS reform have been accepted

14   The government announces its initial response to the report produced by the independent NHS Future Forum following the six-week long 'listening pause'

17 Danny Alexander provokes public sector ire on pensions but argues 'It is absolutely wrong to pretend that public servants can be insulated from the pressures that everyone else is facing'

21 Ken Clarke's plan to offer a 50% sentencing discount to criminals who plead guilty is abandoned

22 As mass strikes loom, Clegg declares his hope of acting as a 'peacemaker' between the coalition and public sector unions

23 Clegg calls for shares in Britain's bailed-out banks to be distributed to taxpayers

24 Cameron claims victory for Britain on the sourcing of the Greek bailout fund

28 The 'good deal' offered to public sector workers means the upcoming mass walkout is 'wrong' according to Cameron

30 Across the country thousands of public sector workers march in protest against proposed changes to their pensions, although unions and government argue over the scale of the walkout

July

1 Labour holds Inverclyde at the by-election but sees its share of the vote drop against a strong challenge from the SNP. The Lib Dems lose their deposit

2 A letter from the office of Eric Pickles to the Prime Minister warning that 40,000 families will be made homeless due to welfare reforms is leaked

4 The 'phone hacking' scandal escalates as it is revealed the *News of the World* accessed the mobile phone of murdered schoolgirl Milly Dowler

6 Cameron bows to pressure and announces public inquiries

into both the alleged phone hacking and the Metropolitan Police investigation into the original claims

10 The 168-year-old *News of the World* hits the newsstands for the last time

16 Metropolitan Police Commissioner Sir Paul Stephenson resigns as the repercussions of the phone hacking scandal widen

19 The Culture Select Committee hear evidence from Rupert and James Murdoch

26 Figures show Britain's economy grew by only 0.2% in the first quarter of the year

27 The Libyan rebels are recognised by Britain as the country's 'sole governmental authority'

August

4   The continuing Eurozone crisis and fears of a return to recession in the US upset markets with nearly £50bn wiped off the value of the FTSE

6   An initially peaceful protest over the police shooting of Mark Duggan is followed by rioting in Tottenham. The disturbances spread overnight across London

8   Cameron returns from holiday as the rioting in London enters its third night and violence breaks out across England, including Birmingham, Manchester, Bristol and Liverpool

11 Following the recall of parliament, the government presents a dissection of the 'insufficient' tactics used by police forces while Ed Miliband calls for police budget cuts to be reversed

15 Cameron provokes controversy by declaring the riots a symptom of a 'broken society' in 'moral collapse'

16 Although falling short of Ed Miliband's demand for a national inquiry into the cause of the riots, the government performs a partial U-turn as Clegg promises a communities and victims panel will produce a report

22 As rebel forces enter the centre of Tripoli, Cameron again returns to Downing Street early from his holidays, declaring 'It is clear from the scenes we are witnessing ... that the end is near for Gaddafi'

26 Clegg draws attention to his difference with Cameron's wish to subdue the influence of European courts by pointedly stressing 'As we continue to promote human rights abroad, we must ensure we work to uphold them here at home'

September

7 Despite a bitter debate, the Health and Social Care Bill passes the Commons with a majority of 65, although four Lib Dem MPs vote against it and 11 abstain

9 In the face of poor news for the economy, Osborne defends his deficit reduction plan as a 'rock of stability' that will protect Britain

12 The Independent Commission on Banking (ICB) issues its final recommendations insisting that the reforms – including the ring-fencing of retail operations from investment arms – be implemented by 2019

14 In a signal that the government is reassessing its economic policy, Clegg unveils plans to speed up major infrastructure projects

15 Following the ousting of Muammar Gaddafi, Cameron and French president Nicolas Sarkozy arrive in Libya to a hero's welcome

18 Clegg assures delegates to the Lib Dem conference that he and his fellow ministers were being 'awkward' in government: 'As our coalition partners are finding out on a daily

basis, we are not here to make things easy. We're here to put things right'

19   Vince Cable's promise of a new 'responsible capitalism' is mocked by the left

21   Clegg admits 'just how tough' the Lib Dems' time in power has been and that the decision which has been 'most heart-wrenching for me – for all of us – was on university funding'

27   Labour surrenders its lead in the polls to the Conservatives for the first time in nearly a year

October

2   A 35,000-strong protest against cuts greets the start of the Conservative party conference in Manchester

6   The Bank of England boosts its programme of quantitative easing by £75bn as Mervyn King warns that Britain is possibly facing 'the most serious financial crisis we've seen, at least since the 1930s, if not ever'

14   Liam Fox resigns as Defence Secretary and is replaced by Phillip Hammond

21   Occupy London Stock Exchange protesters refuse to leave as their makeshift camp leads to St Paul's Cathedral having to shut its doors for the first time since the Second World War

24   Cameron suffers the largest rebellion on Europe for any Conservative Prime Minister since the war as 81 of his MPs support a bid to grant a referendum on EU membership

November

9   Taking no chances, 4,000 police are on duty as thousands of students march peacefully through London in their protest against tuition fees and the 'privatisation' of the university system

16 For the first time since records began youth unemployment exceeds a million

29 In his autumn statement to parliament, Osborne warns he will now have to continue cutting public spending until 2017 after the OBR reduces sharply its forecasts for economic growth

30 A day of public sector action is hailed as 'the biggest strike in a generation' by the TUC but 'a damp squib' by the Prime Minister

December

9 Risking the biggest upset to British-European relations in a generation, Cameron vetoes an agreement among the other EU members aimed at tackling the Eurozone crisis, claiming it failed to provide safeguards for The City. Clegg initially defends Cameron's action but Vince Cable believes the country has finished in a 'bad place' while Ken Clarke describes the outcome of the summit as 'disappointing' and 'very surprising'

11 As details of the negotiations become clearer, Clegg declares he is 'bitterly disappointed' with Cameron's decision, describing it as 'bad for Britain' and fearing it could lead to the country becoming 'isolated and marginalised' within Europe

14 Cameron's actions appear to strike a chord with some voters as well as the Eurosceptic wing of his party, as polls show the Conservatives gaining seven percentage points to lead Labour

Lib Dem MPs abstain en masse from voting for a Democratic Unionist party motion commending Cameron's action

16 Labour wins the Feltham and Heston by-election with an 8% swing from the Conservatives, while the Lib Dems

narrowly hold on to third place with just 88 votes more than UKIP

18 Vince Cable states that he and George Osborne have come to a 'common view' and that the coalition will press ahead with its reforms to the banking system by implementing the ICB report's proposals in full

19 Clegg adopts a combative approach over reform of the Lords declaring 'we have got to get on with it'

22 The outgoing head of the civil service, Sir Gus O'Donnell gives his view that how or 'whether to keep our kingdom united' is set to be one of the 'enormous challenges' facing the country in the coming years

2012

January

5 As a poll reveals only a quarter of those who voted Lib Dem at the General Election would do so again now, Clegg attempts to recapture popular support promising a crackdown on executive bonuses and tax avoidance

9 Cameron stresses his desire to end the 'legal uncertainty' surrounding the Scottish independence referendum, denying claims that the coalition wishes to 'dictate' the terms

10 Details of the £33 billion London to Birmingham high speed rail project (HS2) are announced

Ed Miliband delivers a keynote speech pledging not to reverse the coalition's spending cuts if Labour wins office in 2015

11 Scottish First Minister Alex Salmond accuses the coalition of 'pulling strings and setting conditions' over the timing and conduct of the referendum on independence

16 Clegg announces plans to increase employee share ownership to create a 'John Lewis economy'

18   Cameron describes Argentina's position as more like 'colonialism' in the war of words over the Falkland Islands

23   Vince Cable's recommendations on executive pay awards disappoint those who anticipated the implementation of legislation putting workers on remuneration committees

      Paddy Ashdown leads a Lib Dem rebellion in the Lords supporting an amendment to exclude child benefit from the proposed benefits cap in an embarrassing defeat for the government

24   A poll suggests the Conservatives are now on track to win a majority at the next election

25   Fears of a double-dip recession heighten as ONS data reveal the economic growth slowed by 0.2% in the fourth quarter of 2011

26   Conservative peers join the rebellion on welfare reform as the coalition suffers its greatest defeat yet in the Lords

30   Labour claims victory as the CEO of RBS agrees to forego his £1 million bonus – while the coalition appears divided on the issue

31   Cameron faces criticism from all sides in the Commons over the issue of Europe with Ed Miliband claiming the 'phantom veto' secured nothing for Britain

      The former RBS chief Fred Goodwin is stripped of his knighthood

February

3   Chris Huhne resigns from the cabinet after being charged with perverting the course of justice

5   The coalition's commitment to onshore wind farms is attacked in a letter signed by nearly a third of Conservative MPs

8   Osborne warns that the debate on bonuses and executive pay risks creating an 'anti-business culture in Britain'

10 Argentina submits an official protest to the UN citing Britain's 'militarisation' of the seas surrounding the Falkland Islands

13 Clegg launches the coalition's £1 billion 'youth contract' promising payments to companies that give jobs to unemployed 18- to 24-year-olds

14 Osborne declares that a report that Britain risks losing its AAA credit rating is 'a reality check for the whole political system'

16 Cameron pledges to 'fight with everything' he has to keep the UK together during a visit to Scotland

17 Ed Miliband pledges to make the coalition's attempt to reform the NHS the 'defining issue' of the next election

21 Announcing a new training scheme, Clegg vows to tackle the 'ticking time bomb' of 'Neets' (16 to 24-year-olds who are not in education, employment or training)

ONS figures for January reveal the country's public finances posted their biggest surplus for four years

23 Cameron's 'families' tsar resigns as an advisor to the government amid a police probe into fraud allegations against her 'welfare-to-work' firm

28 Andrew Lansley defends the government's NHS reform bill against claims the coalition was in 'disarray' after Clegg and Baroness Williams write a joint letter to Lib Dem peers expressing support for amendments designed to limit competition

INDEX

347

INDEX

Heywood, Sir Jeremy, 161, 267–8
Hilton, Steve, 55, 114, 127, 128,
    131, 262, 263
Hindu, 282
Holmes, Dame Kelly, 281
Holywell, 13
Home, Sir Alex Douglas, 259
Hope, Alan 'Howling Laud', 117
House of Commons:
    Modernisation Committee, 160
    reduction in membership of, 183
    reform of, 183
Howard, Michael, 11, 76, 114, 130,
    142, 271
Howarth, George, 187
Hughes, Simon, 20, 91, 93–4, 123,
    161, 165, 248, 292, 300
Huhne, Chris, 21, 259
    in negotiating team, 144, 147,
    148–9, 163, 172, 183, 232
hung parliament:
    Cameron attacks idea of, 56–7
    Clegg fends off questions about,
        29
    election results lean towards, 118
    guidance in case of, 160–2
    mathematical certainty of, 131
    in New Zealand, 159
    Osborne raises possibility of, 150
    public said to want, 10
    recognition of possibility of, 105
    see also coalition
Hungary, 18
Hunt, Jeremy, 54
Hunter, Anji, 221, 227

Icelandic ash cloud, 6, 79–80, 159
ICM, 67
ID cards, 140, 231–2
immigration, 74, 88, 89, 90–2, 100,
    141, 272
Independent, 132
India, 273, 280, 281–4

inheritance tax, 16, 152, 181, 300; *see
    also* tax
Institute for Fiscal Studies (IFS), 17,
    18
Institute for Government, 157–8, 160
Iraq, 272
    War, 21, 203, 219
Islam, 285–6
Israel, 272
ITN, 207
ITV, 35, 60–74 *passim*
    exit poll from, 115, 119
    TV debate hosted by, *see* televised
        debates

Jenkins, Roy, 133
John Smith House, 118
Johnson, Alan, 28, 202
Johnson, Boris, 12, 32–3, 34, 90,
    91–2
Johnson, Diana, 238
Jones, Dylan, 257
Jones, Joey, Cameron's interview
    with, 265–6
Justice Committee, 156

Karzai, Hamid, 272, 276
Kelly, Dr David, 219
Kelly, Ruth, 259
Kennedy, Charles, 21, 165, 248
Khan, Sadiq, 114, 204
King, Mervyn, 178, 179–80
Kingston-upon-Thames, 51
Kingswood, 116
Kinnock, Neil, 104
Kirkcaldy and Cowdenbeath, 119
Knight, Jim, 87, 201

Labour:
    anti-war anger directed towards,
        21
    AV commitment by, 185
    AV concessions of, 228–30

ACKNOWLEDGEMENTS

We would like to thank the following:

Our researcher and all round factotum, Tom Roberts, without whom this book would not have happened. All those both identified and unidentified who talked to us about the events of 2010. Peter Oborne and Lucy Aitkens gave vital help getting this project of the ground. Sky News and BSkyB for employing us to occupy front row seats. We have the good fortune to be part of a terrific Sky operation in Westminster splendidly led by Jonathan Levy. All at Simon & Schuster and the Wylie Agency. And thanks go too to those who played host to the authors over the summer – James and Alison Boulton, Mark and Carolyn Ware, Philip Evans and Aline Delcroix.

Our families showed great patience during the short but intense period of writing and it is to them that we dedicate this work.